American Sea Power and the Obsolescence of Capital Ship Theory

R. B. Watts

McFarland & Company, Inc., Publishers
Jefferson, North Carolina

LIBRARY OF CONGRESS CATALOGUING-IN-PUBLICATION DATA (new form)
Names: Watts, R. B. (Robert B.), 1963–
Title: American sea power and the obsolescence of capital ship theory / R.B. Watts.
Description: Jefferson, North Carolina : McFarland & Company, Inc., Publishers, 2016. | Includes bibliographical references and index.
Identifiers: LCCN 2015038525 | ISBN 9780786498796 (softcover : acid free paper) | ISBN 9781476620763 (ebook)
Subjects: LCSH: Sea-power—United States. | Irregular warfare—United States. | Warships—United States | Naval art and science—United States. | Naval strategy. | United States. Navy—History—20th century. | United States—History, Naval—20th century.
Classification: LCC VA50.W38 2016 | DDC 359/.030973—dc23
LC record available at http://lccn.loc.gov/2015038525

BRITISH LIBRARY CATALOGUING DATA ARE AVAILABLE

© 2016 R. B. Watts. All rights reserved

No part of this book may be reproduced or transmitted in any form or by any means, electronic or mechanical, including photocopying or recording, or by any information storage and retrieval system, without permission in writing from the publisher.

On the cover: LCS 1, the *Freedom*. In the aftermath of 9/11 CNO Admiral Verne Clark called for over 70 of these platforms to be built immediately to deal with the irregular threat. Today a handful of them have been delivered, their operational success and mission sets still unclear (Navsource online)

Printed in the United States of America

McFarland & Company, Inc., Publishers
  Box 611, Jefferson, North Carolina 28640
    www.mcfarlandpub.com

American Sea Power and the Obsolescence of Capital Ship Theory

For my parents, to whom I owe all.

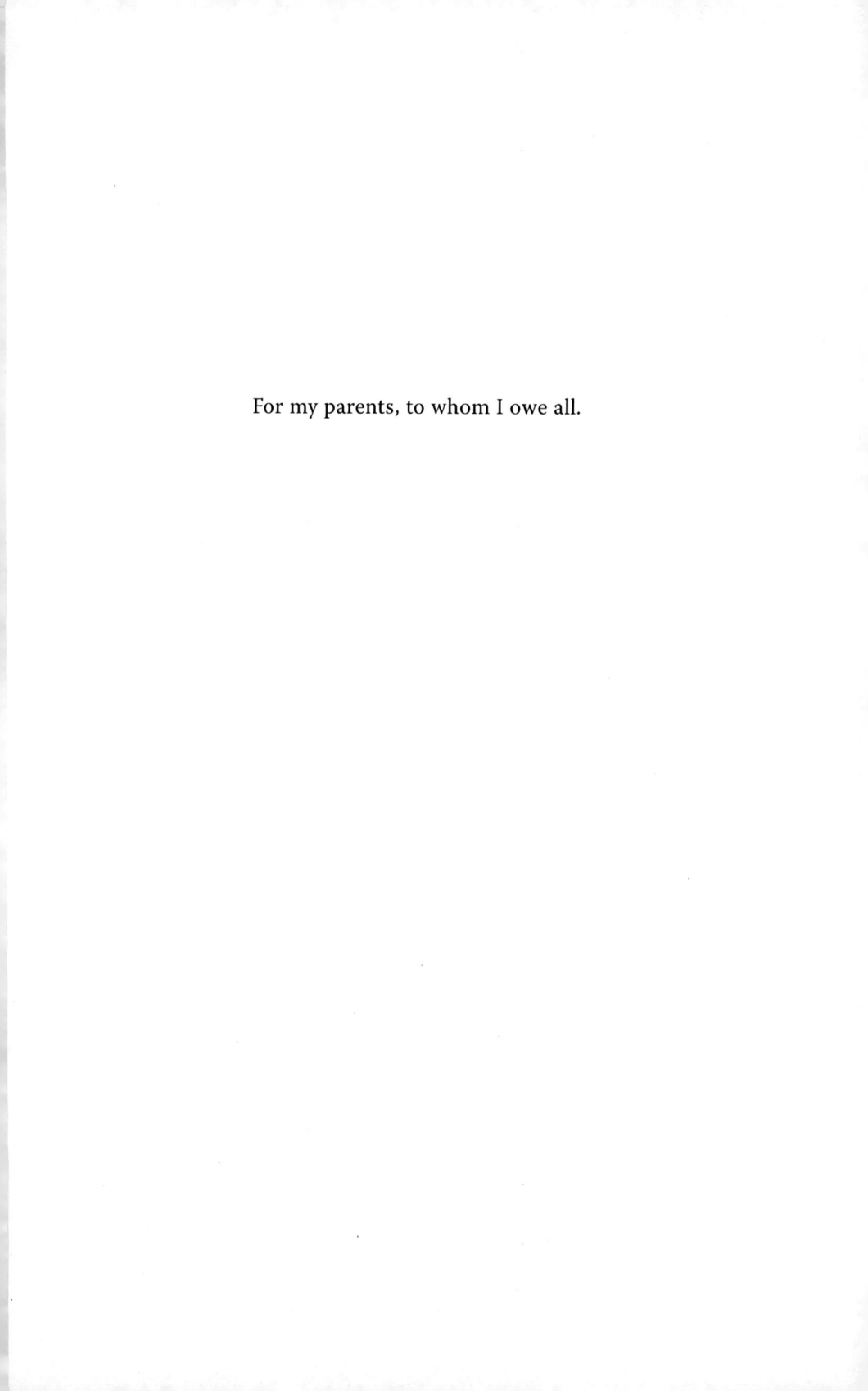

Acknowledgments

Throughout my military and academic careers, the following people have been invaluable in my study and understanding of sea power: Dr. Ernest King, USCGA; Captain Bob Glynn USCG (Ret.); Captain "Mac" McDonough, USCG (Ret.); RADM Richard Kelly, USCG (Ret.); Captain Bill Coleman, USN (Ret.); Captain John Leibman, USN (Ret.); Dr. Carl Boyd, Old Dominion University; Captain Jeff Kline, USN (Ret.); Dr. Peter Swartz; VADM Charlie Martoglio, USN; my colleagues (far too many to list) at the Naval War College, the Naval Post-Graduate School Monterey and, of course, the National War College; my wife, Laurie (USCG Ret.), for her continuous support and inspiration; and finally Dr. Joel Sokolsky, Royal Military College of Canada—scholar, advisor, and friend.

Table of Contents

Acknowledgments vi
Preface 1
Introduction 5

ONE. The Changing Paradigm of War: The United States and Irregular Warfare Theory 15

TWO. The Philosophy: A. T. Mahan and the Foundations of U.S. Naval Thought 30

THREE. War Fighting Theory and Practice, 1914–1941: The Ascendancy of the Capital Ship 40

FOUR. Lessons, Retrenchment, and Theory, 1945–1951 57

FIVE. Theory and the Challenge of Irregular Warfare, 1950–1980 73

SIX. Theoretical Renaissance: The Maritime Strategy, 1980–1990 92

SEVEN. Strategy Adrift, 1990–2001 115

EIGHT. The New Challenge: 9/11 and the Use of Naval Power in Irregular Warfare 134

NINE. The Legacy Lives On 163

Conclusions—The Cycles of History 177
Chapter Notes 181
Bibliography 203
Index 217

Preface

This book is the culmination of almost thirty years of research, writing, and advocating for sea power. Despite the work's central thesis—that the United States is dangerously wedded to outdated theory that threatens to make our Navy unsustainable or, at worst, irrelevant—I have always been and remain a strong proponent of the continued development of naval power and U.S. dominance on the sea. The United States began its history reliant on the sea and has prospered not only by the use of the sea but also through its ability to project influence across the seas as part of its global role as a superpower. We are and must remain a sea power. But our continued adherence to the tradition of the capital ship is increasingly problematic in a world that is rapidly changing around us, and we must change. The story of how I changed from naval traditionalist to advocate for alternative forms of sea power is illustrative of this thesis.

Commissioned in 1985 in the U.S. Coast Guard, I found myself very early in my career working in the policy and planning world as part of a team investigating how the service could integrate the new maritime strategy into part of its wartime mission. Given far too much access for someone relatively new to the military—the Coast Guard has a tradition of giving a great deal of responsibility to and encouraging initiative in its junior personnel—I witnessed firsthand the development and testing of the central concepts of the maritime strategy, as well as new and exciting concepts such as integrated coastal defense and strategic power projection operations performed in conjunction with continental land power. In observing these operations, a number of elements became apparent. Close to home, I felt that as a sea-going service with unique missions that contributed significantly to the national strategy, it was essential that the Coast Guard become as integrated as possible in modern naval operations both at home and aboard. Fortunately a number of my senior mentors were of the same mind and began encouraging "joint" tours outside the service to encourage officers to "speak the language" of sea power. Toward that end, I pursued a number of "exchange" tours with the Navy, first afloat as surface warfare officer, then as an operations officer in a Navy battle group and, ultimately, as a liaison for the chief of naval operations. These tours afforded me the unique opportunity to learn about the various nuances of sea power from a very broad perspective. As a surface warfare officer, I was able to see how sea power was viewed from the "union" perspective of the fleet, while as a Coastie I was able to examine other forms of sea power that were regarded as, at best, unusual (port security and irregular operations, for example). As an "outsider" who had found a seat at the inside table, I began questioning many fundamental assumptions that were ordinarily sacrosanct, much like a visiting relative from out of town. What I found over this prolonged course of study was surprising.

First, there was Mahan. Spoken of almost in reverence, the principles espoused by Mahan—at least principles that began with Mahan—dominated naval theory. This was especially true in the maritime strategy of the 1980s. But how could a naval philosopher of the 19th century be so influential in modern operations? Clearly I needed to know more. This began a prolonged period of study of Mahan and sea power, both formally at the Naval War College and the Navy Post Graduate School and informally through writing on the subject for the U.S. Naval Institute. It was during this course of study that I began to notice a curious phenomenon that, although new to me, was apparently well known to regular Navy officers. While many of the principles first devised by Mahan and modified by his later disciples—large battle fleets of capital ships, forward deployment, and power projection—made sense in historical eras where there was a reasonable peer competitor, without such a competitor there seemed to be less of a need for these types of operations and the assets required to conduct them, namely overwhelming power in capital ships, especially the centerpiece of Cold War strategy: the aircraft carrier.

Theoretically this course of action made sense, but practical application was another matter. Following the fall of the Soviet Union in the 1990s, a logical course of action for the Navy would have been to modify its strategy to meet emerging irregular threats. This would almost certainly require the design of new types of assets and, arguably, the reduction of its Cold War aircraft carrier fleet. This would obviously have been a radical course of action for any branch of the military and not undertaken lightly. In the era of the "peace dividend," I and others expected there to be serious and prolonged debate about the future of the fleet. But there was none. Rather, any challenge to the continued development of capital ship power was met with, at best, derision and, at worst, career suicide. Throughout the 1990s, the Navy published a series of strategies (discussed in this book) to rationalize the continued development of capital ships, strategies that were increasingly bizarre in their context. Carriers returned to combat in the Gulf Wars, but even then only as a supplement to other forms of combat power. In the aftermath of 9/11, their use remains controversial in terms of effectiveness against irregular enemies.

Even today, to challenge the Mahan paradigm is, at best, a dicey affair. Naval officers depart from capital ship theory at enormous risk; those who challenge conventional naval theory in publications often find themselves ostracized or passed over in their profession. What is discussed in this book—that we need to consider altering core theory to meet modern challenges—is known to many, but few will venture to discuss it due to professional consequences. The discouragement of this kind of discussion is immensely harmful to the development of modern strategy to deal with new and emerging threats. Not only is the world changing rapidly, but the requirements of the "decade of war" have proven to be far more than anticipated, especially in the realm of irregular warfare. In continuing to advocate for a fleet that stresses the Mahanian vision, the Navy, the most expensive of military branches, threatens to price itself out of existence. This is especially true as there is no indication that we will return to the conventional world that Mahan envisioned and that our Navy has been designed for, without which the fleet is becoming increasingly irrelevant. We must change our strategic outlook, and to do that we must have an honest evaluation of the theory that, to date, remains largely unchanged.

In order to understand the impact theory has had on the development of current naval force structure and tactics, this book begins with a comprehensive historical analysis not only of predominant theory, but also alternatives that have been proposed and rejected in the development of modern naval doctrine. It then turns to an examination of the evolution that has occurred (or not occurred) since the end of the Cold War, an era that still drives naval force procurement in many regards. The book concludes with an assessment of the new requirements of irregular warfare (including the execution of "smart power" missions) in order to point to development of a new naval theory that will free American naval thinking from the Mahanian legacy in order to better enable it to meet the national and global threats ahead.

Introduction

The United States has been engaged in global conflict since the terrorist attacks of September 11, 2001. Volumes have been and continue to be written about the attacks and the effects they had on the American psyche as well as their worldwide impact. There is little doubt that they were a world-changing event in the societal and political spectrum. For the military, the attacks represented a direct challenge to core strategic assumptions regarding the nature of war itself. For years a number of military professionals and academics had written that the future belonged to asymmetric military actions very similar to those that had been undertaken on September 11, work that had been discussed and debated but that had limited practical impact. In the aftermath of the attacks, it seemed that the future was upon us. But as events unfolded in the days and weeks following the attacks, the future took a back seat to established methods and practices of war.

Despite the fact that the United States was fighting a non-state actor with almost no conventional forces, the initial response by the United States was distinctly American: "shock and awe"–style campaigns into the heart of the terrorist support region (Afghanistan), followed by another conventional campaign into Iraq. Rapid tactical victory on the battlefield was not followed by strategic victory; rather, both these campaigns devolved into prolonged periods of insurgency while the main enemy, Al-Qaida (ALQ), showed no signs of being eliminated as a threat from the global stage. These attacks on sovereign states resulted in prolonged irregular warfare against new opponents. The United States found itself fighting (and continues to fight) in a style of war for which, as a military superpower, it has little taste. Yet the idea of global "irregular" war involving multiple and diverse elements of society is now a reality.

This new reality is not so much a "new" type of warfare as it is different from previous conflicts in both size and scope. Although 9/11 was certainly one of the most dramatic illustrations of an unconventional attack in the modern era, the view that this was a radically new type of warfare is not entirely correct. Historically, unconventional warfare is as old as war itself and is arguably the predominant form of warfare practiced worldwide. Since the conclusion of the Second World War, unconventional and irregular conflict has become increasingly the norm as the world moves farther from "conventional" conflicts between nation-states or wars between major powers. These have varied in both size and scope, ranging from conflicts that were conventional but distinctly limited (such as Korea), to those increasingly dominated by irregular tactics (Vietnam), to conflicts where apparent conventional victory is almost meaningless in the aftermath that dissolves into long-term irregular war (Afghanistan and Iraq).

Although conventional warfare between nation-states is still a very real possibility, globally the prevailing trend in "irregular warfare" (IW) has increased significantly with the end of the Cold War and subsequent breakup of the Soviet Union, requiring that conventional forces adapt to fight against threats and in environments that are increasingly diverse. It must be stressed that in the modern era, irregular warfare is not limited to small-scale actions against armed terrorists or unconventional forces. Technology today allows for rapid coordination of forces and promulgation of ideology that was unheard of until very recently. In its most extreme form, nations—or, more significantly, non-state actors—can pursue "hybrid" or "fourth-generation warfare" where virtually all elements of society (criminal, terrorist, military, etc.) are effectively engaged in irregular conflict. Nations have fought global conventional war in the past against other nations; today, technology and common ideologies can allow for a "total irregular war" to be fought on a global scale.

In the diverse environment of irregular war, the sea can be a significant force multiplier for an unconventional enemy. In a world embracing globalization, as international trade has increased, so has use of the sea. As a medium, the sea is inherently neutral, available for use to any who can take advantage of it. Tactically and operationally, this is a boon to forces engaged in irregular warfare who can use it to covertly transport weapons, to engage in illicit activity in support of conflict, or to rapidly mobilize for combat. This fact would seem to be intuitively obvious. Historically, the sea has always been the vast highway connecting sovereign nations, a region that is largely uncontrolled, unprotected, and subject to all manners of use. The sea can be exploited not only as a resource but also as a means of rapid mobilization for combat operations or, in the case of "weaker" powers, to strike at vulnerable areas of larger nation-states. These factors have been evident since the earliest days of galley warfare and are all the more prevalent today in an era of proliferation of modern technology that makes use of the sea far simpler for a determined opponent. The ease with which the sea can be used by irregular forces has effectively changed the established paradigm of sea power.

As a global maritime power, the United States has a long history of using the sea in both peace and war. The sea has always been fundamental to U.S. national strategy for global engagement; its Navy was designed to maximize the inherent flexibility, mobility, and sustainability represented by conventional sea power. The United States has historically demonstrated that in conventional operations the establishment of "command of the sea" enables not only free transit but also the ability to deploy (and strike) virtually at will. Traditionally this has been accomplished by eliminating an opponent's sea power, composed of principal naval forces. But operations in an irregular warfare environment are far more uncertain than confronting an enemy in conventional war. The role of sea power in irregular war is not irregular war at sea, but rather determining how sea power can affect an irregular campaign strategically. In addition to facing a very uncertain threat, traditional naval forces can also find themselves engaged in various "soft" power missions that are essential to strategic victory in irregular conflict. Since the end of the Cold War, these types of missions have become the norm for U.S. naval forces.

Yet despite the clear trend away from conventional conflict and the advantages the sea provides to an asymmetric enemy, as well as to the means to defeat that enemy, the United States has taken very limited steps in adapting its considerable naval power to meet the irregular warfare threat. This is not apparent from the rhetoric. In multiple posture statements, articles, and even strategic documents, the U.S. Navy has seemingly given a great deal of attention to the phenomenon of modern IW. But the actual capability that is being built in U.S. shipyards tells another story. Today the U.S. Navy continues to build ships for the "large war" scenario and emphasizes doctrine based on principles that stress decisive battle against an equally capable conventional opponent.

The attacks of September 11 dramatically illustrated the vulnerability of the United States to irregular attack and served as the impetus for a major governmental reorganization, which was intended to focus on the challenges of homeland security. Yet while naval power is clearly relevant to this challenge, given the reliance of the United States on the sea and the vast areas of coastline that constitute vulnerability, the U.S. Navy continues to cling to both a doctrine and ship design that promises little real success to meet the IW challenge. Operations overseas against an unconventional opponent have a clearly conventional mindset. The reasons for this are complex, including such factors as tradition, pervasive acceptance of theory, a continuing fear of irrelevancy, competition for funding, and the influence of the industrial complex, among others. These factors have entrenched the U.S. Navy in a position that either downplays or marginalizes the current IW threat both overseas and to the homeland.

The Navy's resistance to the changing paradigm of sea power is deeply rooted in military culture and a conventional strategic paradigm. The U.S. Navy is ultimately a child of its culture; culture drives strategy, doctrine, operations, and the design of ships. Although the Navy is steeped in tradition, its modern strategic culture developed quite rapidly. Arguably the U.S. Navy is the sole remaining naval power, but compared to other historical major naval powers, the U.S. Navy as a global force is quite young, emerging as a significant force only after the American Civil War in the late 19th century and experiencing unprecedented growth in a relatively short period of time. But while the Navy may be young in terms of global strategic force, by the time of its emergence in the late 19th century, it had a well-established culture and tradition that unified its officer corps into one cohesive group embedded in a core set of principles that largely remained unchanged. These principles ushered in the United States as an emerging force on the global stage, and the Navy would play a central role. But how this role was to be accomplished, given the power of other nations at the turn of the century, was something of a mystery. Because of its relatively late entry as a global force (and unlike other European navies, it had a long history of operational development), the U.S. Navy looked to theory to determine its composition and future course.

In order to understand the development of U.S. naval doctrine, it is critical to examine the role of U.S. sea power theory and its evolution. War on the sea dates from ancient times, but strategic sea power theory is a relatively new phenomenon. For centuries, naval force was not considered independent of other forms of warfare, nor was it formally tied (at least in theory) to a nation's strategic success. The military role of navies was quite straightforward: ships evolved as weapons platforms in a relatively consistent manner to fight other ships or operate in support of land operations—either by transporting troops or engaging in offensive operations against shore fortifications. "Theory," such as it was, focused almost exclusively on successfully coordinating operations at sea to find the enemy and concentrate naval power effectively. Although tactics and operational methods evolved over time, for the bulk of naval history, theory was not an important element, as the means for success at sea was relatively apparent to sailors and their commanders.

Ships and fighting methods evolved following a natural progression in the relationship between armament and size. As armament became more sophisticated (and weighty), ships naturally grew to accommodate their weapons. Larger ships with increased firepower were key to victory in battle. In the simplest sense, those powers with large ships and fleets inevitably dominated at sea. So long as technology remained relatively "equal" between all competing naval powers (i.e., all sides were able to build and employ the weapons of the day, something that was possible when ships were wind-driven and guns relatively low-tech), this formula held true. The use of sail power, for example, lasted for centuries with comparatively little change save for the accuracy of cannon. There was little need for the development of comprehensive theory to employ navies strategically.

This changed with the advent of new technologies that threatened to radically alter the "big ship" paradigm. In the aftermath of the American Civil War, these came in rapid succession as the nations of the world engaged in mass industrialization. Steam power made ships more mobile, the rifled breech-loading cannon allowed for far more accurate and rapid fire, and the development of new underwater weapons (such as mines and torpedoes) altered the calculus of the large ship/mass firepower model. Moreover, secondary technologies such as radio for communications and the use of aircraft for scouting (and later attack) added new elements of complexity to naval operations. The rapidity of these developments and the subsequent race among the great naval powers to develop new and larger ships that could potentially capitalize on (or counter) them produced an interesting dilemma: in the absence of a major power clash, how could the effect of these technologies be determined? In an era of worldwide peace—or at least without major power conflict—what was the role of naval power? Into this breech stepped a generation of naval theorists whose attempts to answer these questions and subsequent influence is still being felt today.

Although a number of theorists gained prominence in the era following the American Civil War, none was as significant to the development of U.S. naval power as Alfred Thayer Mahan. The theory he proposed for sea power took the world by storm, directly influencing the development of navies worldwide. As we shall see, Mahan was no radical—rather, he was a U.S. naval officer deeply imbued with the established principles of his fellow officers. But unlike other members of his class, Mahan attempted to define the role of the U.S. Navy in global terms, using naval history to distill principles of sea power that would ultimately argue for the naval expansion of the United States to be on par with those of the other great powers. Writing during a politically contentious period that was fertile ground for his theories, Mahan essentially argued that historically great powers were sea powers, employing large battle fleets to exert influence worldwide—a message that was well received by Great Britain and the United States, which at the time was seeking to enter the world stage as a rising power. Although there was much in Mahan that was already dated by the time of his writing (he largely ignored or underestimated the development of new technologies such as the submarine and airplane), his historical argument for the development of sea power was wildly popular. Mahan's theory became the basis and rationale for the development of a large, "blue water" Navy for the United States and continued development of capital ship power, an action completely in alignment with the culture embraced by his fellow officers. This fact is not new. While much has been written about Mahan as a strategic thinker (in a similar vein as Clausewitz or Douhet), this thesis examines how the U.S. Navy interpreted Mahan and how this interpretation impacted the employment of sea power in irregular conflicts. While it is true that other strategic theorists had similar influence on the core theories of other services—Liddell Hart on U.S. Army tank doctrine, and Douhet on the theories of strategic bombing employed by the Air Force—Mahan's influence is unique in that while the core theories of other strategists were modified over time by their respective services, the Navy's interpretation of Mahan remains relatively consistent despite the changing nature of conflict. This thesis will explain why.

For the U.S. Navy, Mahan (rightly or wrongly) translated into a core theory that came to be almost exclusively based upon a single naval asset—the capital ship. In capital ship theory, this asset is all-important, and preserving and promoting it drives both strategy and doctrine, a condition that began with Mahan and continues to the present day. The definition of capital ship in this case possesses a number of key characteristics: it is large and fast, operates on the high seas, and is capable of projecting significant strike power either against other vessels or shore targets. The capital ship is in itself a symbol of national power and presented as such. These characteristics were present in the earliest battleships developed by the United States and continued as the capital ship morphed into its current form, the aircraft carrier. It is important to note the capital ship theory requires that the asset be able to function in multiple roles; the mere ability to strike is not enough. Capital ships project power through their representative presence as well as being able to perform missions in multiple dimensions against multiple threats. Within these requirements an aircraft carrier would be considered a capital ship, whereas a ballistic missile submarine—certainly far more powerful in terms of the ability to deliver explosive nuclear strike power—would not be, due to its specialization toward one mission.

Historically, it has been argued that Mahan's vision was successfully validated during the naval operations of the twentieth century, culminating in the strategic contribution of sea power during the Second World War. Operational history and theory seemed to be mutually reinforcing in 1945 when the capital ships, components of the "two-ocean war," reigned supreme. In the eyes of the victors, sea power and fleet power were one and the same; the clear lesson to be learned from the global conflict was distinctly Mahanian—great powers maintained great fleets capable of sweeping the seas of any opponent as a means to achieve national objectives. This position, dramatically illustrated in 1945, has effectively never changed for the United States Navy, whose subsequent strategies to the modern day reflect this core principle.

But is this position valid? It is widely accepted (even by the most avowed navalists) that sea power alone cannot win wars; rather, the effective use of sea power is best determined in relation to an overall national or military strategy. But beyond the specific example of a largely ocean war (such as the Pacific campaign during World War II) what is the strategic impact of sea power? Unlike warfare on land, where a single battle or campaign can have decisive results, the effects of naval power are far more indirect and often nebulous. Mahan argued that decisive battle was the main determinant for the impact of sea power—decisive battle that would eliminate the enemy and thus ensure unimpeded command of the sea. It therefore followed that ships must be designed primarily for this battle. But decisive battle at sea is historically quite rare, and the impact of other supporting naval missions is often not apparent until well after a conflict is complete. Throughout history there have been a number of naval battles—Salamis, Trafalgar, and Midway are noted examples—whose strategic impact was obvious. But most of the time, naval forces have either operated in support of broad strategic objectives (for example, the use of naval power to maintain Britain's empire) or in support of operations ashore. Even during the Second World War, supposedly the classic case study for the use of fleet power in battle, the day-to-day role of naval forces was far more indirect than active combat. This is not reflected in current naval theory.

Naval theory is singularly unique both in terms of how it is devised and also in its impact on force composition. Military theory is nothing new—since the time of Thucydides, theorists have speculated on the course and causes of war and used that theory to develop military power for future war or to rationalize force structure. But naval theory has a number of singular characteristics. Historically, military theory has overwhelmingly focused on land conflicts and, moreover, was tested repeatedly in battle—theory that was not successful on the field was often rapidly relegated to the dust bin. For naval power, however, practical tests have been, at best, inconclusive and rare.

As direct fleet battle is a relatively rare occurrence, the actual strategic impact of naval power was (and is) the subject of intense debate. Naval missions that are as nebulous as "presence" or even "blockade" have, at best, secondary impact on the course of a conflict that is either long-term or not immediately apparent. This makes analysis of these missions difficult—and subject to the whims of popular theory if there is no obvious evidence to support "results." This means that the impact of sea power is given to historical analysis such as that performed by Mahan, but this analysis has proven to be vulnerable to individual bias. Mahan, the product of a Navy culture that stressed fleet power and an unapologetic anglophile, wrote a work whose conclusions heavily favored the fleet and used England's path to imperialism as an example to be emulated. His theories were not only accepted but became a cornerstone of naval theorists arguing for the strategic impact of large fleets. Alternatives, such as the fact that irregular warfare has always been part and parcel, to some degree, of maritime conflict and therefore could have significant contribution to sea power theory, were (and are) ignored as not part of the populist trend.

Because actual combat on the sea is a rarity, naval theory is critically important not just for projected operations but also because it has a direct impact on force procurement. It is a historical fact that the design and building of ships takes time and is a fantastically expensive endeavor. This was as true during the age of sail (the HMS *Victory*, Nelson's flagship, took six years to build, used 2,000 oak trees, and cost over 63,000 pounds) as in the industrial age, when cost associated with fleets and naval technology became an even more significant factor in determining composition and use. The average life cycle, from concept to launch, for a modern warship is twenty years—assuming that all political and economic elements that impact its creation are in alignment. Modern warships are usually designed for the war of the future or the immediate future, using speculative threat assessment and utilizing technology that may exist only on a drawing board. Because of this, how they are to be used is almost always based in strategic theory—and if theory changes, so too will the design of the ship, an enormous effort that may or may not result in the ship being built at all. These facts create a tendency to adhere to prevailing theory at all costs.

While other nations may have moved away from capital ship theory, in the post–World War II era, the Navy's adoption of the role as a global strategic force complemented its desire to remain wedded to its theory, a condition that exists to this day. This obviously required a huge investment in personnel and material to design, build, and maintain a capital ship fleet. With such an investment in creating a fleet that is designed to excel in a Mahanian-style open-ocean decisive battle, a change in the paradigm is a significant threat not only to that fleet (and, arguably, national security if proven wrong) but also to careers, funding, prestige, future procurement—the list goes on and on.

Given these factors, it is perhaps understandable that the U.S. Navy is resistant to change. But it is clear that the world has changed. Reliance on traditional theory continues today in current operations despite the fact that the requirements of the current conflict are far divorced from decisive battle at sea. Although global irregular warfare is intrinsically complex, in the strategic sense there are two overriding demands that must be addressed by sea power. First, "terrorists" must be defeated by a broad application of power, ranging from traditional military/strike operations to "smart" or "soft" power focusing on support and development. Second, the homeland must be protected against external threat, including "response"-style contingency operations in the event that atrocity strikes.

Navalists claim these demands can be met using classical naval principles. In theory, the Navy is operating forward in accordance with classic naval theoretical principles, using kinetic power against terrorists ashore through strike operations and protecting the homeland by striking enemies far from the shores of the United States. But the impact of these actions cannot be easily seen or, more importantly, measured. In lieu of immediate or obvious results, one can use theory to argue effectiveness even if this result is debatable. The lack of reaction, response, or presence of an enemy allows for the claim of success when in fact naval power may have had nothing to do with enemy inaction, especially in irregular warfare where the enemy often operates in the shadows. Thus the Navy after 9/11 can claim that terrorists have been "deterred" from attacking the United

States by sea due to the aggressive forward presence it has taken overseas—although in reality kinetic actions against "terrorists" have been extremely limited and other impacts unknown. The danger of this adherence to theory is that while the Navy can claim success, in fact our nation may be increasingly vulnerable to irregular threats that can use the sea with impunity both at home and abroad.

This poses a challenge to the U.S. Navy. Global irregular warfare continues with no end in sight; while the current global jihad initiated by Al Qaida may wane, the fact remains that irregular warfare is now the weapon of choice. Crisis contingency operations occur more frequently, demanding a flexible and often irregular response. While it is true that the Navy has taken some steps to fight in a more unconventional manner with the design of smaller units dedicated to special operations, overall the Navy has not adjusted to the current IW challenge, continuing to pursue a doctrinal course that stresses its readiness for traditional blue-ocean combat in accordance with its established core principles. This thesis argues that the U.S. Navy has not met the challenge of irregular warfare and explains why this is the case. This is a case study examining how the Navy reacts to new threats, be they external foreign enemies, new types of warfare, or domestic challenges to its culture and established theory. This thesis argues that given a different force structure, results could be far more effective.

In order to understand the impact culture and theory have had on the development of current naval force structure and strategy, this book is divided into three parts. It begins by examining the concept of irregular warfare as an evolving phenomenon, including the basis of current irregular warfare theory and how maritime power is important in its development. Next the history of Navy culture is examined in relation to the writings of Mahan, noting not only how his principles became engrained in Navy strategic thought but also how they were modified by his disciples, a fact evident not only in the operations of the Navy but also in the promulgation of its various strategies up to and including the present day. Finally, the new requirements of irregular warfare (including the execution of "smart power" missions, crisis contingency operations, and homeland security) are explored to describe a way ahead for the development of new naval theory to meet the irregular warfare threat.

One

The Changing Paradigm of War
The United States and Irregular Warfare Theory

It is perhaps one of the great ironies of military strategic thinking that historically the most common form of warfare is the one that until very recently has received the least amount of attention, both professionally and academically. Irregular warfare[1] has been a constant in military history, arguably far more so than any form of conventional war. But despite its frequency, it has always been regarded by the military profession as a marginal topic, not to be taken seriously by conventional forces and given very limited attention in strategic planning. This is particularly true of the United States as it emerged from the Second World War as a global superpower.[2]

Given the practical military history of the U.S., this limited attention to irregular warfare might seem surprising. The wars fought by colonial America were distinctly irregular in nature, the "minuteman" or militia mythos a distinct part of the popular culture. Even as the U.S. developed its conventional force, irregular conflicts ranging from the conquest of the American West to the Philippine insurrection were the rule, not the exception, in the U.S. military experience.[3] But as the U.S. emerged as a leader in the industrial revolution in the post–Civil War era, there emerged a distinct "American way of war" that stressed mechanization and mass conventional force that shifted focus away from the irregular mindset, so much so that even where irregular force was appropriate, the first choice was usually a conventional one.[4] The idea of creating an unconventional force to deal specifically with counter-insurgency (COIN) was formally recognized during the Kennedy administration and resulted in the official creation of the U.S. special operations community, which for a brief period of time enjoyed a unique status at the top of the military hierarchy. This timing was particularly fortuitous given the U.S. involvement in Vietnam and the distinctly irregular nature of that conflict. But with Kennedy's death and subsequent loss of sponsorship, the focus shifted away from specialized irregular warfare forces and back toward an attrition strategy using conventional forces. This conventional mindset remains today in all military branches.[5]

For the U.S., the attacks on September 11 obviously provided an impetus to change this focus. Much attention has been given to the irregular nature of the attacks, but what is perhaps more significant in terms of warfare trends for the future is the nature of the conflict that followed. Despite high expectations for the use of military force against the terrorist enemy, the subsequent conventional campaigns did not eliminate the threat; indeed, the argument has been made that they may in fact have enhanced the status of Al Qaida (ALQ) and led to its increased prestige and proliferation globally.[6] The proliferation of ALQ and its philosophy was in accordance with classic insurgency theory, which states that all an insurgency really has to do is survive, as this demonstrates its resourcefulness and power and acts as a recruiting tool.[7] When it became apparent in the aftermath of the invasions of Iraq and Afghanistan that the conflicts had devolved into irregular war, the operational rhetoric began to change. The Department of Defense soon began referring to the "long war" (then "overseas contingency operations") against violent extremists, a term indicative of the fact that there appeared to be no end in sight.[8] Some academics have gone so far as to describe the ongoing "global insurgency," noting that the extremist rhetoric of ALQ is not only spreading but is actively cited in a number of ongoing conflicts which previously had little to do with Islamist philosophy.[9] The attacks of 9/11 illustrated that IW can be successful in setting the conditions for war against a conventional power and subsequently driving the narrative of conflict and as such have made it the war of choice not only for growing global insurgencies against the West but also for those waging internal and regional conflicts worldwide.

Irregular warfare has often been characterized (disdainfully) as "the strategy of the weak."[10] While this may have been true in the past when applied to various insurgencies—and the point is itself debatable, as often these insurgencies have prevailed—the success of the global insurgency against the West indicates that this viewpoint is not only wrong, but also potentially irrelevant. Strength or weakness, traditionally measured purely in terms of force size and the ability to apply kinetic force, is now measured in the success or failure of the global campaign and regionally specific victories of irregular elements. Irregular warfare thus represents a significant challenge, mainly because in the modern era it is often easier for an enemy to succeed in IW than for a conventional force to defeat it.

Irregular warfare's greatest strength is that it is enormously adaptive for a non-professional force fighting against a conventional enemy. Modern technology is as much a force multiplier for insurgents as for conventional combat troops, perhaps more so given that it is adopted far more quickly. The flexible use of secure communication now allows for IW forces to exercise global strategic influence not only on the propaganda front, but also in the potential to coordinate global insurgent strikes, an ability especially pertinent to terrorist groups. The length of this ongoing irregular struggle, the global scope, and the clear threat it poses to the West and the U.S. homeland make this irregular war unique in one very clear respect: it is now a strategic threat, and, with the emergence of ISIS, morphing. This has direct correlation with the United States' reliance on sea power as a strategic shield and capability to project power globally. In global struggles, the U.S. has used sea power's flexibility and sustainability repeatedly to ensure victory. But this use has been distinctly conventional and reliant on long developed traditional theory. How can it be used in the modern context of irregular warfare?

Before examining the impact of irregular warfare on naval theory and sea power, it is important to define irregular warfare as a concept. This task is fraught with difficulty, mainly because while most strategists agree that IW is an old (and consistent) concept that continues to exert influence on the spectrum of warfare, where exactly this concept fits (and its ultimate impact) in the modern era is a matter of intense debate. Many argue that IW, especially given the events post–9/11, is the new method of warfare and characteristic of future conflicts, while others (especially navalists) see IW as nothing but a distraction from the bigger picture, which will inevitably return to nation-state warfare where conflicts between battle fleets will take center stage.[11] This argument is nothing new; as we shall see, it was pursued vehemently in the aftermath of many of the irregular conflicts or operations conducted by the U.S. in the past. Regardless of which of these respective arguments will ultimately prevail, the fact that irregular warfare is a global phenomenon in the present requires an examination of the basic tenets of IW and how it will affect future concepts of sea power. This begins with history.

Modern U.S. Strategy and Irregular Warfare: A Brief Troubled Recent History

While irregular warfare is not new, serious study of the concept as an enduring challenge to established conventional military theory is very recent. Given the history of U.S. military actions following the Second World War, this is perhaps surprising. The longest protracted war ever fought by the United States—Vietnam—was almost exclusively an irregular-style conflict fought largely in a conventional manner with multiple lessons in the strategic, operational, and tactical realms.[12] Yet in the aftermath of America's defeat in Vietnam, there was a tendency to look at the war as an aberration with few subsequent lessons that could be employed in the context of the broader conventional conflict with the Soviet Union. Given the character of the then-ongoing Cold War and the humiliating defeat in Vietnam, this is perhaps understandable.

It is not the purpose of this study to review the lessons of Vietnam, but one point of interest regarding the U.S. military's attitude toward irregular warfare is the debate surrounding the nature of the war itself. Although the overwhelming number of historians and analysts characterize Vietnam as an irregular war, in the mid–1980s, Col. Harry Summers published his work *On Strategy*, which interpreted the war from a Clausewitzian viewpoint applied toward modern conventional operations. Summers's thesis was that the misinterpretation of the war at the time as an irregular conflict was the primary reason for defeat: that it was, in fact, a conventional conflict and should have been fought as such, in a traditional nation-versus-nation manner.[13] As an example of the unpopularity of irregular warfare, this thesis was seized on by many in the military as well as the conservative political establishment, leading to the foundation of an entirely new school of historical thought commonly referred to as "Hawk Revisionism."[14] Whether this school is correct is not the point; the rapid rise of it and its popularity, on the other hand, are illustrative of how unpopular IW is in many military circles. But while for many military officers the end of U.S. involvement in Vietnam seemed to be the end of irregular warfare, history would show that the practitioners of IW were not done with the U.S.[15]

Since the conclusion of the Second World War, the United States has been involved in at least four conflicts that could be described as "irregular" wars: Vietnam, Lebanon, Somalia, and Bosnia—and, of course, Afghanistan and Iraq.[16] Of these, only Bosnia could be described as a "victory" of sorts.[17] The final strategic results of the wars in Iraq and Afghanistan, clearly irregular in nature, remain undecided.[18] Yet despite the heavy involvement of U.S. forces in these conflicts, the concept of IW remained something of a misnomer in the military. Although IW received various surges of attention in the early and late 1990s (going under various names such as Low-Intensity Conflict (LIC), 4th Generation, or Hybrid War), the concept was not taken seriously by the military services—especially the Navy, whose strategies continued to focus almost exclusively on traditional forward and conventional blue-water operations.[19] But the Navy was not alone in its rationale for continued reliance on Cold War-style missions and forces; although it has a unique strategic culture in emphasizing decisive battle against a large conventional opponent, this culture was largely shared (and justified) by the defense establishment as a whole. There are a number of important reasons for this.

The sudden collapse of the Soviet Union forced the Department of Defense to radically redefine its focus. The end of the Cold War effectively heralded an almost complete reversal of the main planning scenario that had dominated the West for over forty years. While the United States and the Soviet Union never actually engaged in open warfare, the potential for global conflict and various acts of brinksmanship during the course of the Cold War drove all elements of planning, training, and procurement for the respective superpowers and their allies. In terms of strategic planning, the general theory held that if such a conflict were to occur, it would happen on a global scale and in accordance with accepted guidelines of state-versus-state nuclear or conventional war.[20] The theoretical U.S.-Soviet conflict dominated military and geopolitical theory for so long that it became a standard by which all other wars were measured. As time went on, the accepted scenario of the East-West conflict shifted from one that would result in an inevitable (and globally catastrophic) nuclear exchange to one that favored a prolonged conventional war, a theory that continued up to the sudden collapse of the Soviet Union.[21] The fall of the Berlin Wall and the rapid dissolution of the Soviet Union brought with it the collapse of this dominant theory. The sudden and dramatic end of this period resulted in wide speculation as to the type of warfare that would be waged in the future. The vacuum created by the lack of a major state enemy caused many analysts to speculate that the entire character of warfare changed with the end of the Cold War, some going so far as to say that warfare between nations was a thing of the past.[22] By extension, the very idea of war itself seemed outdated.

Despite idealistic rhetoric concerning the spread of a global peace and the potential of a "peace dividend,"[23] it soon became readily apparent that geopolitical conflict was not a thing of the past. Saddam Hussein's largely conventional invasion of Kuwait and the subsequent Western response clearly indicated that war between states was not something that was outdated, at least as far as the world outside the East-West paradigm was concerned. The Western response to the invasion of Kuwait was almost purely conventional, illustrating that conventional forces still had a place in the world's arsenals.[24] But compared to global trends in warfare, this was a somewhat rare event. Continuing and increasingly violent "brushfire wars" in Africa and Asia took on new significance both in terms of frequency of occurrence and severity. During the Cold War these "low-intensity conflicts" (LICs) were viewed by Western analysts as parts of the grander East-West global conflict, usually through the direct or indirect sponsorship of one of the opponents (in hindsight this black and white analysis was almost completely wrong).[25] These irregular wars had been with us all along but had been marginalized in terms of the larger East-West conflict; in the post–Cold War era they took on new meaning and importance for global security. They were now sources of violent extremism. The brushfire wars of the 1990s were unique in that they were characterized by increasing use of advanced technology that allowed conflicts to spread rapidly (with associated increased violence), the increasing involvement of non-state actors as central figures rather than peripheral combatants, and a far greater reliance on ideological rationale (especially religious) for conflict.[26] These factors demonstrated an increased flexibility and diversity in warfare that was (and is) difficult to quantify. In short, what the demise of the U.S.-Soviet rivalry brought about was not so much peace, but rather complexity.

This complexity brought with it an enormous challenge to established strategic thinking within the Department of Defense and the analytical community that supported it. Simply put, conventional war was cemented in the American tradition. Even the most cursory analysis of the LICs of the 1990s illustrated that mass conventional force was not the answer for successful conflict resolution.[27] The collapse of the Soviet Union left a void for the potential future use of conventional force. Massive demobilization was obviously not in the interest of DOD or the defense industry. With no obvious threat that could immediately justify the huge bureaucratic structure of DOD and the military branches, a threat had to be defined to rationalize maintaining a significant portion of the force structure that had been established to fight the Cold War. From a purely bureaucratic standpoint, time was of the essence given that the fall of the Soviets had revived the classic "guns or butter" debate common to discussions of military funding. Politically, if the traditional enemy that had defined the defense establishment was gone, the U.S. military was in the uncomfortable position of facing massive cutbacks and perhaps even disestablishment of a well-defined (and well-funded) organization.[28] Conventional war, the rationale for virtually the entire structure of DOD, had to be redefined to illustrate relevance. The approach that was eventually adopted was twofold: providing a rationalization for the collapse of the Soviet Union that was tied into the defense establishment and devising future scenarios that would justify the maintenance of that force. It should be noted, however, that the point is controversial. While there is no doubt that viewing the Soviet Union as the enemy was beneficial to the defense establishment, this is not to imply that the actions taken by the Department of Defense and other agencies were aligned with some form of conspiracy to keep the United States militaristic. As a global world leader, the U.S. would be expected to face some form of threat in the future; in accordance with established norms, this would traditionally be considered to be some form of conventional threat.[29] But study of and emphasis on IW suffered.

The rationalization for the collapse of the Soviet Union took an interesting turn that was pursued aggressively, both militarily, as a reason for continued reliance on high-tech conventional power, and politically, as part of the Right's historical interpretations of its own actions. This has become a popular mythos in many conservative circles of the United States. Rather than examine the myriad of social and political factors that led to the downfall of the Soviets, DOD's position—backed by a conservative establishment dedicated to the memory of the Reagan administration as well as a myriad of defense contractors—maintained that the Soviet Union had collapsed because of military pressure, recognizing that it could not "win" in the face of U.S. high tech weaponry (the Strategic Defense Initiative, or SDI, being the most commonly cited system), the Soviets had simply given up.[30] Given the widespread social and economic problems of the Soviet Union, this thesis is, at best, dubious but still argued vehemently today by both politicians and military officers who view the Reagan administration as the apex of government effectiveness.[31] This is simplistic; the collapse of the Soviet Union was immensely complex and clearly not due to one factor.[32] But it did serve as a starting premise for future strategic planning at DOD.

Technological superiority was the mainstay of Western conventional forces and seemed to be a significant component in victory in the Cold War, so this element was continually stressed in post–Cold War strategic documents. The success of coalition forces in the first Gulf War seemed to reaffirm this viewpoint. In the aftermath of the fall of the Soviet Union, the main thesis of joint planning documents stressed the rise of a new "revolution in military affairs" (RMA) that promoted the use of information networks, cyber war, and continued development of high-tech weaponry under the guise of the concept of Net Centric Warfare (NCW) and ultimately Transformation.[33] "Transformation" was an official Pentagon program initially defined by Defense Secretary Donald Rumsfeld prior to 9/11 and continued with various degrees of success until his retirement in 2006. The basic concept of Transformation was increased reliance on high-tech and networked weapons and systems that would act as a force multiplier for conventional forces. It should be noted that while it seems this would be ideal for confronting irregular forces, the bulk of the systems that incorporated these principles were designed for traditional, conventional conflict. Although these concepts seem to be in alignment with IW, the reality is they were applied almost exclusively to the development of conventional force.[34] In the accepted view of the time, conventional power had defeated the Soviet Union; "transformed" conventional power could deal with all future threats. It is perhaps significant that the first articulation of the concept of net-centric warfare, a key element of transformation, was devised by a Navy vice admiral.[35]

The conventional mindset was formally reflected in official documents that related transformation to established conventional power. All services (but particularly the Navy), expressed this view in the official Quadrennial Defense Review (QDR), released almost on the eve of 9/11. For the purposes of sea power and IW, its content is telling. A comprehensive review of the entire U.S. military conducted every four years by law, the QDR provides guidance for the individual branches and DOD as to the way ahead for force procurement and training. Each branch assigns officers to the QDR staff who are theoretically neutral in their analysis but often are representative of their respective service cultures and traditions.[36] What the 2001 QDR says about IW for naval forces is illuminating. For the Navy, IW was defined not as a priority singular mission, but rather as a set of peripheral missions that are part of the traditional Navy lexicon, such as mine and amphibious warfare.[37] Missions for the Navy, including those defined as "irregular," are almost exclusively "kinetic" and executed under a broad strategy of conventional naval combat against a forward opponent.[38] Non-kinetic "peace operations" (which are a key component for the successful prosecution of IW) are noted in the document, but only in terms of how they detract from conventional capability.[39] The message was clear: non-kinetic operations were not part of the Navy's conventional lexicon and could in fact be harmful to its overall mission by detracting from procurement and training necessary to fight a conventional war. This trend to support established theory and conventional power is nothing new nor is it unique to the Navy. But unlike the other branches, which adapted relatively quickly to the challenges of IW in the immediate aftermath of 9/11 and the onset of global conflict both in Iraq and Afghanistan, as well as in operations in support of the GWOT, the Navy stubbornly held to its conventional mindset. We will examine this point later in greater detail.[40]

It was not until the post-9/11 era and the subsequent conflicts in Iraq and Afghanistan that irregular warfare received formal attention and serious study from the Department of Defense and its components. And there is no doubt that IW as a subject has exploded; dozens of offices were established at the Pentagon to study the subject while the civilian and academic world produced hundreds of works examining Al Qaida, the conflicts in Iraq and Afghanistan, and the "new" irregular threat.[41] But even this trend had mixed results, perhaps most importantly in the strategic and bureaucratic realms. Organizationally, the Defense Department responded to the new "Global War on Terror" (GWOT)[42] by assigning responsibility to one of its combatant commanders—special operations command (USSOCOM)—as the coordinator for global irregular and counter-terrorism operations.[43] At first glance this would seem to be a logical step. There is no doubt that SOCOM possessed both the talent and expertise to deal with the combative elements of IW, but its influence was only effective to a certain point. Special operations have never been a core focus for the U.S. military, and SOCOM lacks any major forces beyond those that are assigned in the special warfare community.[44] This assignment of responsibility can be seen in both positive and negative lights; on the one hand, the U.S. dedicated significant assets and the right expertise to the problem (at least on the ground); on the other, by assigning primary responsibility to the special operations community, the more conventional forces could effectively wash their hands of the IW mission and focus on traditional operations.

For purposes of this study, this is significant, because assuming IW lies in the realm of special operations allows continued emphasis on the conventional force structure for missions outside of the IW realm—a logical action, if in fact there were other conventional enemies to fight. While it is true that the military plans for the future in the design of its forces, the fact remains that conventional power is being reduced worldwide; in terms of sea power, most nations are cutting back on their fleets and technological capability at sea to fight conventionally, not increasing it.[45] Yet the U.S. military—and especially the sea services—continue to return to a conventional mindset, assuming that IW is either transitory, a specialized area of warfare, or both. In modern times it is neither. This is evident when examining the core principles of IW.

Irregular Warfare: Definitions and Debates

Irregular warfare is an enormously diverse and complex phenomenon. As we have seen, prior to the attacks of 9/11, conventional warfare theory still held sway for the bulk of U.S. military planning and strategic theory; warfare outside the conventional realm was considered the purview of very specialized units and special operations forces or was addressed by limited adaptation of conventional forces for short periods of time.[46] Both Iraq and Afghanistan challenged this line of thought. While these conflicts began as conventional wars, they swiftly shifted to irregular conflicts that defied easy categorization. The U.S. is learning an ancient lesson: irregular warfare is variable, often region-specific, and very messy.

Irregular warfare is a remarkably diverse phenomenon, often defying textbook approaches in successful prosecution. In the simplest terms, geography and timing are critical; the lessons learned from one war often do not apply in the face of new cultures, terrain, and technological advancement. Because IW is so diverse, theory matters. Theory drives both force composition and, perhaps more importantly, training to deal with the vast diversity of conflicts that are broadly defined by the term irregular warfare.[47] The scope of IW in the modern era is also important. If irregular warfare were a limited phenomenon (as many in the pre–9/11 era argued) then the old approach—the use of highly trained SOF conducting operations for limited objectives—would seem appropriate. But the attacks of 9/11 and the subsequent Global War on Terror automatically propelled irregular warfare into the strategic realm. The enemy in these conflicts—of which Al Qaida and ISIS are the current but probably not the last examples—represent a global, not a localized threat. This factor increases the spectrum of conflict enormously as IW represents a significant strategic challenge on the global stage. In short, irregular wars are no longer the quaint "little wars" of times past.

That the U.S. military has not adapted effectively to the challenges of IW would seem apparent from the prolonged campaigns fought in Afghanistan, Iraq, and other theaters in the GWOT. What will become equally apparent is that while the subject has been addressed extensively by both official and academic sources in the aftermath of 9/11, there is still a great deal of debate with regard to what actually constitutes IW. This is important in terms of sea power in that if the concept cannot be properly defined it is fair to say that it will be almost impossible to adapt current sea power theory (and eventually doctrine, to say nothing of procurement strategy) to effectively meet the needs of the global conflict.

The problem of definition has certainly not been ignored by the U.S. military's doctrinal lexicon, but the results have been something less than satisfying. The *Irregular Warfare Joint Operating Concept* currently defines irregular warfare as:

> ... a violent struggle among state and non-state actors for legitimacy and influence over relevant populations. Irregular warfare favors indirect and asymmetric approaches, though it may employ the full range of military and other capabilities in order to erode an adversary's power, influence, and will.[48]

What is striking is how remarkably generic and all-encompassing this definition is; at first glance, it would seem that IW potentially encompasses everything that conventional warfare is not—although the definition does state that conventional kinetic means may be required to conduct IW (further confusing the issue). From a doctrinal or practical standpoint, this presents challenges to the strategist or practitioner as it provides little specificity as to how military forces are to deal with the concept.

The official definition of IW is not the only one in existence, nor is this definition universally agreed upon. Indeed, the diversity of work in both the professional military and academic community surrounding irregular warfare prior to 9/11 was one of the factors that contributed to its low regard with the traditionalists who favor the conventional approach—if an phenomenon could not even be defined, it was difficult to plan for (or even be taken seriously, for that matter).[49] The problem of definition became even more difficult as the tactics and techniques of irregular warfare were moved beyond local and regional conflicts to the global stage by international movements such as ALQ (and now ISIS), terrorist groups that are capable of adapting to a wide range of regional conflicts and circumstances. What was complex before became even more so, and increasingly controversial.

There are, however, a number of definitions that bear examination in relation to strategic force (and sea power). In *The Sling and the Stone*, T.X. Hammes provides a definition of the characteristics of what he calls "fourth generation" warfare (4GW) that attempts to further refine IW's strategic elements:

> Fourth Generation warfare uses all available networks—political, economic, social, and military—to convince the enemy's political decision makers that their strategic goals are either unachievable or too costly for the perceived benefit. It is an evolved form of insurgency. Still rooted in the fundamental precept that superior political will, when properly employed, can defeat greater economic and military power, 4GW makes

use of society's networks to carry on its fight. Unlike previous generations of warfare, it does not attempt to win by defeating the enemy's military forces. Instead, via the networks, it directly attacks the minds of enemy decision makers to destroy the enemy's political will. Fourth generation wars are lengthy—measured in decades rather than months or years.[50]

The theory of 4GW postulates that irregular warfare becomes far more strategic when an insurgency utilizes all available means in a culture or society to indirectly target a conventional power's vulnerabilities outside the classic military realm. This is a modern trend,[51] possible due to the global proliferation of communications and media technology that allows for instantaneous communication between irregular elements as well as exploitation of social media. Hammes notes the increasing trend in conflict toward these types of operations, citing the successes of modern insurgencies that have utilized these tactics, including the Sandanistas, the tribal networks in Afghanistan, the Ba'thists in Iraq, and of course the operations of Al Qaida.

Frank Hoffman expands this examination of irregular warfare through his theory of "hybrid war." Hoffman agrees with Hammes that warfare has become increasingly more complex through its increased use of societal elements but argues that irregular warfare in the modern sense is far more than insurgency or counter-insurgency. Rather, it is a multi-nodal or multivariant phenomenon where an enemy will attempt to utilize all elements traditionally found on the use of force spectrum—including a combination of conventional, irregular, and insurgent or terrorist forces. The highly networked nature of hybrid conflicts allows this combination of diverse elements to be successful where they had failed in the past.[52] This is not simply a matter of "compound war," where conventional and irregular forces operate together; rather, it is a blurring through technology, networks, and shared ideology (Hoffman uses the Second Lebanon War in 2006 to illustrate a classic example of hybrid war that effectively neutralized a conventional opponent). Hybrid wars blend the lethality of state conflict with the protracted and fanatical fervor of traditional irregular war.[53]

Despite its diversity, irregular warfare is still war and as such possesses a number of characteristics that are similar to conventional conflicts. First, in the finest tradition of Clausewitz, the ultimate goal of IW is to change the enemy's political position. Clausewitz most famously noted that the political is at the heart of conflict; the enemy fights for a reason; identifying that reason and determining effective ways to attack it are at the heart of a successful strategic campaign. In the modern military lexicon, this is usually identified as the enemy's "center of gravity" (COG).[54] Where COG differs in IW is that it is often more diverse (ideologically, culturally, religiously, or a combination of the three), consequently making actions designed to change it equally diverse.[55]

Second, like conventional war, IW has the tendency to reflect the society of which it is part. Again, this is quite similar to a conventional mindset that argues that states ultimately train and fight in accordance with the principles of their national characters. In the academic and professional lexicon, much has been made of the "western way of war" (which stresses technology and the delivery of massive firepower) and how this directly affects force composition and the use of conventional military power in the U.S.; much the same could be said of the Afghan Mujahadheen, who fight in accordance within established tribal boundaries and methods.[56]

Third, like conventional war, IW undergoes evolution in consonance with society and the practical impact of operations in the field.[57] It is here, perhaps, that we see the greatest divergence; whereas in conventional war an opponent may opt to negotiate or surrender with the loss of territory, cities, or armies, irregular forces (driven by an ideological component) are far more likely to go underground and adapt. Irregular wars therefore truly become "the long wars."[58]

Regardless of the particulars of these individual theories, there are a number of common points on which they agree that invite emphasis. Modern irregular warfare is remarkably diverse, complex, and effective both operationally and strategically. The diversity of irregular warfare—as well as its new effects strategically—demands a response that is similarly diverse. Like many of the elements of irregular warfare, a successful response to it is still in the theoretical stages. As we shall see, much of this response is focused on areas that are not traditionally part of the military realm, including application of various elements of "soft" power designed to target the insurgent base of support in the population.[59]

Sea Power and Irregular Warfare

Discussion to this point has dealt with the individual tenets of irregular warfare and various modern elements that make it a strategic phenomenon. While all this may be well and good, what do these factors have to do with the application of sea power?

First and perhaps most importantly, sea power in itself is a strategic element of national power and as such is designed to deal with strategic threats—of which IW is most certainly a modern manifestation. In the past, where IW was largely a localized or regional phenomenon, the argument could be made that it was best relegated to those forces (almost always land-based or special operations type assets) for action. This is no longer the case. The U.S. Navy has been designed as and has always prided itself on being a strategic force; one can make the argument that this claim to be strategic is invalid if sea power cannot address a means of warfare that is used to implement a strategic threat, especially one that potentially employs the sea. The fact that irregular warfare has moved into the strategic realm both at home and abroad demands that sea power adapt to it if it is to remain a relevant strategic force.

Second, this threat is not limited to actions taken against the United States overseas. As the great global commons, the sea can be used by all, including irregular forces conducting operations directly against the United States. The sea is a force multiplier in terms of mobility and flexibility for an irregular enemy as much as (if not more so) for an opponent using unconventional means as one using an established Navy. Given the relative ease by which ocean transit can be accomplished and the fact that the vast majority of the world's oceans are unregulated and unmonitored, the sea presents an excellent venue from which to launch an attack either against forces deployed overseas or against the homeland of the United States. Technology that has made the sea such an effective element of globalization has also enabled it to be used far more easily as a method for war—and as the attacks of 9/11 illustrated, that war has now come to the homeland of the United States. Navigation, seamanship and the expertise to employ weaponry, formerly solidly confined to the realm of trained experts, is now far less complex when relying on modern seaborne and military technology (such as readily available GPS). U.S. naval power has always been the great defense against these forms of operations and developed to such an extent that a conventional threat is almost inconceivable; this is not true with the new challenge of irregular warfare.

Third, on a more operational level, the very diversity represented by the challenge of irregular warfare requires an equally diverse response. Although many authors and strategists disagree on the finer points of what constitutes an irregular conflict, there is almost universal agreement that various non-kinetic methods—ranging from "soft power" to applied application of combat power—must be utilized for a conventional power to emerge victorious. Sea power possesses the inherent mobility and flexibility to rapidly apply various degrees of power along the force continuum from peaceful to kinetic. As such, when properly applied it can be a tremendous force multiplier for a nation fighting an irregular conflict.

Given these factors, it would seem that the U.S. Navy would be quick to adapt to the challenges of the IW threat and modify traditional missions to meet that challenge. To date this has not occurred. The reasons for this are complex and deeply rooted in the cultural psyche of sea power theorists and advocates who, despite the increasing need, remain wedded to a traditional conventional mindset, a mindset that has been developed, indoctrinated, and defended since the Navy became a global force at the turn of the 19th century. This is evident when we examine the history of U.S. sea power theory.

Two

The Philosophy
A. T. Mahan and the Foundations of U.S. Naval Thought

At the turn of the 19th century, the United States Navy underwent a massive expansion that fundamentally altered it from a relatively low-tech coastal defense force to a modern fleet capable of global deployment. Coinciding with the entrance of the United States into the world scene as a global power, the timing of this expansion was fortuitous, but it was not inevitable. The pieces were certainly there: an expansionist nation, new technology, increased militarism—but there was no unifying rationale for the United States to become a competitor on the high seas. This was provided by Mahan.

Any study of modern sea power must begin with the man who first defined it, popularized it, and subsequently provided the bedrock rationale for U.S. naval theory. Alfred Thayer Mahan and his writings literally gave birth to the modern concept of sea power, from which sprang the modern battle fleet, an effect never seen before or since from a single work of strategy. While Mahan's theories remained influential well past his death, Mahan the man may perhaps be seen as something of an anachronism. Writing in the late 1800s, Mahan as a historian wrote from the distinctive 19th-century Western view of benign imperialism, a style that is today often regarded (at best) as quaint but misguided.[1] He was a naval officer with an admittedly limited operational background during a time of international modernization, an officer who despaired over modern technology and how it affected the traditions of the Navy. But due to a unique combination of international events, changing Navy culture, and luck, Mahan and his writings became the bedrock upon which the U.S. Navy (and others) launched sea power in the modern era. Often misinterpreted even in his own lifetime and frequently criticized both as a historian and strategist,

Mahan and his philosophy remain central for advocates of the modern battle fleet and the principles with which to employ it.

Mahan has been called many things—prophet, propagandist, imperialist, and philosopher, among others.[2] The scope of his work touches on each. Although he wrote as a historian, his work is important not for is contribution to history itself but rather for its effect on the development of major-power navies. Mahan's work as a historian has been roundly criticized on a number of points by academics throughout the years, including very limited focus, questionable research methods, and a simplistic comparison of American national characteristics with those of the British.[3] In fairness to Mahan, he was not a professional historian (coming to the profession late in life and somewhat incidentally) and was writing from as much a philosophical viewpoint as a strictly academic one.

Moreover, Mahan's attempts to apply strategic historical lessons to a modern problem was a new (and radical) approach to the discipline.[4] In this sense, few historians before or since have had his lasting impact; Mahan stands alone in philosophical and practical impact on the development of sea power and by extension the course the great powers steered in developing it. A naval officer who disliked going to sea, a historian with no formal training, his work revolutionized the use of history as an applied science and popularized a movement toward blue-water fleet navies worldwide. Within his lifetime his writings became gospel for both military and civilian leaders bent on imperialistic colonialism, providing justification for a massive naval arms race among the great—and emerging—powers. His work has been cited as having the same impact as that of Darwin[5]; while this may perhaps be an exaggeration, there is no doubt that his work has not only survived in the modern lexicon but also has undergone resurgence, his theories often cited by navalists[6] as demonstrating principles of eternal relevance for the use of the sea.

To understand Mahan as a theorist, it is critical to examine the man and his times. Mahan was very much the product of a specific and highly focused culture, a "band of brothers" imbued with the love of their profession above all else.[7] In this context the link between his profession, philosophy, and times become apparent over time, for initially there was little indication that Mahan was anything other than an average naval officer of the era. The early years of Mahan's life and professional career provide little indication of his future potential. Born into an Army family, young Alfred spent most of his young life at West Point, where his father served as superintendent. There is no indication that he took to a military lifestyle or that he was particularly influenced by his father's teachings or writings (the elder Mahan was the author of two minor classics on land tactics).[8] Despite the family background, he entered the Navy as a midshipman at sixteen. Mahan's time at Annapolis was unremarkable; by all accounts he was not a popular midshipman, undergoing "silencing" (a form of hazing where the midshipman is ignored for having committed some perceived infraction) for reporting a classmate for talking in the ranks. Mahan may have been part of the "naval aristocracy" at Annapolis, but he was not part of the "club."[9] Regardless of his social status, he did well academically, graduating second in his Annapolis class of twenty in 1858.[10]

The life of a naval officer in the late 1800s was first and foremost dedicated to sea duty. Mahan's seagoing career is fairly typical for the period and not particularly distinguished; indeed, for an advocate of sea power, he demonstrated a distinct dislike for sea duty, widely regarded as the seminal goal for the naval professional.[11] During the Civil War he served in several afloat assignments on blockade duty, a mission renowned for long and tedious monotony. It should be noted that although the Navy had expanded considerably to meet wartime needs and was experimenting rapidly with new technologies, it remained very much a wind-powered force. A traditionalist like many of his Annapolis classmates, Mahan expressed considerable affection for sailing ships while disliking for the conversion to steam—an odd opinion for a strategist, given the increased strategic and tactical mobility this technical innovation brought to the Navy, but very much in character for officers of his generation.[12] Following the war he had the opportunity to serve on cruises to both Europe and Asia, events that would have unforeseen consequences on his future career.

Sea duty was anything but glamorous for U.S. naval officers, its characteristics generally reflective of the service as a whole. The U.S. Navy in the post–Civil War era was stagnating in a period of slow, bordering on indifferent, modernization. The ironclad battles of Hampton Roads during the Civil War had worldwide impact on the design of fleets, but it was a lesson that the peacetime Navy was slow to adopt. Traditionalists steeped in the Annapolis vision of the old sailing fleet dominated the Navy both before and after the war. There is no doubt that navalists—a remarkably small and philosophically unified fraternity—favored a larger fleet and a greater role in national affairs.[13] But among naval officers the type of fleet that should be developed was very much in question. Modernization remained a contentious issue. During the war the newly designated naval corps of engineers had exercised great influence on the design of ships using new armor, engines, and ordnance required for the successful prosecution of the conflict, but in the peacetime Navy it rapidly lost influence.[14] But within the service a full-scale culture war between engineers and officers of the line was brewing, line officers (the bulk of the naval officer corps consisting entirely of Annapolis graduates) viewing the new technology as a threat to their finely honed skills in maneuvering sailing vessels. The traditionalists—admirals all—held sway, resulting in a postwar Navy composed of wooden ships haphazardly converted to steam, which was considered (at best) an auxiliary power source.[15] No real doctrine or construction plans existed for the Navy beyond a force that was capable of coastal defense or commerce raiding, missions that seemed appropriate given the relative isolationist stance the nation took during the period of reconstruction.[16] So long as there was disagreement over the composition of the force and appropriate missions for a future Navy, there was little if any hope for the service to expand beyond a very small and increasingly dilapidated third-rate force.

Interestingly, prior to his historical research that led to his writing career, Mahan echoed the traditionalist sentiment of the time that the United States did not need a large Navy so long as it was capable of expanding within its own borders, an attitude typical of the Annapolis fraternity mindset.[17] This would change dramatically during Mahan's self-imposed study while he was deployed overseas, a study that would ultimately serve not only to completely alter his thinking (and others') regarding the need for a large fleet but would also serve to bridge the gap between the technologists and traditionalists. Perhaps in an effort to stave off the boredom associated with long voyages, Mahan began a dedicated study of military classics with an eye toward an examination of the use and impact of naval power. This led to revelation. In his own words:

> It suddenly struck me, whether by some chance phrase of the author I do not know, how different things might have been could Hannibal have invaded Italy by sea, as the Romans often had Africa, instead of by the long land route; or could he, after arrival, have been in free communications with Carthage by water. This clew, once laid hold, I followed in the particular instance. It and the general theory already conceived threw on each other reciprocal illustration; and between the two my plan was formed by the time I reached home in September 1885.[18]

Mahan would subsequently pursue this line of thought to examine how sea power (a term he coined) influenced the historical development of nations, using the example of Great Britain as his model (the obvious choice, coincidentally loved by the traditionalists.) While his theory approaches the geopolitical in many respects and relies on messianic imperialism and a number of social-darwinist assumptions of the late 19th century that have largely been discredited,[19] he concluded through his analysis that great powers and empires owed their unique status to their respective abilities to use the sea freely as avenues of ever-expanding commerce and colonization. This could only be possible if the means of expansion (merchant or trading power) were protected, accomplished through the ability to exercise "command of the sea." The means of achieving and maintaining this command were through the development of a large battle fleet.[20] Although it was assumed that that this battle fleet would be "modern" in the sense of times (as was the British ship of the line during the period he examined), Mahan did not focus so much on the composition of the fleet but rather the use—in accordance with timeless strategic principles that he claimed to have distilled from his study.[21]

Although there were many elements to Mahan's theory of sea power (some of which, such as "national character," seem at best quaint to us today), the core of his thesis was simple. For a nation to become a sea power (and therefore a great power), it required an economic manufacturing base, overseas colonies, and a flourishing merchant marine.[22] To ensure the safety and security of these elements required a large fleet composed of the most powerful ships available. Therefore, great powers had great navies. To be a great power, build a Navy. As his model for historical examination was a British Navy composed of large and powerful ships of the line, a modern extrapolation of the historical theory indicated that only a fleet of capital ships could exert its influence worldwide. It would perhaps appear obvious today that as a naval officer Mahan would focus on his own profession as a means for international greatness and promote this to the public, but this must be considered in the context of the times. Prior to Mahan's writings, military branches—especially the Navy—were remarkably insular. Public opinion was simply not a factor for the vast majority of naval officers, who operated more or less in an independent aristocracy.[23] Services did not need to be "sold" to the public and generally held such activity as properly conducted by politicians operating in a realm that was unfamiliar and usually held in contempt. In the United States this gradually changed with a well-orchestrated public relations effort in Congress by the navalists in the late 1800s for new and larger ships, an action that opened the door for further efforts.[24] Mahan provided this by breaking with this tradition by writing for the public, a public that quickly became enamored with his work. While his seminal work, *The Influence of Sea Power on History*, was billed as a work of history, there is no doubt that it was also a call to his countrymen to develop as a naval power. It was meant to be read and to influence the reader toward a singular conclusion. In this it was completely and overwhelmingly successful, not only among those who knew the sea but also those who heretofore had not given it much thought as a path to international greatness, including not only a political base but also an enthusiastic populace who ultimately would pay for the rapid naval expansion required to fulfill Mahan's vision.

It is no secret that as a populist, Mahan's timing was impeccable. In terms of his appeal to the public, the time was remarkably ripe for Mahan's theories of geopolitical expansion. The United States had fulfilled the philosophy of Manifest Destiny in its successful westward expansion, an expansion that was ending at the time of Mahan's writing. The sea was the logical next step for those who saw global expansion as a natural extension of this movement. In the late 1890s, by happy coincidence, these personages were firmly entrenched in the U.S. political system or were in positions of influence and power. Many, such as Theodore Roosevelt, John Hay, Henry Cabot Lodge, and Albert J. Beverridge were not only intimately familiar with Mahan's theories but also knew him personally.[25] The influence of these men served to present Mahan's theories as a potential blueprint for practically implementing expansionist policies through sea power.

The sense of international expansionism these men represented would have been difficult to rationalize (or collectively express) without Mahan.[26] Traditionally, the U.S. had been reluctant to engage in foreign adventures; although it had been an active on the international stage since its founding, actions taken overseas were done hesitantly and with great political sensitivity. Since the Revolution, Americans viewed themselves as a cut above the "old world" and generally held expansion (with the exception of that conducted in the Western hemisphere) in disdain. This was most famously characterized by Washington's often misquoted admonition against becoming involved in entangling European alliances, remarks that Americans took to heart.[27] The impact of this should not be underestimated; even when directly challenged by Barbary pirates, U.S. politicians still moved cautiously in a conflict that lasted over 30 years before—with a certain irony, given the heretofore resistance to building and deploying warships—finally being decisively solved by sea power.

Mahan's theories were a direct challenge to Washington's admonition, transcending it through his description of sea power as a reflection of national character. Moreover, they were unique in that they provided a straightforward rationale that was both easy to understand and popular. But what is it about Mahan's theories that made them so appealing?

First, and perhaps foremost, Mahan's ideas made sense to the layman. Mahan benefited by being the "first" to write naval theory (or, for that matter, naval history in the strategic sense). Beyond popular histories that dramatized the exploits of naval heroes, there was no real "history" of naval power that was readily available to which Mahan could be compared in the sense that the significance of events was explained strategically.[28] Mahan's relatively easy writing style, his use of historical examples to justify his thesis, and the lack of alternatives all served to strengthen the logic of his arguments—arguments that, in the grand scheme, people wanted to hear. It was this populism that also made Mahan eminently appealing. Mahan was no dry academic; he wrote passionately, and if one were inclined toward supporting his thesis, it was easy to be convinced. This was true not only of politicians eager to find a scientific rationale for the leap from Manifest Destiny to imperialism, but also of Navy men for whom Mahan was not only a rationalizing factor in justifying a large fleet but also a source of professional pride. Mahan provided not only the "how" for politicians but also "why" the Navy should develop as a global force.[29]

The key to this, as both political and military men were well aware, was popular support. Navies cost money; indeed, the development of a fleet was far and away the most expensive element of military power that could be developed by any nation (both then and now). Popular support for this in the U.S. prior to Mahan was decidedly mixed; even Jefferson, in the face of a clear threat to U.S. interests in the Barbary Wars, was loathe to commit the financial backing necessary for the development of a relatively small fleet.[30] Westward expansion aside, the popular U.S. will was not for global expansion. The Monroe Doctrine was very much a reflection of this attitude, a cautious warning to the "old world" that the U.S. would not tolerate further European involvement or expansion in its own sphere of influence. For the bulk of the U.S. public, Washington's warning remained sacred.

Mahan changed all this. His call for the development of a blue-water battle fleet as a necessity for greatness effectively negated the common issue of cost (how could a great nation *not* afford the development of a fleet?) and effectively modified Washington's disclaimer. The United States was not becoming involved in old-world entanglements or alliances; it was rising above them through the development of sea power.[31] The social Darwinism of his arguments aside, Mahan argued that a great *people* took to the sea to expand their benign influence for the civilizing benefit of all, an ancient English mantra that was believed by an increasing number of Americans eager to step into that role. This fit in well with the proselytizing role that was becoming increasingly popular in America.[32] To quote Democratic Congressman Richmond Pearson Hobson, writing in 1902:

> The finger of fate is pointing forward. America will be the controlling World power, holding the scepter of the sea, reigning in mighty beneficence with the guiding principle of maximum of world service. She will help all nations of the earth. Europe will be saved by her young offspring grown to manhood.[33]

It is important to note that Mahan's influence was not confined to the shores of his mother country but rather was a global phenomenon—in point of fact, Mahan was first wildly popular in Europe before being discovered by his fellow countrymen.[34] His work was eagerly read by the rulers of the old-world great powers, all engaged in territorial expansion schemes of their own. With limited continental space and a dwindling amount of territory available for colonization, the sea seemed the answer to continued greatness in the inevitable conflict between the powers. Subsequently, there was a rush to capitalize on Mahan's theories that took the practical form of a rush to build capital ships, actions that would inevitably draw in the United States as an emerging power. Mahan did not start the great powers in a rush to develop battle fleets—the process was already under way at the time of his writing—but he did help to rationalize and accelerate it.[35] The end of the 19th century saw a tremendous resurgence in imperialism worldwide, due in part to the emergence of new powers (Germany and Japan) that wanted a seat at the table with the older, established empires. The demise of the Spanish overseas empire, the opening of Africa from exploration to exploitation, and the designation of "spheres of influence" in Asia all drove the new imperialism.

The old-world empires were based on colonization, completely in alignment with Mahan's writings.[36] This may seem to be, at first, a somewhat obvious point—if empires desired overseas colonizes, they must obtain the means to reach those colonies and project some form of power, actions that could only be accomplished through building navies. Colonial nations had all developed maritime trading power on the seas, but this was obviously vulnerable in wartime, perhaps more so in the era of modernization. This capability had to be protected. The interpretation of Mahan's history seemed to provide the answer: the development of the modern battle fleet of capital ships. And if the great powers were building them and were potential enemies of the emerging United States, it stood to reason that the United States had to develop them as well.[37]

Politicians and the populace were not the only ones to greet Mahan enthusiastically. Mahan's impact on the naval profession was even more profound than on the popular imagination. As noted, Mahan's time was one of rapid change for the navies of major powers. The industrial age brought a boom to the shipbuilding industry, not only in the ways and means of production but also through the application of new technologies at sea that increased the versatility of naval power enormously.[38] Mahan saw this in his lifetime with the transition from sail to steam power (an event he somewhat romantically lamented). Great powers raced to develop this technology and built capital ships largely as a matter of national pride, as an expression of the ability to create and project force. This was a race in which the U.S. Navy had fallen woefully behind. Despite clear advances made during the Civil War, with its ships reduced in number and dilapidated in the postwar era, there was little if any thought given to strategy for the use of a blue-water fleet beyond the traditional missions of commerce raiding and coastal defense.[39] In the culture war between technologists and traditionalists, the traditionalists—those who wrote doctrine—held power by virtue of their rank and position and were unlikely to be swayed from these missions by anything other than a major revelation.

Mahan provided this revelation in a manner that was satisfying to all sides. As a work of history, his study effectively sidestepped the technological issue (for which he would later be much criticized), stating that he was attempting a higher goal—to distill from the lessons of history various naval principles that would transcend technology.[40] Proponents on both sides seized on this point. Mahan's message was that ultimately sea power was all about command of the sea obtained in battle—battle fought by fleets and therefore by capital ships. This argument soothed the fear of the traditionalists that they would be marginalized in the new world by stressing that understanding of technology was not essential for senior officers directing a strategic force in accordance with the unchangeable principles of sea power. In a similar sense, Mahan's strategic argument was seized on by the technologists (particularly the rising stars of the classes of 1874–1880, who were arguing for reform and modernization), who noted that a force required to fulfill Mahan's vision had to be not only global but also competitive in the technological realm.[41] A fleet had to be modern, strategic, and utilize the most up-to-date technology in order to fulfill the Mahanian vision. In this sense Mahan had bridged the gap between the warring factions, clearing the way for the development of a fleet of capital ships for the U.S. Navy within its own ranks.

The end result, both strategically and culturally within the Navy, was the establishment of a "hierarchy" of vessels that fit the needs of both the traditionalists and the technologists, a philosophical concept that would have significant impact on the development of future naval theory.[42] At the top of this hierarchy was the capital ship (represented by the dreadnought during Mahan's time—a ship that, ironically, he criticized as being too mission-focused).[43] In Mahan's history, capital ships of the line fought their equals in an almost prearranged form of set-piece battle, an image that pleased the traditionalists as emphasizing their skills at strategic and operational maneuver. For the technocrats, this was a practical reality as opposed to a philosophical point—as guns got bigger, it seemed obvious that a proper opponent could only be a large ship with equally large (or larger) guns.

Not all technologists agreed with this line of thought; in theory, new naval technologies in propulsion and ordnance could make the capital ship invincible (according to the school of thought that argued for large, heavily armed and armored battleships, which was in the majority) or increasingly vulnerable (argued by those who favored the development of the torpedo boat, alternative anti-ship technology such as mines and later aircraft, and smaller, specialized vessels).[44] Using rationales based on Mahan's writings, the "size is invincible" school won out, fully supported by the traditionalists. Thus was born the "big ship" paradigm that came to dominate not just U.S. Navy thinking, but the thinking of great power navies worldwide. In a relatively short period of time the unity of the traditionalists and technologists under the umbrella of Mahan had created a strategic culture.

Although history would prove many of Mahan's theories wrong (or at least misguided), there was a definite logic in Mahan that seemed to "fit" the subsequent race to develop large blue-water navies. Mahan had successfully demonstrated that historically fleet power and sea power were inexorably mixed in a formula for national greatness. New naval technologies that increased the mobility and firepower of modern vessels offered the chance to make the Mahanian vision a reality. And ultimately Mahan provided a unifying force to a number of diverse political elements that all sought the same thing: international greatness for the United States. The weakness in this form of thinking, however, was that war itself had to cooperate—in anything other than a traditional great power battle (reminiscent of the 18th century), Mahan's vision of the fleet of capital ships ruling the seas through decisive battle might be more complicated and far less effective than envisioned. This would become increasingly apparent in the wars of the 20th century.

Three

War Fighting Theory and Practice, 1914–1941
The Ascendancy of the Capital Ship

The interwar period of 1918–1941 was critical for the solidification of capital ship theory, despite the fact that theory derived prior to the First World War did not live up to the reality of global combat. The navies that were poised to fight in 1914 were distinctly Mahanian both in design and doctrine, but the war that followed was almost completely counter to Mahan's thesis, resulting in an intellectual backlash against the navalists. Yet as the "lessons" of World War I were reevaluated, capital ship theory enjoyed an almost immediate resurgence in the United States and continued to dominate fleet doctrine and construction. This was the first example of a trend that would become critically important in the interwar era and the ultimate war fighting philosophy of the U.S. Navy: the revisionism of lessons learned in combat to fit preconceived theory that favored the development of the capital ship.

The manipulation of Mahanian theory was not a new phenomenon in itself. It could be argued that even in the final days of his life, what had been adopted as Mahanian theory no longer echoed Mahan's thoughts, a fact he noted immediately prior to his death.[1] Many of the pre-conditions for Mahan's theories and the complexities of it were swept aside by enthusiasts who echoed the single message that favored the capital fleet and decisive battle at the expense of all other priorities. But until the First World War, this theory had been speculative; during the war, practical experience in combat threatened it, demanding action if the theory was to remain the primary basis for the future development of U.S. naval power. Subsequent events would demonstrate that dominance of this theory was such that even the lessons of global combat—representing enormous complexity in themselves—could be rationalized in favor of maintaining capital ship fleets designed to fight the decisive battle.

Mahan Interpreted and Reinvented

As the world's foremost naval theorist, Mahan was—at least for a time—widely regarded as the primary voice for naval expansion in the United States. While it is true that Mahan's advocates used his work to justify capital ship construction and fleet expansion, his theory is not so simplistic—and his thesis was not without its contemporary critics or controversy. Historically, fleets have always been one of the most expensive elements of military power, and in the modern era this was no exception. The building of fleets required a massive commitment of national resources whose subsequent economic benefit in infrastructure and employment was not spread equally across the nation (a fact often noted by anxious politicians).[2] Those who advocated continued development of naval technologies pointed out that Mahan's thesis was based on academic historical analysis, not an examination of modern naval trends. And there was also the question of other forms of power; critiques pointed out (correctly) that winning wars with sea power alone was a difficult proposition.[3] These critiques, while significant, could be argued or dismissed in the rush to modernize. But in a somewhat ironic turn of events prior to the First World War, Mahan's greatest critic was—Mahan.

Mahan was well aware of his shortcomings as a modern strategist and of his position within the naval hierarchy. As a retired military officer he was certainly influential as a theorist and frequently consulted by both politicians and military men, but ultimately he wrote no policy nor did he control the direction of the Navy—a direction that was increasingly departing from the core elements of his theory.[4] In the wake of his popularity, Mahan's "model" became, interestingly enough, not so much the work of Mahan as it was that of those who wished to use historical analysis to rationalize the development of a large capital fleet.[5] Mahan had made the leap in identifying sea power as a strategic element directly linked to national power, but how this was carried out in the minds of navalists was not entirely in accordance with what he proposed his vision to be. Although he was in favor of the rapid expansion of the Navy, the rush to develop capital ships (in this case, modern dreadnoughts and eventually battleships) presented problems, both economically and in terms of mission efficiency. Mahan was well aware that many naval missions were best accomplished by a smaller-caliber vessel or a more diverse fleet and, moreover, that there were only so many national resources that could be dedicated to naval expansion. Mahan reflected this critique in his own speeches and articles, writing:

Unless the country—and the Congress—are prepared for practically unlimited expenditures, bigger ships mean fewer ships. Now there are strong military reasons why numbers of ships are wanted; and in view of the steady increase in size, due to increasing demands of each technical factor on the battleship, the time has arrived when the military experts should be directed to consider what the limits of size should be.[6]

This position did not sit well with the navalists. While Mahan never lost his stature as the prophet of sea power, he did lose his influence in the latter years of his life within naval circles and the political establishment supporting them.[7] His comments on the development of a large battle fleet composed of many different sizes and types of ships over a large fleet composed primarily of larger capital ships were ignored by the movement he helped create.[8] This movement was composed of the union of two diverse groups that were remarkably unified in their desire for the creation of capital ship power, each with their own respective agendas and their own means of influence. The first group was external to the Navy and composed primarily of politicians, leading public figures, and influential men of business and media that embraced Mahan.[9] As noted, Mahan's theories were popular in political circles that favored international expansion for the United States. Motivations for this group were mixed, including a new expansionist version of the Monroe Doctrine, proliferating theories of racial superiority, and a new spiritual idea of manifest destiny.[10] It should be noted that this expansion was not entirely altruistic but also had tremendous domestic potential as the building of capital ships had the additional benefit of creating the large industrial base required to build and maintain a fleet, a distinct economic boom to congressional districts.[11] Once this base was created it was difficult to curb, both economically and politically. The nation had been committed.

This commitment to naval expansion took the form not only of the construction of a capital fleet, but also a solidifying of theory surrounding that fleet. This was driven by the second group of the Mahanian movement, naval officers dedicated to using Mahan's theories for their purposes of transforming the fleet. It must be stressed that the transformation they proposed was quite radical both in form and theory. Prior to Mahan's writings, the fleet had primarily been composed of smaller vessels. It is important to note that "smaller" in this case does not mean coastal; the U.S. Navy had always operated overseas representing national interests, but this was normally conducted singularly with frigate-style vessels or vessels operating in squadrons or groups. The missions these vessels performed were far more "irregular" in style than traditional fleet combat.[12]

This mode of U.S. Navy operations was now marginalized in favor of the theory of decisive battle using capital ships.[13] In the early 1900s the new "big gun club" quickly established a unique "hierarchy" of ships where the battleship—the biggest guns—reigned supreme; smaller vessels or vessels that performed roles outside the main purpose of decisive battle were subordinate to this overall goal.[14] Mahan's own call for a "mixed caliber" fleet composed of big and small ships that could function in other roles was politely brushed aside. The prophet had been overtaken by the zealots. It was the beginning of a trend where Mahan's theories would be used to rationalize capital ship types, starting with the battleship and eventually morphing into the current trend of rationalizing the aircraft carrier.[15]

The transformation of the U.S. Navy prior to 1914 was both rapid and decisive. On the eve of the First World War, the United States Navy had transitioned to a force that was distinctly Mahanian in nature. The force was not unbloodied. Rapid victory in the Spanish-American war—a war that was almost wholly reliant on sea power—seemed to vindicate Mahan's theories. The successful deployment of Theodore Roosevelt's "Great White Fleet" of modern dreadnoughts carried the message that the United States had arrived on the world stage as a contending global power.[16] And there seemed to be no end in sight for expanding the Navy as popular enthusiasm continued to call for the building of a larger and more effective fleet, a mood similar to that of the naval arms race in Europe. Yet in a relatively short period of time it all seemed to end as the world moved toward the war that would be the first real test of Mahan's theory.

The Test of Combat and the Navalists' Counterattack

On the eve of the First World War, all of the major combatants possessed (or strove to possess) fleets of capital ships and sought to employ them in methods that were distinctly Mahanian.[17] Not only were these fleets designed for decisive battle, but the philosophy of the bold offensive was firmly ingrained in the naval mindset worldwide. British and German naval officers dreamed of "De Tag," the decisive battle that would resolve everything.[18] As is well documented, the results were far less conclusive. The only major engagement between the capital fleets—Jutland—was at best indecisive. The Battle of Jutland has been subject to volumes of research and analysis that won't be discussed here; for purposes of this study, Jutland is significant because the results—for whatever reason— were vastly different from those envisioned by prewar navalists who favored capital ship development. Despite prewar theory regarding decisiveness, it soon became apparent that the potential for strategic catastrophe bred caution and prevented the fleet from being committed in action. Following the initial encounter, the respective fleets of capital ships spent the remainder of the war bristling at each other, but accomplishing little else.[19]

The First World War resulted in two critiques of Mahan that proved significant for the future use of his theory. Mahan, like other so-called militarists, suffered the public backlash against the carnage of trench warfare that characterized the First World War, and his reputation suffered.[20] Mahan was not alone in this; this trend was especially evident in the besmirching of Clausewitz, who was unfairly characterized as the "Mahdi of mass" by Liddell Hart and others.[21] The unfortunate reality is that in the years prior to the First World War, militarists in all specialties cited military philosophers such as Clausewitz and Mahan as inspiration for their doctrine while ignoring the advent of modern battlefield technology, with tragic results.[22]

Backlash against Mahan took a number of forms. In the realm of international relations, Mahan was criticized as being directly responsible for the worldwide naval arms race that favored the development of ever-larger capital ships and thus directly contributing to the outbreak of the war. This portrayal is somewhat unfair. There is no doubt that Mahan was an unapologetic imperialist, but he was simply one of many, a man of his era. Mahan certainly influenced policy, but he did not have his hands on the reins of power. That the world was heading for conflict in 1914 was the product of many factors, of which Mahan was but one influential element. Regardless of the ultimate unfairness of this, Mahan had been tainted and with it much of his glorified call for a larger U.S. Navy. No longer could imperialistic rationale be effectively cited as a motive to build a fleet—at least for the time being.

But while Mahan might be categorized as but one of many imperialists whose influence led to the war, the technological critique of his theory was far more pointed, especially in the strategic sense. Arguably Mahan's theories should have died with the final shot of the battle of Jutland and the strategic success of the German U-boat offensive, both of which ran counter to his theories and predictions. In essence, naval warfare had become three-dimensional, something that Mahan did not credit as significant.[23] In Mahanian philosophy the capital ship reigned supreme, its only counter being another capital ship. Both submarines and aircraft altered this calculus considerably. Not only were fleets vulnerable to new

Three. War Fighting Theory and Practice, 1914–1941   45

technologies (requiring, in turn, defensive technologies and tactics to respond to the new threat), but for the first time, fleets were vulnerable in port. Forward operating areas near enemy coasts were now especially vulnerable for capital ships—whereas in the past enemy fortifications had been the only challenge, now land-based aircraft (and submarines) could keep a fleet effectively at bay. Suddenly areas where the battle fleet could exert its influence with limited fear of harm had shrunk considerably. And as the First World War demonstrated, fear of loss was far more strategically significant than had been envisioned. The battle fleet was simply far too important (and expensive) to risk in anything other than decisive battle—something an enemy could easily avoid if he so desired.[24]

In Mahan's defense, he had recognized the changing world. Near the end of his life, he commented that the new technology was making him feel irrelevant, and in all fairness it must be recognized that very few theorists recognized the practical wartime adaptability and impact of the new technologies.[25] But in his case rejection was not only due to militarism per se but also focused on the theoretical. Rather than sail off to decisive battle as anticipated, the fleet of U.S. battleships deployed for combat sat idle at anchor alongside their British allies at Scapa Flow, smarting in stalemate after the indecisive battle of Jutland. The capital ship move to the sidelines in the face of new threats. Prior to the war, new technologies had been viewed almost exclusively as to how they would impact the course of the inevitable decisive battle of capital ships.[26] During the war they became much more: they became the focus of the strategic war at sea.

The First World War at sea was almost completely non-Mahanian, revolving around the supply of battlefield armaments and logistical support from the sea, a role in which the capital ship played almost no part. Moreover, other elements of Mahan were discredited; protection of colonies played no role whatsoever, and as noted, the role of the battle fleet was relegated to simple existence, a threat to be used against a corresponding threat. In the aftermath of the war Corbett's "fleet in being" and limited command of the sea theories seemed, at least initially, far more relevant for the future of naval combat.[27]

Corbett was a British academic who taught sea power theory at the Royal Naval College. His theories focused on battle in the strategic sense, applying Clausewitzian principles in arguing that "command of sea" was illusory so long as the enemy could maintain an effective challenge in some form—the "fleet in being." In the final analysis Corbett's writings were far more reflective of the reality of the First World War. The war at sea was fought by smaller ships against a new, elusive opponent, waging a campaign that was distinctly irregular. In short, Mahan's theories and the fleet that resulted from them had disappointed. With the civilian backlash against all things military and the increasing sense of isolationism in the United States,[28] it seemed that Mahanian theory was dead.

Mahan died in 1914 and so did not see what was widely regarded as a repudiation of his theories. But this rejection did not last; even as Germany was negotiating at Versailles, forces in the United States were in motion to revitalize Mahan's theories and continue the development of a capital fleet. For dedicated navalists this task would not be easy; Mahan had been proven wrong in many cases, so continuing his rationale as a basis for fleet development would ultimately require a reevaluation of Mahan and a focused effort to discredit many of the lessons of the first great modern war at sea. For purposes of his subsequent use by generations of naval strategists, these critiques were, however, almost irrelevant.[29] Mahan as a geopolitical figure was regarded by subsequent generations as part of an era that was almost quaint in its naiveté. Mahan was (and is) cited for his strategic ideas on command of the sea, not for any tactical or operational innovations he espoused. What had to be addressed was the apparent failure of his theory during the global war.

There was no doubt about the position of the U.S. Navy. Despite the surprising turn of events in the war at sea, navalists in the United States remained dedicated to the building of capital ship fleets and their extension of Mahanian theory, arguing the case for new battleships passionately even before the treaty of Versailles was signed.[30] The reasons for this were complex. Naval men, after all, were not blind to reality; the U.S. naval officer class was one of the most highly educated in the military and had experienced the changes in war at sea firsthand.[31] But in the minds of many—especially for a service that came to the war late—one experience did not invalidate years of carefully developed theory. Mahan's ideas were not only deeply engrained in the naval mindset but also continued to meet a number of important needs for the Navy as a whole. The fact remained that naval officers were culturally committed to the theory of offensive battle that required the development of large and modern battle fleets composed of capital ships.

The newly unified groups within the navalist establishment agreed that the future remained with capital ships for various reasons. Technologists argued that although the war at sea had demonstrated the potential for new technologies that challenged the primacy of the capital ship, theoretically given the time allotted with peace it was possible to develop technology to counter anything that had been demonstrated in combat. The fact that the Allies emerged victorious supported this view. Although the submarine had been a significant threat, it was, after all, ultimately defeated. This fact lent credence to the argument that technologies and tactics had been or could be developed to return the capital ship to the top of the hierarchical pyramid. The enthusiasm of this argument was bolstered by the fact that professionally, the real influence in the Navy lay in technology that could be developed for the capital ships. A group that had previously been held in low regard by the naval hierarchy now found its voice.[32]

Outside the Navy, in the political realm, the building of capital ships remained supported by increasingly influential industrialists and their political allies. The relationship between military force and the civilian industrial base that supports it—what Eisenhower called the military-industrial complex—took on a whole new dimension with the development of capital ships.[33] Modern naval vessels, always expensive, necessitated an entirely new industry in their demands for steel and iron production. The development of this industry soon became a national imperative—and source of heretofore unimaginable wealth for the industrialists who supported it, which led to political power. The merging of national and military culture under the auspices of the new imperialism was still a factor, especially as the military had proven its capability for global influence. The argument now transformed into a "defensive" one. Naval officers noted that capital ships had to be built to counter new, emerging threats worldwide (a trend that continues today). In perhaps one of the oddest rationales ever presented to Congress, naval officers argued that battleships could be needed to meet "future British aggression," an argument that left Congress incredulous (even Theodore Roosevelt was skeptical).[34] Regardless of potential criticisms, the Mahanian mindset ran within the Navy hierarchy; the pacifism that seemed to be infecting the rest of the nation was not evident within naval ranks.[35]

The problem, of course, was how to convince everyone else outside committed navalist circles. Fleets cost money, and in the aftermath of the war, this money was not forthcoming, especially as the results of the war at sea were readily apparent for critics to view and analyze. There was no denying that the theory of decisive fleet battle had been shaken by the results of the war. How to address this fact? For an emerging naval power such as the United States, the answer to this question was critical, especially for the Americans, whose naval experience during the First World War was comparatively limited. The inactivity of American battleships and the fact that smaller ships fought the U-boat threat at sea was not lost upon fiscally minded congressmen.[36] The failure of the battleships had to be addressed. Jutland was the key: the Mahanian battle that should have decided everything but failed to live up to expectations.

As the only example of true fleet combat during the war, Jutland subsequently became the most analyzed battle in U.S. naval war games and texts. But "analysis" in this case was not entirely unbiased. From the outset, nationalist overtones were prevalent. The battle was obviously British and German, not American, so it was viewed increasingly as a "we could have done better" scenario. As time went on, this analysis became more critical (and disdainful), focusing on tactical decisions made during the battle instead of the strategic applications of capital ships.[37] Throughout the study, there was no doubt that those who favored continued capital ship development held sway using a method of analysis that was prejudiced toward their own cultural interpretation of events and the future of naval war, reaching the inevitable conclusion: the Americans could do better.[38] Doing better required a fleet of modern capital ships.

But analyzing the battle of Jutland and devising a "we could have done better" tactical solution only took the argument for capital ships so far—after all, the bulk of the war at sea did not involve capital ships, and there was no doubt that World War I innovations in the air and under water threatened the supremacy of the battleship fleet. The war at sea had been a surprise that dominated strategic thought; given that the British Isles had almost been starved out by the German U-boat campaign, it simply could not be ignored. The new technologies that threatened the future development of the battle fleet had to be addressed.

This was precisely the tack taken by American planners. In reviewing lessons learned from the First World War, many theorists and naval professionals pursued the strategy of ignoring or maligning the new technologies while espousing Mahanian theory that "could" work in the future.[39] In both the case of the submarine and the airplane, an unusual rationale was used to minimize their potential impact on future naval conflict.

The German U-boat campaign was undoubtedly the most decisive element of war at sea and, interestingly, the one that had the most impact on U.S. naval operations throughout the conflict. It was also the one that touched closest to U.S. national interests because it directly threatened "freedom of the seas" and the commerce that depended on it.[40] As a national interest, there was little doubt that the submarine would be the postwar focus of many outside of traditional Navy circles. Defeating the

Three. War Fighting Theory and Practice, 1914–1941

U-boat had dominated practical naval operations throughout the war, so much so that a wave of new tactics, techniques, and ships were designed and tested in an effort that ultimately proved successful. How successful it would be in the future, however, remained problematic, especially as the means for "defeat" had been anything but clear. The U-boat in World War I had been defeated by the institution of a mass convoy system (against traditionalist objections), the building of smaller vessels that could chase and engage the submarines on the surface, and even the use of a fledgling naval air arm.[41] Capital ships had played almost no part in this campaign. As the U.S. had no desire to build a fleet whose central focus was anti-submarine warfare, the problem had to be addressed.

This was accomplished through a two-prong approach, from both cultural and technological perspectives. Culturally the effectiveness of the U-boat was widely viewed by the former Allies as at best a fluke, a tactic resorted to by a desperate power incapable of waging traditional (and therefore civilized) combat.[42] Widely characterized as barbaric during the war, the Germans' use of the U-boat as a commerce raider in the formal postwar analysis was almost completely disregarded as one step above piratical, and actions were taken to limit repeats of this form of warfare through international treaty. Shortly before the London Naval Disarmament Conference in 1930, President Hoover stated, "For many years I have been convinced that ships which carry foodstuffs should be free of all interference during times of war ... on the same level as hospital ships."[43] This indirect reference to commerce-raiding submarines was generally regarded with approval. U.S. planners rationalized that their nation would never resort to such a dishonorable practice and persuaded themselves that other powers would follow suit.[44] Interestingly, Hoover's subsequent calls for a Navy for defensive purposes only was castigated by navalists in Congress and in the press.[45]

Treaties were, however, often transitory, and despite limitations, submarines certainly weren't going away (and on the eve of the Second World War were in fact quite advanced; the U.S. Navy's "fleet" or "Gato" class of submarines were as advanced as any comparable naval power), so the threat had to be addressed, especially in response to a small clique of naval submarine enthusiasts and skeptical Congressmen.[46] Superficially the "lessons" of the First World War seemed to provide an answer. Although the German U-boats came perilously close to victory, at the end of the day they ultimately had been defeated, a fact that was repeated time and again by capital ship enthusiasts.[47] It would seem logical (given the restrictions placed on submarines following the war) that the tactics used to defeat the threat during the First World War would more than suffice in dealing with the threat in the future. These "lessons," however, were not completely accurate when viewed in their entirety. It was a commonly accepted fiction, for example, that the U-boat had ultimately been defeated by ASDIC (sonar) and aggressive patrolling tactics—an idealistic view at best, given that the device had been developed late in the war, with very mixed success, and that "hunter-killer" groups were wholly ineffective.[48] The Americans were so enamored with the technological solution that the argument was made even during the early months of the Second World War that convoying, the tactic that had proven its worth in the First War, was unnecessary.[49]

As individual platforms, the submarines came under increasing criticism by classical surface navalists. Technologically the capability of submarines advanced considerably in a very short period of time, especially in the interwar years. But compared to the new and sophisticated destroyers being built as scouts and escorts—many now equipped with scout aircraft specifically designed to find submarines—pundits argued (with some justification) that submarines remained extremely fragile, difficult to operate, specialized, and vulnerable when detected, and, since the detection problem had been technically resolved, arguably were no longer a significant threat so long as proper defenses were maintained.[50] There were, however, flaws in this argument. The individual vulnerability of the submarine was certainly true, but this rationale ignored future advances in submarine technology that allowed them to travel faster and farther and remain submerged to greater depths, technology that was being pursued worldwide. More importantly, this argument also ignored the increased use of secure communications that allowed for the development of coordinated submarine tactics. These factors would be key in the famous wolfpack tactics designed by Doenitz.[51]

Despite the arguments against the platform, submarines continued to advance and were accepted (however begrudgingly) as part of the naval arm in the United States. This did not mean, however, that their practiced use was effective or, for that matter, realistic. This is especially evident in prewar doctrine developed by the United States for the use of its submarines—doctrine heavily influenced by surface officers who seemed intent on demonstrating the ineffectiveness of the platform.[52] As commerce raiding was no long acceptable, the role of the submarine in fleet doctrine was to act as a scout or in an anti-warship role.[53] In interwar tests they did not perform well. Submarines made poor scouts due to their slow speed underwater, limited communications ability, and low height of eye, which made spotting fast-moving surface ships difficult. Moreover, as if to prove the point regarding their ineffectiveness, fleet war games in the interwar years operated under rules of play that made it virtually impossible for a submarine to attack successfully. Surface attacks were almost always ruled unsuccessful due to "spotting" by invisible aircraft (rulings were made by umpires from the fleet; whether or not the submarine had actually been seen was a moot point), and submarine commanders were trained to fire their torpedoes while deeply submerged, using passive sonar targeting methods—a technique that had zero success during the Second World War.[54]

These factors served to minimize the submarine in the eyes of U.S. naval planners in the interwar period. The alleged poor results with U.S. submarines in war games could be extrapolated to apply to foreign navies as well, indicating that the threat of the future was well contained, thus clearing the way for the continued development of the capital fleet.

Fleet Expansion: The Capital Ship in Multi-dimensions

The three-dimensional element of naval warfare that developed during the First World War was not limited to undersea operations. Air power had proven itself during the land battles of the First World War and was just beginning to come into its own as a force at sea at war's end. The clear potential aircraft offered at sea, both as scouts and weapons, logically led to the development of platforms designed to make the air arm a permanent part of the fleet. Aircraft carriers, at first rudimentary platforms, soon developed into capital ships in their own right. Their development and doctrinal use in the interwar years, however, did not foretell the force they would eventually become nor how they would ultimately replace the battleship as the primary means of executing Mahan's vision.

The ship with the most potential to extend combat power on the surface was initially developed as an emergency means to deal with the great nemesis of the First World War: the submarine.[55] The British had employed aircraft successfully as scouts flying from land bases and logically rationalized expanding this role at sea in an anti-submarine role. By war's end, the Royal Navy was operating 12 rudimentary aircraft carriers that conducted over 120 attacks on surfaced U-boats, demonstrating one of the few combative counters to the U-boat that was actually effective.[56] This effectiveness, however, did not result in a rush to build aircraft carriers. The use of aircraft at sea against a wartime threat was one thing, peacetime doctrine another. If the submarine was eliminated as a threat (as many argued), then the development of carriers in this role was at best an overallocation of scarce resources. Other roles clearly existed, but how effective aircraft would be in these roles was controversial.

The aircraft-versus-ship debate has become legend among the respective military branches. In popular folklore, General Billy Mitchell's famous bombing test (or as some saw it, a public affairs display) forever altered the calculus at sea, decisively ending the era of the capital ship.[57] In the well-known (and well-documented) story, the flamboyant Army general bragged that his aircraft could annihilate fully armored dreadnoughts. The challenge became both a public and political one. At one point the Secretary of the Navy vowed that he would stand on one of the targets during the test to prove the ship's invulnerability (a challenge he neglected to take).[58] Mitchell made good on his claims, destroying the targets in a spectacular display that reportedly left a number of observing naval officers (who were fully aware of what the test implied) in tears.[59]

In hindsight, Mitchell's claim that aircraft forever changed war at sea was certainly correct, but at the time, the demonstration heralded something less than a total revolution. The destruction of the dreadnoughts notwithstanding, capital ship theory remained dominant in the interwar years. There were a number of important reasons for this, not the least of which was an immediate counter-offensive by navalists challenging Mitchell's results. Mitchell's test, although spectacular, had been conducted against stationary targets unable to defend themselves—facts that were pointed out repeatedly by Navy admirals who hinted darkly at conspiracy.[60] Those who advocated Mahanian theory argued that new propulsion methods allowed capital ships to be exceptionally well armored and also that larger ships boasted nests of new anti-aircraft weapons that made any successful attack increasingly unlikely. Moreover, Mitchell's aircraft were heavier land-based planes and capable of carrying heavy ordnance, something that was (at the time) impossible at sea. The battleship had been challenged and theory shaken, but it was not dead, at least in the minds of the navalists and their civilian allies.

This is not to say that the utility of aircraft was not recognized within the Navy. However, their acceptance represented more of an evolution than revolution in the interwar years. In exercises, naval aircraft were invaluable in solving the age-old problem of successfully finding the enemy for the decisive engagement, and lighter fighters brought to sea seemingly could provide an effective shield against any enemy bombing attack launched from a hostile shore. The increasing ability of aircraft to carry

Three. War Fighting Theory and Practice, 1914–1941 53

ordnance indicated they had significant potential as a strike weapon, a point that remained controversial in naval circles until the onset of World War II.[61] The role of strike aircraft was the subject of intense debate in the interwar years, primarily focused on whether or not aircraft could actually deliver their bombs and torpedoes effectively in combat. Where one stood on this issue was usually in accordance with one's belief as to whether the aircraft carrier or battleship was the dominant capital ship. The issue was not easily resolved; even as late as 1944, some Japanese naval officers were arguing for the continued development of super "unsinkable" battleships rather than aircraft carriers.[62]

It is true that in doctrinal discussions, the aircraft carrier had mixed reviews prior to the onset of World War II.[63] This did not, however, stop the development of carriers. It is a commonly held view that the rise of naval airpower was in direct conflict with the Mahanian mindset that justified battle fleets composed of the dreadnoughts that the "big gun club" cherished.[64] This is not completely correct, although there is no doubt that the role of the aircraft spurred considerable debate in naval circles.[65] There are a number of important reasons for this, not the least of which being that the use of aircraft at sea was largely theoretical; without the test of actual combat, pundits for larger and more powerful battleships remained well positioned in the naval hierarchy to make their views count. Where there was agreement was on the challenges of the decisive battle. Theory—and the lessons of Jutland—demonstrated that the side that found the enemy first and was given time to concentrate would win overwhelmingly in the decisive battle; aircraft seemed to provide a tool to enable this to occur.[66] Accordingly, carriers were injected into fleet doctrine, which was modified to account for the new capability—but in a way that was distinctly Mahanian, looking for a decisive battle for the capital ship fleet.

This was reflected both in the construction of carriers and their doctrinal role as part of the battle fleet. Smaller carriers operating against submarines (such as those the British had developed in the First World War) were viewed distastefully; if the submarine had been largely eliminated as a threat (as many envisioned), there was no real use for these ships, which were subsequently never developed to any great extent in the prewar era.[67] A small number of aircraft had limited use in complementing the battle line; the capital ship fleet needed large numbers of aircraft to perform the dual roles of scouting and spotting for the battle-line gun engagement and providing fleet defense against enemy air attack, elements that became part of doctrine after a number of theoretical war games and fleet exercises.[68] For aircraft to fulfill these roles, the ships carrying them had to possess two overriding capabilities: they had to carry enough aircraft to be effective in all missions, and they had to be able to keep up with the main force. These requirements demanded that carriers be both large and fast, elements that appealed to the Mahanian mindset. In following this formula, carriers became, perhaps inadvertently, capital ships in their own right.

By the mid–1930s, aircraft carriers had become a recognized part of the battle fleet, but their role was quite limited and their numbers small. Fleet doctrine still stressed concentration of the main battle line against an enemy force, all efforts directed toward bringing the opposing fleet into the one decisive engagement of capital ships—the key component of concentration Mahan held dear. Aircraft were an important element of this strategy. With aircraft acting as both scouts and "spotters" for battleship gunfire, theorists argued that the power of the gunnery line could be considerably enhanced, not only in finding the enemy but also effectively directing shots to target.[69] Tests using aircraft in these roles seemed to bear this theory out, and carriers were quickly adopted as "auxiliaries" for the battle line.[70] Strategy drove numbers. As war games at the Naval War College in Newport continued to theorize about future decisive battles (originally against England but increasingly against Japan), battleships remained the focus; only a handful of carriers were required to support the battle line.[71] This was reflected in construction—on the eve of the Second World War, the United States had four fleet carriers on the naval rolls, all of which were stationed in the Pacific.

The role of strike—that for which the carrier would become famous in very short order—was more doctrinally problematic. That aircraft were a threat to surface ships was clear, but how much of a threat was dependent on the aircraft's ability to carry effective ordnance and survive an attack. Recognizing this, the growing fleet air wing sought to develop means of offensive strike, creating innovations in both dive bombing and torpedo technologies that were in place prior to the outbreak of war. It must be stressed that despite extensive testing, there was still a large uncertainty as to how these technologies would work. It was generally held, for example, that ships in shallow ports would be safe from torpedo attack, as most prewar torpedoes sank to ninety feet before leveling off for attack—a problem solved by the British at Taranto and the Japanese at Pearl Harbor through the design of new torpedoes.[72] The emphasis placed on these technologies, however, was mixed, due to the inherent division between naval officers who saw air power as the wave of the future and a primary

Three. War Fighting Theory and Practice, 1914–1941 55

emphasis and those who continued to view the battleship as the primary focus for the Navy, with aircraft in a supporting role. Ultimately this debate would be decisively resolved in the reality of combat.

The ultimate results of interwar theory and doctrine were significant. On the eve of World War II, the United States possessed a Navy that would prove to have a number of defining characteristics. Strategically, it emphasized the primacy of the battle line in forward, offensive operations on a vast strategic scale. The Navy had studied the future use of its capital ship fleet in an extensive series of war games at the Naval War College that stressed the fleet's use in global combat. Initially begun as a series of training exercises against England (although not a politically realistic opponent, England did possess the largest fleet), these games evolved into a strategic planning vehicle for a war against the Japanese.[73] The war plans that emerged from these games envisioned a rolling series of offensive battles across the Pacific, ultimately ending in the naval isolation and defeat of Japan. Carriers were certainly a part of this, but the main focus was how to mass and support a large fleet of battleships as they moved across the Pacific in battle.

Carriers were certainly a part of naval doctrine but were still largely undeveloped in terms of their future use. The Navy had developed a rudimentary strike capability, largely due to the efforts of the growing aviation community. In time, this strike capability, launched from carriers, would become the dominant element of naval warfare, but in 1941 this capability was still regarded by many Navy traditionalists as a secondary support role for the main gun engagement. Navy strike aircraft in 1941 were few and largely obsolete compared to those possessed by the Japanese; this was, however, gradually changing through the efforts of a number of senior naval aviators.[74] Finally, in what could be regarded as an "irregular" conflict, the Navy had largely ignored the ASW problem, relying on untested technology and tactics. This was a particularly interesting development, as the United States was effectively engaged in anti-submarine warfare (at least unofficially) when it began its "neutrality patrols" in 1940. The Navy had built a number of destroyers for this purpose and outfitted older ships with sonar, but the results were mixed. Strategically, it was felt that if the United States was to enter the war, the submarine problem could be easily addressed. This would be proven otherwise in the first months of 1942.[75]

The fleet that was developed in the interwar years was the "right" fleet theoretically, but one that was wrong for the practical war that followed. It would thoroughly evolve to meet the demands of combat. The three greatest elements of the war at sea in both the Atlantic and Pacific—the carrier, anti-submarine warfare, and economic warfare using the submarine—were poorly served by Mahanian theory. The battleships struck at Pearl Harbor, regarded as the centerpiece of fleet power, would eventually be raised and return to a vastly different world, relegated to a secondary role in the new naval war.

Four

Lessons, Retrenchment, and Theory, 1945–1951

From 1945 to 1951, the Navy faced its greatest test as a force founded on Mahanian theory. It had excelled during the Second World War, emerging as the most powerful force on the seas. In four years of brutal combat, the Navy met every challenge and fought in every theater, demonstrating the importance of sea power in a worldwide conflict. This is not to say that there were not mistakes made or battles lost; in many cases (particularly in the Atlantic theater) the conflict was (as Wellington characterized his famous victory) a "near-run thing." Yet in terms of theory it seemed that in 1945 the Navy could rest on its laurels. The Mahanian vision and investment in capital ships had been fully justified. This was at once a Mahanian dream and his nightmare. It was a dream in that the war seemed to validate the principle of command of the sea—but a nightmare in the form of the future dominance of the atomic bomb.[1]

As a result, this triumph was short-lived for sea power advocates. The victory achieved by the Navy did not herald a new era where sea power was the primary focus of the United States' military power. Although the U.S. would take on the role of global policeman in the aftermath of its victory, how this mission was to be carried out was very much a matter of debate. Sea power—particularly, as argued by the navalists, in the Mahanian sense of capital ship fleet power—had been an essential component in the Allied victory. But the world of 1945 was very different from that of 1941. New technologies dominated the American military mindset, as did new theories as to how to deal with the emerging communist threat and America's role in the new bi-polar world.[2] There was little clarity as to how new technologies, especially atomic weapons, were to be used. Internally the Navy began to see its traditional role usurped. The Navy had been a strategic global force since the early 1900s with its development and deployment of a large battle fleet that could act strategically, based on the writings of Mahan. The other branches had no such precept; the traditional American distrust of a standing military had kept them small except for times of war. But with the eventual emergence of the national security state in the aftermath of the war, other military services sought to take on a global role as strategic elements of national power. These actions would be as much a challenge to traditional Mahanian theory as any enemy in combat, perhaps even more so. For the Navy to survive as a capital-ship force, it had to retrench, reorganize, and above all stress the value of its Mahanian vision to an increasingly skeptical public and a growing number of opponents within the new national security apparatus.

Mahan Vindicated or Vilified: The World War II Experience

The Second World War was a global conflict that hinged in many respects on the successful application of naval power. The story of how America successfully rose to the challenge of world war and ultimately emerged as a global superpower is well known; it is not the purpose of this discussion to reexamine the various campaigns of the war in detail, but rather to examine the ultimate impact of the war on fleet battle doctrine and the success (or failure) of the application of Mahanian theory. The impact of the war on theory was enormously significant, as success served as a rationalization for the continued use of Mahanian fleet doctrine in the postwar era of the "Pax Americana." But while much of the conflict did seem to be a fulfillment of Mahan's vision, there was also an inherent contradiction in how the lessons of the conflict were applied by the U.S. Navy. Termed the "two-ocean war" by historian and navalist Samuel Elliot Morrison,[3] the respective theaters of the Atlantic and Pacific presented very different challenges for the use of naval power—one that was one distinctly Mahanian in its reliance on capital ships engaging in decisive battle and one that was far more irregular in its scope. Both visions of sea power, each essential to overall victory in their own right, presented a very different model on which to base the postwar Navy.

For navalists, the Pacific war came closest to Mahan's vision of obtaining command of the sea through decisive battle and the role of the capital ship. In character, the war in the Pacific fit Mahan's model, demanding a large fleet for success. The sheer size of the Pacific campaign was daunting; at war's end, the U.S. Navy had expanded almost one hundredfold and was continuing to build a fleet the size and power of which were never before seen in world history.[4] While it is true that many of the (often unheralded) elements of the campaign were distinctly non-Mahanian (most notably the extremely successful submarine guerre de course against Japanese shipping), the Pacific was a "carrier war" both publicly and practically. Carriers had come into their own during the war as the central element of naval power and as such gradually shuffled the battleship aside as the ultimate expression of the Mahanian capital ship. This shift away from battleships to carriers was a product of wartime necessity, but one that was philosophically aligned with the mindset that the capital ship reigned supreme. The "big gun club" still had its advocates; contrary to popular mythology, carriers did not spell the end of battleships, which were constructed until war's end.[5] But while the heavy firepower of the battleships still played an important role in providing support to the island-hopping campaign in the Pacific, the carrier had become the new focal point for capital ship theorists.[6] Carrier task forces[7] ultimately swept the enemy from the seas in decisive battles such as Midway and Leyte, enabling almost total command of the sea and the air above it, leaving the United States poised for victory—much as Mahan had foretold.

But while strategically the Pacific hinged on carrier operations and fleet engagement, in analyzing the war in the Pacific, one must ask whether the success of the Navy was the result of a long adherence to Mahanian theory or was the result of a unique combination of circumstances that favored a capital ship war. Although for navalists the Pacific came very close to fulfilling the Mahanian vision in that the Pacific war was, in their view, decided by decisive battle at sea, it could be argued (and was, in the postwar era) that the war against Japan was a very specific case that ultimately favored a Mahanian-style war.[8] Japan, like Britain, was an island nation wholly dependent on sea power in both peace and war. Unlike Britain—Mahan's case study—Japan had industrialized very quickly and did not have well-developed trade relationships with other nations, relying instead on exploitation and extraction, leaving it isolated in war.[9] Because Japan was denied natural resources required for industrialization, perhaps more than any modern nation, the sea was Japan's Achilles heel, requiring war to be waged on the sea as a matter of necessity. While there was certainly a continental element to Japan's war (in China), this never delivered the promised resources the Japanese hoped for, forcing them to look elsewhere across the sea for other sources of materials.[10] For this it needed to develop and maintain a large modern fleet.[11]

Japan's development of a capital ship battle fleet was influenced by other factors. The sea was not only a vehicle of expansion but also of protection. Geographically the vastness of the Pacific demanded that any enemy wishing to strike at Japan effectively develop major sea power, sea power that was composed of capital ships that could transit those distances. Protection of the home islands (in addition to its expansionist plans) demanded that Japan's strength on the sea be at least equal to any potential enemies'. Ultimately this strength was substantial; in 1941 the Japanese possessed a modern fleet of six fleet carriers, ten battleships, 150 heavy cruisers and destroyers, and a host of smaller support vessels.[12] Defeating this force required the Americans to match it both materially and in operational acumen. In some respects the Japanese themselves unwittingly encouraged the Allies' focus on the development of the capital ship in their failure to present any effective irregular threat that required smaller ships or defensive measures.[13] In building a traditional fleet and fighting a traditional war, they demanded a similar response in turn—a response that, given the vast industrial power of the United States, was decisive. This was war as Mahan and his advocates had envisioned.

The Atlantic war presented different challenges both geographically and strategically. The campaign was, in many ways, an antithesis of that fought in the Pacific and, like the First World War, almost completely non-Mahanian in nature. While the enemy did not possess a significant battle fleet that could challenge the Allies on the surface (at least after the conclusion of the Bismarck campaign), this is not to imply that Germany was not a sea power. Once again, the threat came from an "irregular"-style enemy, one that was far more deadly than that fought in the past. The Allies had largely written off the submarine as a threat, but the Germans had developed and refined the platform both technically and strategically. The U-boats employed by the Nazis were technologically superior to their World War I counterparts and employed new group tactics in a highly coordinated strategic campaign—a campaign in which submarines were used in a distinctly irregular manner not against military targets, but against commerce.[14] The ASW campaign against them dwarfed that of the First World War both in offensive capability and the requirements to bring it to a successful conclusion. In hindsight, this could have been avoided; the Allies in the interwar period considered the submarine no longer a threat and thus had failed to develop effective tactics and countermeasures.[15] This was especially apparent for the United States during the first months following its entry into the war, when a handful of German U-boats in the "Drumbeat" campaign successfully sank more 400 ships along the Atlantic coast, a disaster of far more military significance than

Four. Lessons, Retrenchment, and Theory, 1945–1951

Pearl Harbor.[16] This should have sent a signal that the war in the Atlantic was fundamentally different, but it was ignored. Interestingly the first operational tactic employed by the Navy—to form "hunter-killer" groups of destroyers to "offensively patrol"—while completely in character with offensive naval tradition, was almost completely ineffective against the threat, leading the Navy to launch an ineffective public relations campaign denying the scope of the problem.[17] Ultimately, it would be a combination of strategic measures including convoys, new anti-submarine technologies (improved sonar, depth bombs, and ASW aircraft) and especially intelligence that would bring the U-boat to heel.[18]

The geography of the European theater and especially the nature of the enemy largely dictated the role of sea power in the Atlantic. Compared to the Pacific, the Atlantic campaign was a "small ship" war where the primary role of sea power was to ensure access and supply for land forces. Capital ships certainly contributed to this mission, but there was little need for carriers beyond the ability to hunt for submarines, a task that could be accomplished by the smaller variety.[19] Achieving command of the sea in these campaigns was essential to overall victory in allowing for the movement of vast material across the Atlantic to wage the war successfully, but this was ultimately gained through defeat of the irregular threat with capital ships in a distinct supporting role. Capital ships prevented the Axis invasion of Britain by acting in a defensive posture and provided support to landing operations, but engagement in decisive battle was rare. Russia was able to get to Berlin without a major naval force. The lesson, again, seemed to be that against a modern continental power, command of the sea was not as relevant as it had been in previous wars. This is obviously a very different type of lesson from that envisioned by Mahan's advocates.

The overwhelming naval victory in the Second World War left Mahanian theorists in a quandary. The aircraft carrier emerged from the war as the centerpiece of naval power for the United States; the Navy had begun the war with four aircraft carriers and ended it with over 100.[20] As an industrial superpower, the United States was in the unique position during the war of building more ships than it could actually man, a condition never seen before or since.[21] Even after demobilization, the fleet was historically enormous. But how to use that fleet in the postwar era—and what lessons to take from the war—were problematic. The capital ship fleet had been designed to fight on the high seas against a similarly armed opponent, and in the aftermath of the war there was no immediate sea power to engage. This initially did not seem to be a concern for the Navy; the

Mahanian vision had proven itself, and despite the lack of any remaining threat, the Navy seemed content to assume that the case for a large fleet had been made. In the Navy's view, even the factors that contributed to its greatest victory were secondary. The island-hopping campaign in the Pacific was unnecessary given that Japan was being economically strangled, and even the extensive bombing campaign, while speeding the victory, had been a minor factor.[22] This was naïve, for not everyone saw the reasons for victory quite as clearly as the navalists. Emerging domestic forces stood ready to challenge the Navy's vision. And this time, the stakes for the future composition of the fleet would be much higher.

Threats at Home and Abroad: The Fight for Service Unification and Strategy

In the broadest strategic sense, the Navy had two distinct models that had offered success in 1945—a Mahanian-style capital ship fleet based on the aircraft carrier and decisive battle, and a second force designed to support the projection of U.S. combat power on land or fight against an irregular threat with smaller or more diverse vessels.[23] These two models presented certain challenges to navalists dedicated to maintaining a capital ship fleet. Within the Navy there was overwhelming support for the continuation of the carrier as the centerpiece of naval doctrine and emphasis on the Mahanian mindset—given the size and scope of the Pacific victory, it is difficult to see how this could have been otherwise. Conversely, the very concept of "decisive battle" had rapidly become a misnomer, as there literally were no enemies left that could hope to engage in such a battle. The world that emerged from the global conflict had no historical parallel; the bi-polar division of the world into two superpowers (U.S. and Soviet) presented not only diametrically opposed ideologies but also a distinct difference in their respective bases for strategic power.[24] The Soviet Union was dominant as a conventional land power, while the United States retained primacy on the sea.[25] While the Soviets had continued in their development of submarines, the postwar Soviet surface fleet was not as yet a significant challenge to the United States; indeed, if all of the Communist navies in the world had combined strength (as part of the unified Communist movement that most felt existed), a portion of the U.S. Navy would have been sufficient to handle the threat.[26] This fact was well known in the defense establishment.

The Cold War was a sudden reality that demanded new forms of

Four. Lessons, Retrenchment, and Theory, 1945–1951   63

thinking and a global outlook, areas in which the Navy—as an experienced strategic service—had the potential to excel. In 1946, State Department Soviet expert George Kennan penned his famous "long telegram" that characterized the Soviet regime as repressing its citizens and intent on worldwide domination and expansion. Kennan suggested that the Soviets only responded to military power since they were "committed fanatically to the belief that with the U.S. there can be no permanent modus vivendi, that it is desirable and necessary that the internal harmony of our society be disrupted, the internal authority of our state be broken, if Soviet power is to be secure."[27] Kennan recommended a series of blocking maneuvers (political, economic, and military) directed at what he saw was global Communist expansion. This doctrine was formalized by President Truman the day after his election in 1948 under the broad strategy of "Containment."[28] By adopting this strategy, Truman built public support that effectively guaranteed the continuation of the national security apparatus begun during the Second World War and, with it, continued reliance on a substantial standing military force.

    The strategy of containment was in many ways a boon for navalists who remained committed to Mahanian theory. "Containment" implied "encirclement," and while there were many components to the strategy (especially on the diplomatic front, in providing aid to friendly Western governments, rebuilding Europe under the auspices of the Marshall Plan, and solidifying alliances that would eventually become NATO), militarily the options available to the United States were quite limited on land. But not so on the sea, where a glance at a globe demonstrated that potential Soviet expansion could be checked everywhere, including the Atlantic, Pacific, Mediterranean, and the Black and Baltic Seas, a point made repeatedly by naval planners.[29] Navy rationale noted that as the sea surrounded the Soviet Union, control of that sea represented Containment in the broadest and most practical sense.[30] This would be conducted through a series of global alliances with friendly Western navies (none of whom possessed capital ship power similar to the U.S.) and the development of new, powerful capital ships that would be the mainstay of the allied forces to both deter Soviet aggression and support potential military operations ashore. The Navy now had its rationale for continued development of its fleet: the containment of Soviet land power.

    The composition of that fleet, however, was another matter that soon came to the forefront of the broader debate regarding the future role of the services. The Navy's own theoretical arguments did not help in this regard; after all, the primary role of capital ships in the Mahanian sense was to engage other capital ships, which the enemy was clearly lacking. The only sea power threat the Soviets possessed was their ability to strike at the West with their considerable fleet of attack submarines, a force that had been developed during the Second World War and that represented the primary Soviet naval arm until the mid–1960s.[31] As this threat was remarkably similar to that posed by the Germans during the Second World War (and in point of fact many of the Soviet submarines were based on captured German design),[32] logically any response to the Soviet submarine threat should build on what was successful in the past—the "small ship" model.

This was not in alignment with the Navy's thinking. Accordingly, the Navy approached this with yet another modification of theory, arguing that carriers were the perfect vehicle to conduct "offensive" ASW against the Soviet support system, targeting bases and yards and attacking submarines before they could deploy.[33] Moreover, the Navy would not be operating alone in this campaign but rather as one part of an alliance system of navies engaged in containing the Soviets—knowing quite well that the only capital ships available in the alliance for this strategy were those that belonged to the United States. Carriers would operate forward in accordance with the traditional offensive mindset, within potential strike range of Communist targets acting to support alliance navies and forming a bulwark against any Communist aggression.[34] Whatever traditional distaste Americans may have had for "entangling alliances," the fact remained that these were now the bread and butter for the Navy and a solid rationale for its overseas operations.[35] This fit in nicely with Truman's diplomatic Containment goals, including the formation of NATO. In what would emerge as a bipartisan congressional issue, even the Republican Right—traditionally composed of isolationists—began to see these in a similar light when shown that alliances were a fiscal bonus as the enormous cost of Containment became apparent.[36]

The fact that the Navy favored capital ships as an instrument of containment was a foregone conclusion given its culture, Mahanian mindset, and its World War II combat experience. The success of fleet operations during World War II generated a certain sense of complacency in the Navy, confident that its reliance on theory had been effectively proven and thus would continue as the mainstay of U.S. naval policy in the future.[37] But this concept faced challenges from a number of domestic arenas. In its new role as a global superpower (and global police force), the United States was flexing all forms of military power that in the face of limited resources and budgets presented a direct challenge to the postwar Navy. At the heart

Four. Lessons, Retrenchment, and Theory, 1945–1951

of this was an intense and contentious debate that struck at the core of Mahanian theory. The key to this debate was the role of strategic air power; at stake for the Navy was the fate of the capital ship fleet. Although the conflict between air and sea power came as something of a surprise to the Navy, it had in fact been brewing within the defense establishment since the later days of the Second World War.[38] New roles, global responsibilities, and an uncertain budget climate brought the debate to the surface.

During the Second World War, the United States engaged in a massive campaign of strategic bombing in the European and Pacific theaters, a campaign that was closely aligned with the prewar theories of the air power theorist Douhet.[39] Although the Army Air Corps had inflicted massive damage (and caused considerable casualties) through its campaign of strategic bombing against Germany and Japan, the actual effectiveness in terms of contribution to victory was very much a matter of debate. The air campaigns required enormous time and resources dedicated to the building of bases, developing aircraft, training crews, and devising a sophisticated logistics chain—but the results against the targets in enemy industry were far from decisive, and the even more nebulous "morale" very difficult to quantify.[40] Despite these difficulties, proponents of air power—especially Army Air Corps officers who were fighting for an independent Air Force—characterized the campaign as decisive on all counts, citing a massive study to prove the point.[41] Opponents pointed out that despite the destruction inflicted in both theaters by bombing, the respective enemies showed every determination to keep fighting until the very end, an end ultimately brought about by a combination of forces on land, sea, and air.[42]

The stakes in this debate were far from theoretical. In 1945, the Army Air Corps was intensely lobbying for the formation of an independent Air Force whose core mission would be power projection through strategic bombing.[43] "Containment" for air power advocates translated into a ring of bases surrounding the Soviet Union from which a strategic bombing campaign could be conducted along the lines of that waged against Germany in World War II. Given the size of the Soviet Union, its large air defensive capability, and its dispersed industrial power, this type of campaign would obviously require considerable expansion of the Air Force, a fact completely in alignment with the air power advocates.[44] Expansion of one service would mean reduction of others—especially other services that had a claim to the use of air power. This became the core argument of the new Air Force—that "balance" among the services meant little if one service adopted the main war fighting burden.[45]

Under the prewar system this domestic battle would have been one simply for influence among separate entities, but in the postwar years, the defense establishment was undergoing a complete realignment from a loosely knit group of branches under the War Department to a more tightly molded system under the new Department of Defense, an act intended to increase civilian control of the military and streamline planning and operations to align with the new global role of the United States.[46] In this new "joint" environment, the branches competed for money, influence, and power whose allocation would ultimately be decided by the Secretary of Defense.[47] This represented an opportunity for the new Air Force, which proceeded to wage a campaign against the other services reminiscent in intensity as those fought during the recently concluded war.

The Air Force's initial salvo was directed at the naval air arm. As the "owners" of air power capability, the Air Force proposed that all planes flying from carriers should be manned by Air Force pilots and that any "support" naval missions flying from land (scouting, ASW, etc.) should not be naval missions at all but rather should be conducted by the Air Force.[48] This proposal took the Navy by surprise but was quickly countered; officially the rationale stated that training for "naval" missions was quite different from that conducted by the Air Force, so therefore it was argued that these missions (and pilots) logically belonged with the service most familiar with war at sea.[49] In the broader bureaucratic sense, the Navy was fully aware that allocating these missions to a force whose primary focus was strategic bombing would quickly put these missions in a secondary status with the Air Force, if they were to survive at all in an austere budget environment. The Air Force lost the initial fight—but it was only the beginning. Air Force officers next convinced advocates in the office of the Secretary of Defense to vastly limit the role of the Navy in its senior strategic planning documents, citing anti-submarine warfare as the primary role of the Navy, effectively eliminating the mention of carriers in grand strategy.[50] Within the Pentagon the Navy reacted with immediate alarm, pointing out that the strategic bombing strategy proposed by the Air Force required a base network that did not in fact exist and until such time as it did, aircraft carriers represented the only flexible capability for bombing potential Communist threats. Again the Air Force lost the fight, but the campaign was far from over.

What changed the calculus in the argument was the proposed use of the new atomic bomb. It is a popular myth that the U.S. emerged from the Second World War as a fully developed atomic power.[51] This is not the case. Although two bombs had been dropped on Japan in the final days of the war, in the aftermath there was no consensus as to how these weapons should be used in the future—or even if they would be part of future war fighting at all. The bomb was decisive when used but suffered from serious limitations. Both politicians and military planners noted that tactically the weapons were limited in terms of targeting, delivery, and above all in availability.[52]

Moreover, there were serious moral considerations that weighed heavily in their use. The idea of massive destruction of civilian targets was one that was viewed distastefully in many quarters of the Pentagon and within government, so much so that there was serious consideration given to treaties that would ban the weapon completely in future conflicts.[53] This attitude hardened with intelligence that the Soviets were developing their own weapon, but exactly when this effort would come to fruition was controversial. The Air Force argued that the Soviets could be a significant atomic power with the capability to strike the United States as early as 1947, while the Navy argued for a much longer time frame.[54] This factor was key; if the Soviets had a strategic bombing force, then the United States needed one that was superior. In this argument, the Air Force was successful, largely through the efforts of General Curtis LeMay, who personally had led the air war against Japan and who molded the newly created Strategic Air Command into a force that was capable of striking decisively at the Soviets—at least according to his popular testimony.

LeMay's efforts refocused the debate into one that was far more challenging to the Navy's vision of a capital ship fleet. Relying on congressional allies and a savvy public affairs campaign, the Air Force brought its plan for strategic bombing with atomic weapons to the forefront of the public eye. The key to the argument was not the war waged "now" but one that would be fought in the very near future. Between two nuclear-armed opponents, atomic weapons made war potentially very fast and very devastating and was theoretically fought almost solely by air power—a fact that was pointed out repeatedly by the Air Force in very public venues.[55] It was aided in this argument by an entirely new class of civilian academic strategists and theorists with influence in government, few of whom had experience in sea power or, for that matter, much interest.[56]

Given that it was widely accepted that a nuclear strike would be decisive and war-winning (or at least war-ending) and the subsequent expense required to develop and maintain the nuclear force, these theorists argued (not unreasonably, within the limits of this scenario) that there was little need for a large and expensive Navy in an atomic war. Within this somewhat limited scenario, the argument made a certain degree of sense. While it was true that ships provided flexibility in conventional war, they were also slow to reach their operational areas, and their strike capability was limited compared to the growing force of strategic bombers. Testimony by war heroes Lieutenant General Jimmy Doolittle and General Curtis LeMay spoke directly on this point to sympathetic congressmen who were enthused by the dual benefit of budget savings by cutting other services and the development of new, high-tech weaponry that seemed to promise unlimited strategic dominance.[57]

The Navy was slow to recognize the challenge that this new strategic thinking presented to its theory and force structure.[58] Although naval officers had been intimately involved in the technical development of atomic weapons, the Navy's initial view of the weapon itself was that it was not as much of a "game changer" as the Air Force implied.[59] Most Navy planners questioned the long-range strategic bombing strategy as either operationally difficult, morally questionable, or both. In their view the atomic bomb was first and foremost a military weapon to be used against military targets. Tests at Bikini Atoll had shown that nuclear weapons were not much of a threat to a prepared and dispersed battle group, so defense against an enemy using nuclear weapons was possible at sea. Therefore, the most logical means of delivering nuclear weapons, from the Navy's viewpoint, was directly against military targets by the most flexible means available—tactical aircraft flying from bases or (more ideally) from carriers. Accordingly, the Navy proceeded to mold its rationale for continued capital ship development, envisioning carriers operating in the following roles in both the conventional and nuclear environment, using operations against the Soviets as a theoretical baseline:

- Support the withdrawal of U.S. and Allied forces [in the face of a Soviet offensive]
- Destroy enemy naval forces, naval bases, and installations.
- Conduct and provide necessary air cover for mining operations.
- Destroy enemy aircraft and facilities at bases which threaten U.S. control of sea areas and locations.
- Hinder enemy advancement of air bases and stockpiling of material in enemy forward areas.
- Support and participate in the strategic air offensive as ordered.
- Support Allied and U.S. ground forces.
- Interdict enemy lines of communications (LOCs).
- Provide supplementary air defense when necessary.
- Participate in the air battle.[60]

There were obviously some familiar themes in this grand strategy—forward operations, support of land battle, offensive operations, and a fundamental reliance on carrier air power as the centerpiece of naval doctrine.[61] This strategy was not only theoretically consistent but also historical; in effect, the Navy was preparing to re-fight the Pacific campaign with a new target—this time, the Soviets in Europe. Absent from the list was a major emphasis: given that the Soviets had no offensive surface power to speak of, the Navy's role would now be one of power projection much like that conducted in the Pacific in the latter days of the war. Ships would still have to be built and prepare for offensive blue-water operations (should the Soviets develop that capability), but for the time being the focus would be on the forward offensive not just against enemy sea power, but land power as well.[62]

Of course the carriers that were required for the Navy's vision of future war did not exist at the time of the drafting of the strategy—but they were in the works and would become the focal point for the conflict that would ultimately define the course of the Navy for generations. But what was obvious to the Navy was that its vision was far from the one proposed by the Air Force, who viewed the Navy's proposals as a direct threat to its main mission (if not existence as a strategic force).[63] Subsequently, the Navy's new strategy and the force plan required to implement it were quickly swept aside in the subsequent public relations blitz launched by the Air Force in an attempt to replace the carrier force with a strategic bomber and effectively end the U.S. reliance on Mahanian theory as an element of strategic war fighting.[64]

The Revolt of the Admirals

The fight that had been simmering between the Navy and Air Force regarding the role of each in the postwar world came to a very public climax in 1949 with the a series of hearings on service unification, strategy, and procurement, commonly referred to as the "revolt of the admirals."[65] Facing increasingly a shrinking budget, a hostile Secretary of Defense, and a strategy increasingly questioned by a public saturated by the Air Force public relations campaign, the Navy finally fought back in a series of congressional hearings that ultimately defined the strategic course of the Navy. The fight was the Navy publicly crossing the Rubicon of sorts; once committed to its modern capital ship theory, there would be no turning back.

Had the fight between the Navy and Air Force simply focused on strategic bombing, the ultimate showdown might have been averted. But in a short period of time, a number of factors combined that required immediate and dramatic resolution. Carriers had always been viewed with hostility by the Air Force as a threat to their hold on U.S. air power; in 1948, a study by the Air War College openly questioned the ability of aircraft carriers to strike with atomic weapons.[66] This subsequently led to a comment by the chief of staff of the Air Force that carriers had limited use in atomic war. In 1949, Louis Johnson replaced Forrestal as Secretary of Defense. Forrestal had always been sympathetic to the Navy and its capital ship theory; not so Johnson, who was aggressive, argumentative, and solidly aligned with the Air Force viewpoint both strategically and fiscally.[67] Moving quickly to cement his authority in the new position, one of his first acts was to cancel the construction of the new flush-deck supercarrier *United States*, a platform that represented (in the Navy's view) the future of the Navy as a capital ship force.[68] In rapid succession he reallocated the funding for the carrier to the Air Force's new B-36 strategic bomber, effectively nullifying the Navy's role in strategic forward operations.[69] The fact that the Air Force's public claims for the effectiveness of the B-36 (and of strategic bombing as a whole) were at best questionable did not affect Johnson's decision. He was deaf to the Navy's arguments for a balanced military global force.[70] This proved to be too much for the navalists, who prepared a counterattack. The issue wasn't simply the fate of one carrier, but rather the future roles and missions of the Navy itself.

In April 1949, an "anonymous document" was forwarded to several congressmen and senators detailing a list of the perceived weaknesses of the B-36 program, questioning the Air Force's claims regarding strategic bombing, and implying that Secretary Johnson had a direct financial interest in the procurement of the B-36.[71] Authored by Cedric Worth, special assistant to the undersecretary of the Navy, and naval aviator Commander Thomas Davies, the accusations created a firestorm in the press and led to immediate hearings, a deep embarrassment both for the Air Force and the new Secretary of Defense. The scope of the charges soon moved the hearings beyond the deficiencies of the B-36 to service strategy and unification as a whole, bringing the fight between the respective services to the full view of the public.

The "revolt of the admirals" did not begin well for the Navy. The Air Force reaped the benefits of years of successful public relations and lobbying, remaining in the public eye and imagination with its promises of high tech and decisive war fighting.[72] Air Force generals came to the hear-

Four. Lessons, Retrenchment, and Theory, 1945–1951

ing table well prepared, openly scoffing at Navy claims as unrealistic and outdated and hinting at aristocratic conspiracy. Supposed improprieties by the Secretary of Defense were quickly discredited, casting doubt on the Navy's claims. This cleared the way for a now completely hostile Johnson to counterattack with his political ally, the new Secretary of the Navy (Matthews).

The Army aligned itself with the Air Force, chairman of the Joint Chiefs Omar Bradley going so far as to call the Navy admirals a bunch of "fancy Dans" and implying limited war fighting experience.[73] But the Navy was not passive in its defense. A succession of admirals, well prepared by the newly formed analytical group Op-23, led by Captain Arleigh Burke, created doubt in the mind of the senators regarding the strategy of strategic bombing. The final testimony, by Admiral Denefield (the chief of naval operations) took the committee by surprise with its passion, demanding that the United States consider all options for future operations against the Communists—testimony that, despite promises of congressional immunity, cost the CNO his job.[74]

In the short term it seemed that the Navy lost more than it gained in the Service Unification hearings. But in the longer term, the hearings set the course for the future of capital ship theory within the service. Naval aviation was effectively saved with the continued authorization of new supercarriers, now supported by congressional advocates impressed by the Navy's arguments. Strategic bombing and the Air Force would still capture the public's imagination as well as the lion's share of the budget, but it would no longer be regarded as the only path to success in the Cold War. Within the service itself, the "revolt" brought together disparate elements that had questioned the course the Navy was taking. Many "blackshoe" (surface line) officers had questioned the rise and emphasis given to the aviators; the "revolt" demonstrated that without carriers, the Navy would have little say in the future of grand strategy, likely relegated to a smaller ship anti-submarine force.[75] Open testimony represented the first solid political representation of formal Navy strategic thought. The battleship was effectively dead as a representation of the capital ship paradigm; although one can make the argument of internal division in the Navy between aviator and surface ship "unions" regarding the tactical use of vessels, there was no doubt that there was unity regarding the development of the carrier battle group as an extension of capital ship/Mahanian theory.

Although the Navy ultimately got its carriers in the wake of the "revolt," the vindictiveness of the hearings and how close it had come to losing the centerpiece of its theory left an indelible impression. It could no longer be assumed that the navalist position was widely accepted in the political realm. The Navy would now have to fight for its position in the defense hierarchy. This meant continuously reinforcing its message. The Navy learned quickly, commencing a long-term and aggressive public relations campaign to stress the importance of carriers and the vital importance of the Navy in containing Communist aggression. The USSR had not arrived yet as a significant ocean force, but it would soon, and it was vital that the Navy develop strike power that would be the centerpiece of a sea-going alliance to counter it when they inevitably became a threat. The public was reminded of the glories of the past through the *Victory at Sea* television series, the first of its kind to bring World War II footage directly into the living room.[76] Turning to Hollywood, movies such as *Aircraft Carrier* and *The Bridges of Toko-Ri* vied with the Air Force's efforts (*Strategic Air Command*) to continually remind the voting public of the considerable power and contribution of the U.S. Navy against past—and potentially future—enemies.

Ultimately the experiences of 1945–1951 that culminated in the "revolt of the admirals" taught the Navy an important lesson that it has never forgotten: that capital ship theory, the bedrock of naval doctrine, was vulnerable. Despite success in global combat, despite a core group of true believers within the service, the theory that seemed so obvious to navalists could and would be challenged by competitors who would go to great lengths to present alternatives that, to an increasingly aware public, made sense. It was a historical fact that fleets require massive investment of national resources, but for the first time this commitment hinged on how successfully the Navy could portray its own effectiveness in an increasingly aware and fast-paced political arena. The United States emerged from the war with a growing national security apparatus whose competitiveness for resources would become increasingly intense. For the Navy, this meant "circling the wagons" and defending its core theory—often at the expense of anything else, including irregular-style operations. This solid (and defensive) commitment to capital ship theory would remain the standard for the next sixty years.

Five

Theory and the Challenge of Irregular Warfare, 1950–1980

The period from 1950 to 1980 represented an era of new and varied challenges for a Navy that was becoming increasingly designed for a global role in a bi-polar world where the U.S. was one of two superpowers. At the beginning of this period, it appeared that the way ahead for the fleet in the future was clear. The Navy emerged bloody but unbowed from the unification hearings, its capital ship theory intact and solidified within the service. Although there would be skirmishes between the services in the future over unified strategy and allocation of resources,[1] by the mid-1950s the Navy was relatively secure domestically. But senior officers had learned the harsh lesson during the unification hearings that relevancy in a changing world was no longer a foregone conclusion. The military strategy of the United States could no longer be determined by the individual services acting in loose concert but rather was a highly scrutinized course of action devised at the highest levels of government, with significant long term effects both domestically and internationally.[2] The U.S. was now a superpower, its military strategy the focal point of a vast alliance directed against a common enemy. The Navy needed to adapt to its role as a representative of that power.

It seemed that capital ship theory was ideal for the new U.S. role. Mahan's central thesis was that great powers employed great navies; the U.S. had eclipsed and replaced Britain (Mahan's model) as the world's superpower, an empire that had maintained its supremacy through the quality and size of its Navy. Moreover, the U.S. and its allies had a clear and recognizable opponent in the Soviet Union. The West made no secret of its view of a projected war with Soviets, employing a grand strategy that remained remarkably consistent.[3] The Navy's response to the threat was based solidly in established theory, displaying a consistent Mahanian element in emphasizing capital ships conducting offensive operations and ultimately seeking decisive battle. This theoretical element became more influential as time went on and the experience of the actual combat faded. New technologies, new weapons, and a new world order were all considered and debated well within the paradigm of capital ship theory, which remained the centerpiece of naval planning.[4]

Had global war with the Soviets been the only threat, this theory might arguably have met the requirements for effective naval operations during the Cold War. But the world had become far more complicated for the United States in its new superpower role, and the requirements for the use of the Navy were often not as "clean" as the traditional theorists desired. The war against the Soviets never became a reality; rather, the next two decades were marked by irregular conflicts of a very different nature that challenged the core conventional theories of all the services.[5]

This was especially true for the Navy, which found itself operating on the periphery of these irregular conflicts, attempting to adapt platforms and tactics to missions that were contrary to both their design and theory. In the test of combat, capital ships had a mixed record of success as the Navy attempted to adapt from a theoretical construct to a practical one, using combat power in a variety of support roles for which it was neither designed nor intended. It was this element of adaptability—successful in some cases, mediocre or poorly executed in others—that would present its own unique challenge to classical theory. This is evident when examining the Navy's planning for the theoretical conflict while actively fighting irregular wars of a very different nature.

Practical Application of Cold War Theory

The onset of the Cold War was militarily unique from a number of perspectives. While it is true that the U.S. never fought the Soviet Union in open combat, there is no doubt that the potential for conflict existed throughout the entire Cold War period; even with the benefit of hindsight, it is difficult to dispute that deliberately provocative events conducted by both sides during the period brought the world perilously close to open war.[6] If we assume that such a war was possible (as the planners of the Cold War most certainly did), the seminal question for the Navy was how to design a force that could effectively engage in such a war and thus to deter war and provide strategic and political stability. The debate centered on two key elements: should the Navy be a deterrent force relying on rapid

Five. Theory and the Challenge of Irregular Warfare, 1950–1980   75

deployment of nuclear power, or should it focus on its conventional warfighting mission?

The answer, initially, was not an easy one for the traditionalists. As we have seen, naval power in peacetime is always subject to a great deal of speculation as to how advancing technology can potentially impact its use during the next war; indeed, the history of naval power itself is one of technological and theoretical development in peacetime and its subsequent test in combat. Publicly, the Navy had committed itself in the aftermath of the "revolt of the admirals" to being a part of the strategic nuclear force, stating that carriers would be the mainstay of a tactical nuclear deterrent that could supplement deep strike operations by Strategic Air Command.[7] Naval policy officially reflected this position, as did subsequent design of ships and aircraft to accommodate atomic weaponry. This included the development of an entirely new weapons system, the Polaris ballistic missile submarine, an incredibly complex (and expensive) nuclear launch system that required such specialization that its officers and crew were often considered a separate "navy within a navy" designed and managed by its enigmatic head, Admiral Hyman Rickover.[8]

A great deal has been written about Rickover and the development of the nuclear Navy. For purposes of this discussion, Rickover's tenure had several implications. First, the traditional Navy paid a great deal for the new strategic capability of Polaris, often to the detriment of the surface fleet in terms of funding and subsequent de-emphasis of traditional missions.[9] Second, Rickover's singular vision of a nuclear fleet—in a sense, a nuclear Mahan—constantly challenged any attempt to develop platforms outside the nuclear paradigm. Capital ships were fine, so long as they were nuclear—an extremely expensive and limiting proposition, even for the traditionalists.[10]

But despite its integration into the nuclear arena, the USN did not become a specialized nuclear force to the extent displayed by the Air Force, which increasingly de-emphasized its tactical battlefield role in favor of its bombers and missile forces.[11] Within the Navy, there was considerable debate concerning over-reliance on nuclear weapons as a core component of naval strategy.[12] There are a number of reasons for this that must be considered from a cultural as well as a practical perspective. Although the Navy was uniform in its desire to possess large capital ships of increasing power and complexity, there were also subdivisions within the force into various "unions" (air, surface, and subsurface) that viewed power projection and the use of this fleet very differently.[13] Nuclear strike and vessels designed specifically for this mission limited the options available to these groups considerably. Traditionalists pointed out (correctly) that wholesale specialization in the nuclear mission would effectively limit or nullify many of the missions that the Navy historically performed.[14] Even in a nuclear war environment, the Navy was not thinking in terms of "mutual assured destruction" (MAD) but was rather more aligned with the future doctrine of selective use (NUTS).[15] Carriers armed with tactical nuclear weapons answered both requirements; the Navy could have it all by building these platforms—so long as the defense establishment agreed.

This concern was not limited to the Navy. The United States' official policy of massive retaliation was a debatable policy position on moral, strategic, and realistic grounds even before the Soviets reached nuclear parity. Soviet actions that would serve as a trigger for the use of such devastating power beyond a mass conventional attack were a key issue, as was the practicality of delivering such a strike while limiting damage to allies. This was especially important to NATO allies: how to defend Europe without actually destroying it? To Europe, even a "limited" war with the Soviets amounted to total war if tactical nuclear weapons were used.[16] Moreover, the decision to use these weapons was a political one that was centralized and made at the highest levels and not by operational commanders, as many in the military had envisioned when the weapon was first introduced. As these weapons rapidly improved in both technical capability and availability, the actual terms of their use became less and less certain.[17] As the Soviet Union slowly achieved a degree of nuclear parity with the United States and mutual use became a very real possibility, it became increasingly obvious to U.S. strategists that alternative scenarios had to be considered that were outside a nuclear exchange that would spell complete destruction for both sides.[18]

In scenarios where military power was used against the Soviets (outside the nuclear paradigm), the Navy saw itself in a particularly envious position vis a vis the other services. Practically, the Navy had extensive experience with deployment for contingencies (such as presence, power projection, etc.) that did not require a nuclear option or where the use of nuclear weapons would be limited or inappropriate. The Navy had always viewed nuclear weapons as an option—but only one option. War had to be viewed holistically, fought with capital ships that were able to meet all contingencies outside a total nuclear strike. This required a robust and flexible operational capability, a requirement that served the theorists well. In terms of Cold War planning, the Navy was in an excellent position to adapt to various contingencies with its capital ship fleet, because in the global context, it could act effectively in both roles, as a nuclear or con-

Five. Theory and the Challenge of Irregular Warfare, 1950–1980   77

ventional strike force. Carriers, although capable of deploying tactical nuclear weapons, also employed a robust air wing capability that had been purposefully diversified to provide a variety of strike options for a wide range of contingencies.[19] The key for success would be to determine how this capability fit into the broader strategic context.

This context was provided by the formation of the newly formed NATO and the Navy's subsequent integration with its planning efforts. From its earliest days, NATO was very much a maritime alliance, with forces from all navies dedicated to cooperative planning for a wide range of contingencies that varied from nuclear to small-scale conventional operations in Europe.[20] As the largest and most capable maritime force in the alliance, the U.S. Navy was particularly active in positioning itself for support of projected NATO operations in all theaters, at the center of which was the inherent flexibility of the carrier battle group.[21] In the strategic sense the purpose of these forces was twofold: to provide flexible strike support options to land forces resisting the Soviet offensive (including cover for an evacuation of Europe if necessary), and to keep the sea lanes clear by conducting offensive forward operations against Soviet submarine bases.[22] The shift from the overwhelming nuclear response of "Massive Retaliation" to "Flexible Response" (first proposed in 1962) did not fundamentally alter these mission sets nor de-emphasize the forces dedicated to them; rather, it strengthened the argument that additional conventional naval power was required to successfully defend NATO. Moreover, in addressing potential contingencies, the Navy began a very subtle shift toward returning to its classical roots, focusing increasingly on sea control operations rather than support of combat operations ashore.[23]

To some extent, the Soviet Navy—perhaps inadvertently—served to reinforce the Navy's desire for a return to its traditional role. Despite a robust naval history, the Soviet Union in the post–World War II era was not widely regarded as an effective naval power. Given that Imperial Russia had maintained a large fleet and the fact that the Soviet Navy had a long and distinguished battle record during the Second World War, the critique is an interesting one. Nitze and others noted that the combat effectiveness of the Soviet Navy had to be viewed in context of its support to land combat, not as a high seas force.[24] Events in the postwar era alternatively emphasized and de-emphasized naval power, actions that offered various interpretations of Soviet strategic motivations for Western analysts.[25] In the immediate aftermath of World War II, Stalin, inspired by the Allied capability for invasion at Normandy and elsewhere, dramatically increased Soviet naval expansion, using surface and subsurface war prizes as a basis for a new fleet.[26] This building program was effectively halted following Stalin's death. Although the Soviets never lost their taste for submarines, Stalin's eventual successor, Khrushchev, ordered surface construction scrapped following a number of spectacular accidents.[27] The limitations of this decision (from the Soviet perspective) were made abundantly clear during the Cuban Missile Crisis, an operational humiliation for the surface fleet, which had very limited assets to escort missile-laden merchants in the face of overwhelming U.S. Navy power.

In the immediate aftermath of the crisis, the fleet began a rapid rebuilding and modernization program that presented (in the eyes of Western analysts) a number of new challenges. Strategically, the Soviet Union developed its own second-strike capability through the construction of a number of rudimentary ballistic missile submarines, which, although inferior to the United States' fleet, posed a significant threat if deployed in mid-ocean within firing range of the United States.[28] Second, the Soviets began a relatively robust construction program of modern ocean-going combatants that began making an appearance on the world stage in various diplomatic missions abroad, most notably in ports that had traditionally been the operating area of the U.S. Navy, including the Indian Ocean, Mediterranean, Caribbean, and many third-world nations.[29] Third, the Soviets began to publicly rationalize the development of a Navy as a strategic force, most notably through the writings of Fleet Admiral Gorshkov.[30]

The composition and public strategy of the Soviet Navy presented something of a dilemma. Gorshkov and others stressed that the primary mission of the Navy was defense, most notably in protecting the strategic ballistic missile submarine (SSBN) force.[31] This stated purpose did not sit well with U.S. naval planners steeped in the offensive. Naval advocates were quick to point out not only the offensive nature of the ships being built (including a large number of nuclear attack submarines and guided missile cruisers and frigates) but also that strategically the idea of Soviet "defense" often translated into offensive operations to protect the homeland.[32] The idea that any Navy, especially one as large and modern as the Soviets were building, would simply sit and wait for an opponent seemed beyond belief.[33] The material design of Soviet ships seemed to support this view.

Soviet modernization efforts in the 1960s and beyond served the interests of the Mahanians well. The Soviet fleet was a great mystery; although today in hindsight it is recognized that most Soviet warships were hopelessly outclassed by their U.S. counterparts, during the Cold

Five. Theory and the Challenge of Irregular Warfare, 1950–1980

War this was neither apparent nor a popular speculation.[34] Technologically, Soviet naval development seemed to be supporting the arguments of U.S. navalists that the fleet was designed for offensive purposes. Whereas the Americans focused on airpower and carriers, the Soviet fleet emphasized surface combatants armed with anti-ship missile technology that was variable and numerous; at its height, the Soviet Navy boasted over twenty different types of missile, each of which seemed to be a serious if not overwhelming threat.[35] Some analysts pointed out that missile technology was not "defensive" in nature.[36] The Soviet traditional reliance on mass firepower (extrapolated from land doctrine) seemed to indicate that the fleet's purpose was offensive, designed to overwhelm carriers with mass barrages of missiles. This fit in nicely with the Mahanian model; even if the Soviets were numerically inferior (fulfilling the role of a "fleet in being"), sitting in port would accomplish nothing. If the Soviets were to pursue a "defensive" doctrine, the idea that they would extend their defensive zone outside their home waters was not contradictory; in point of fact, this idea of a "buffer" was exactly the logic Stalin used in his continued occupation of Poland and East Germany.[37] It was logical (or at least desirable for U.S. planning purposes) that the enemy would sail out and seek offensive action wherever possible with a fleet designed specifically for this purpose: a sea-denial Navy—a sea that the U.S. and NATO needed to use. This assumption served as the basis for a number of contingencies that were strictly "naval" regarding the future war, focusing on at sea combat with a fleet finally "worthy of the steel" of the USN.[38] The planners had their Jutland.

Scenarios speculating on a future war at sea varied as the Soviet Navy grew. The most significant of these for purposes of fleet rationalization and subsequent construction of capital ships was the "limited war at sea," a strategic view of the future war that tied the course of a land war directly to actions that occurred at sea.[39] In this model, war could not only begin at sea with a NATO-Soviet confrontation, but could also (theoretically) be limited to a maritime conflict in the open ocean. There were certain advantages to this for the respective combatants, especially if nuclear weapons were employed; the sea represented the ultimate clear "battle space" where combat could occur freely with allegedly no effect on civilian populations nor damage to the infrastructure of either side. Combat could arguably be contained on the sea, the issue resolved without significant land combat.

The logic behind this was relatively simple: as NATO was clearly reliant on the sea for reinforcement, victory at sea for the Soviets would effectively cut the vital sea lanes and force the alliance to sue for peace, a factor that seemed obvious to U.S. naval planners.[40] NATO victory at sea, on the other hand, would show resolve—and ensure that the alliance was fully capable of defense, which could forestall or halt a Soviet land offensive before it began.[41] Both of these factors relied on two assumptions: that the Soviets had the capability to defeat NATO—mainly U.S.—forces at sea (in hindsight, the point is extremely debatable) and that the Soviets would in fact choose this option over a massive land offensive if they decided to go to war. Although highly speculative (the model not only assumed the Soviets would use their fleet offensively, but also that victory at sea would be war-winning for either side—and that there would be no strategic nuclear exchange), the limited war at sea scenario was used with various degrees of success in rationalizing the continued development of capital ship power from the 1960s until the mid–1980s.

The impact of this train of thought was undeniable. Throughout his tenure as CNO (1970–74), Admiral Elmo Zumwalt repeatedly testified before Congress that in an open war at sea the Soviet fleet would dominate, overwhelming U.S. carriers and their escorts with their surface, air, and missile capability.[42] Zumwalt's testimony was strictly along classic navalist lines, assuming that the Soviets would sail out aggressively to challenge U.S. command of the sea in a Jutland-style battle, a scenario that was recognizable to sympathetic congressmen who rarely challenged what motivations the Soviets might have to risk their fleet in such a venture. This also went against the NATO vision of the use of the Soviet fleet, which envisioned the enemy creating a defensive buffer closer to the land mass of Europe, forming a naval perimeter.[43] Regardless, the testimony had both immediate and long-term impact. New construction was authorized, but more importantly, capital ships—now an increasingly large fleet of cruisers as well as carriers—began to undergo technological upgrades that enabled them to compete against a serious surface threat.[44] Systems such as Aegis, Harpoon, and Tomahawk, all initially designed to improve surface strike power and survivability in a war at sea scenario, were born.

In the context of a global war with the Soviets, the ultimate objective of the Cold War Navy was twofold: to obtain superiority at sea for its unfettered use and to take the fight to the Soviets through the aggressive application of naval power in both conventional and nuclear war. Both elements were distinctly Mahanian in nature. Considering that the Soviets were a land power with limited naval resources, directing strategy toward this end was a remarkable achievement, especially as it necessitated the continued buildup of large and expensive capital ships, arguably to the detriment of land power that could be used against advancing Soviet armies.

NATO was a huge commitment for the Navy from the outset, yet even in planning for various contingencies the navalists pursued a Mahanian viewpoint for a force founded on capital ship theory; no matter what maritime strategy that was adopted by the alliance, the Navy possessed the capital ships and would use them accordingly. What was particularly remarkable about this approach was that NATO sea power was focused primarily on defeating a submarine threat—something that capital ships were not particularly suited to deal with. Although the Navy answered this with continued development of ASW technology and building some new destroyers, the bulk of the direct ASW mission to meet this threat was largely to be provided by the Europeans.[45] While all the Allied navies worked together toward this one common goal, none of these navies could come close to matching the striking power of the USN, which was delegated to other, more offensive roles. NATO maritime strategies were clearly centered on this power. U.S. ships were subsequently constructed for these scenarios—and not for warfare that was unconventional or irregular.[46]

The New Irregular Warfare Challenge

Had NATO been the only commitment for the U.S. Navy, there arguably would have been little to challenge capital ship theory in the immediate postwar era. But the potential war with the Soviets was not the only conflict faced by the United States as it grew into its role as a global superpower. Regional wars—at the time largely viewed as peripheral to the overall West-East conflict—raged throughout the period, committing U.S. forces to engage in widespread conflict in both Korea and Vietnam as well as lesser engagements in a host of other conflicts and hot spots worldwide.[47] With the exception of Korea, these were distinctly irregular, requiring operational and material adaptability outside the realm of traditional theory. How the Navy responded to these challenges was indicative of its commitment to its theory.

Why were regional wars a challenge during the Cold War period? At first glance this would seem unusual; after all, the U.S. Navy in the postwar period was not only the largest and most modern on earth, but also exercised almost total command of the sea. Historically, naval forces have always demonstrated a remarkable ability to adapt to local operational and tactical challenges, exercising the ability to conduct a wide range of missions. And potential new challenges were certainly not unknown to senior Navy officials; Arleigh Burke put it best when he said:

What the country needed were fast moving forces configured for limited war, and a forward strategy so as to present our allies and the Communists with tangible evidence of our capacity to resist aggression. In these situations we must take advantage of the ocean highways to project the force necessary to eliminate the menace where it occurs. The Navy is more than a "first line" of defense. It frequently is and must be the spearhead of our military actions overseas. It is the first line of impact in many occasions.[48]

But the Navy of the Cold War period was not the Navy of the past. The potential conflict with the Soviets and emphasis on capital ship development had created a Navy that was very specialized toward conventional, global combat.[49] Materially, Cold War naval forces were neither designed for nor trained for operations outside the Soviet paradigm. This is especially true in an irregular warfare context, which as noted often requires execution of support missions that are far more nebulous than traditional ocean combat.[50] The Navy, with its guns, missiles, and air strike capability, was focused on an entirely different type of war, a focus that demanded not only increased emphasis on advanced weapons systems but also technological and tactical training designed to maximize the effectiveness of those systems. Ships and crews trained in this paradigm could not easily "shift" to a new role and hope for effectiveness in the new environment. Fighting in irregular wars required an entirely new focus in both ship design and training. It is true that in 1962 the Navy began to make plans for irregular warfare in the design of special operations forces, some small boat units, and retraining of SeaBee technical assist teams.[51] But making this shift was far more complex than simply buying new weapons systems and training for their use. If viewed in the strategic (and bureaucratic) sense, shifting focus to irregular war, no matter how prevalent these conflicts might be, could potentially threaten the core purpose of the fleet, a very dangerous proposition if viewed in the context of the never-ending competition for relevance and resources fought between the services.

In many respects the greatest challenges posed by irregular war lay in the domestic arena. The irregular conflicts of the postwar era required adaptability to be successful, but the act of adapting presented unique bureaucratic and strategic challenges. Simply put, irregular wars could not be ignored—but the core mission of global war had to remain a priority.[52] As regional wars became more prevalent, however, the Navy found itself in an increasingly precarious position regarding its long-term strategic goals that relied upon conventional combat against an equally equipped opponent. The Navy had argued forcefully during the "revolt of the admirals" that it was a full partner in global war and had constructed its fleet

Five. Theory and the Challenge of Irregular Warfare, 1950–1980   83

accordingly. Theory argued that a capital-ship Navy was the most effective way to fight in this war, but it was an expensive proposition. Funding had been committed to building and maintaining this type of fleet, a form of sea power that was not a proper "fit" for irregular war. But conversely, the Navy could not turn its back on irregular operations; capital ships sitting idle at the pier could foster the argument that these ships were irrelevant in modern conflicts that were becoming the norm rather than the exception. The Navy had capital ships and had to use them. As combat operations overseas became more of a national focus, the Navy could not simply turn its back on war without the very real risk of its contribution to the national strategy once again being publicly questioned. To do so would once again have raised the specter of relevancy, an area where the Navy was vulnerable.[53] The Navy had to make the case that it could do it all with its capital ships.[54]

The fundamental question for Navy planners was to what degree traditional theory (and the assets designed around the core tenets of that theory) should adapt to the irregular challenge. Too much commitment to the irregular warfare mission would surely result in another public challenge to capital ship theory. Carriers were a very expensive way to fight an irregular war, especially as their contribution to irregular mission areas outside strike operations was debatable.[55] Although the Air Force had suffered setbacks in the wake of the unification hearings, it was still a competitor, and the price of capital ships was increasing exponentially. The Navy was therefore forced into a very delicate balancing act of committing some of its resources to irregular conflict while maintaining others for the inevitable showdown with the Soviets. The Navy either had to demonstrate some relevancy in irregular war, or the threat had to be marginalized—or both. Practically, this was accomplished by developing policy that committed some capital ships to support missions while simultaneously developing smaller, irregular warfare forces that were useful in the current irregular conflict—but to quickly disestablish those units and their supporting doctrine when no longer needed, reemphasizing the need for capital ship power. This was the beginning of a pattern that would continue until the present day.

Theory Under Fire: Korea and Vietnam

The first open conflict of the Cold War did not seem—initially—to be a significant theoretical challenge.[56] On 25 June 1950, the Army of Communist North Korea surged over the 39th parallel in a massive coordinated offensive against the South. Supported by the Soviets and Chinese politically and materially, the mass attack represented the first "hot" action of the Cold War. Within days the United States responded, conducting air strikes against the advancing land forces of North Korea from carriers that had been rushed onto the scene. Tactical air support for land combat operations soon expanded to a broader campaign of strikes against more distant military targets and infrastructure.[57] For the next three years, the Navy would continue in this vein, supporting operations ashore and using tactical air power to strike at vulnerable military and infrastructure targets along the Korean peninsula. These operations gave the Navy a far greater status in the defense hierarchy. In addition to its combat operations (many of which, especially the amphibious landings at Inchon, had direct impact on the course of the war), American forces operating in Korea were dependent on the Navy for a host of reasons, not the least of which was that all supplies were transported by sea.[58]

As first, Korea seemed to be distinctly conventional. Initial Navy combat operations were conducted along familiar lines, employing air strike and bombardment in support of land operations. But these operations also represented a subtle theoretical shift that was to have significant implications for future U.S. naval strategy. Because the Navy exercised almost total command of the sea in Korea, it was possible for carriers and their support forces to operate in forward areas for sustained periods of time, an element that was relatively new (having been exercised for the first time in the final months of World War II). This was a theoretical evolution; historically, while capital ships had always operated "forward" in battle, their usual employment was near home waters until needed, their loss being too great a risk to rationalize continuous deployment forward against an enemy.[59] Against a conventional or equally matched naval enemy, these types of operations would not have been possible, but in an environment where the Navy exercised total sea dominance, forward deployment could become a reality both in theory and practice.[60] Sustained forward basing and deployment was distinctly Mahanian in terms of exercising command of the sea, but it did not come cheaply. Throughout the Korean conflict, the Navy maintained at least three aircraft carrier groups continuously "on station" to conduct strike operations with relative impunity.[61] In addition to losses in aircraft (which mounted as the North Koreans became more skillful at anti-air defense), the cost in men and material of such sustained operations was substantial—and detracted from combat power available for the larger perceived conflict against the Soviets. Moreover, the presence of carriers, while certainly tactically effective, did not deter Chinese intervention.

Five. Theory and the Challenge of Irregular Warfare, 1950–1980 85

As the war came to a stalemate, sustained operations against military and industrial targets became routine. How effective these operations were is a matter of debate. Tactically there was no doubt that carrier air power contributed to support of direct combat operations, but attacks against infrastructure were far more difficult to quantify.[62] Once again there was the matter of cost; carriers operating off shore not only were expensive (especially when compared to the use of land aircraft), but their operations did not have a measurable impact on the North's ability to wage war as the respective powers settled into a prolonged stalemate. North Korea had no sea power to speak of that could challenge the fleet, but more importantly did not seek to challenge U.S. control of the sea in any way.[63] Carriers had performed their mission admirably in the initial war of maneuver, but their impact was increasingly marginalized as the war went on with no indications that their efforts were bringing the enemy any closer to defeat.[64] Their presence was not a deterrent to the Chinese decision to intervene, nor did their impact move beyond the tactical. This was important not only in practical but also theoretical terms. Traditional theory held that while control of the sea did not in itself ensure victory, its loss for an enemy would surely spell defeat.[65] Mahan had been clear on this point. But Korea seemed to defy the formula as the enemy was seemingly indifferent to U.S. control of the sea. Korea was a war fought with limitations on operational forces, with limited strategic objectives that affected how sea power could be employed. This was a new, practical reality of warfare and a lesson for NATO. Control of the sea, so vital in a large, conventional war, ultimately might or might not matter to a committed land enemy where the sea was largely irrelevant.

The Korean War was not popular with either an indifferent public or the U.S. military writ large, which was frustrated with the lack of discernable outcome.[66] At its conclusion, the war did not seem to offer many lessons to a Navy increasingly committed to global conflict with the Soviets. There was a number of positives; the war demonstrated that naval flexibility offered operational advantage in a war of maneuver and could be a very effective force multiplier in crisis.[67] Additionally, sustained forward deployment for crisis was now a practical reality and quickly became part of the Navy lexicon. But the unspoken truth remained that the decisiveness of naval power in a protracted regional conflict, especially one where an enemy by all accounts fought with no consideration of surrender or defeat, was unproven. In the broadest sense, this brought into question the importance of the sea itself to regional war. This would become evident ten years later as the United States became increasingly involved in Vietnam.

America's involvement in Vietnam would ultimately challenge the core assumptions of U.S. military strategy and have a long-term and lasting effect on all services, fundamentally altering America's view of the use of military power.[68] Apart from the huge cultural shift fostered by Vietnam, the military would find itself overextended, underfunded, and marginalized in its aftermath. For the Navy the conflict that (somewhat ironically) began with an engagement at sea in the Gulf of Tonkin would result in yet another and far more serious challenge as it argued for the relevancy of its theory, an argument that would only bear fruit in the 1980s with a renewed commitment to classical naval theory as part of the Reagan agenda.

None of this was apparent in 1964, but from the outset it seemed that the Navy's potential contribution to combat operations in Vietnam would be far more difficult to quantify than Korea. While both were regional conflicts, they were quite different in scope and character.[69] Although North Vietnam possessed a conventional Army, operations with that Army were almost wholly irregular in nature; land battles were few, and those that were fought were conducted in terrain and with methods that were highly resistant to classical application of strike power.[70] As in Korea, the Navy deployed significant carrier power off shore to strike at military targets of opportunity in support of land forces and conducted a long-term strike campaign against infrastructure.[71] Unlike Korea, however, the irregular nature of the war made these types of operations ultimately of dubious effectiveness and increasing frustration, as little or no long-term result was apparent.[72] Vietnam was a classic irregular conflict where defining targets that were important to the enemy was difficult, a fact that was well known in the defense establishment.[73] Yet despite this fact, the Navy continued a classic response well into the late 1960s at tremendous cost in men and material.

In many ways the Navy fought two distinctly different wars in Vietnam, wars that were given very different priorities. The initial and sustained response to the conflict was much like that conducted in Korea: carriers operating off shore and exercising total command of the sea, providing tactical and strategic strike power against military targets and infrastructure. The carrier war off shore was clearly the priority in terms of manpower, funding, and emphasis.[74] But along the coastal zones and inland, a new type of naval combat evolved that was quite different, involving new tactics, techniques, and materials that put the Navy in a very different role—one that had some degree of effectiveness but directly countered traditional theory. This was the "brown-water" interdiction

Five. Theory and the Challenge of Irregular Warfare, 1950–1980

campaign reminiscent of the days of the use of gunboats on rivers in Asia and coordination with irregular forces ashore. In response to a perception that the North Vietnamese were using coastal routes to supply insurgents in the South, the Navy commenced Operation Market Time, an effort to interdict arms shipments along inshore sea lanes of communication (SLOCs).[75] The Navy outfitted and trained a small "brown-water" force to operate inland along Vietnam's numerous rivers and inlets to interdict supplies, provide support to land forces, and conduct special operations.[76]

On paper, the Navy's inshore operations seemed to be a bold initiative to adapt to the irregular environment of Vietnam, directly addressing the threat while operating in concert with both land and local forces. The reality, however, was somewhat different. This was perhaps obvious from the outset from the attention the Navy gave to the mission and its priority in the grand scheme of prosecuting the war.[77] The brown-water mission was almost unknown to most Navy admirals, who increasingly focused public attention on the carrier war. Staffing standards for the force were particularly low; many in the service regarded it as a "dumping ground" for low-performing officers in the fleet.[78] Immediately offshore, the "Market Time" forces consisted of ships that were small, old, and outdated; coordination of these forces was assigned to a Coast Guard commodore under the theory that he had necessary "coastal" expertise.[79] Despite a very high operations tempo—the brown-water force conducted over 400,000 board-and-searches during its time in Vietnam and was involved in over 2,000 firefights—the operation received little attention and was largely regarded as a sideshow.[80] Even highly decorated officers from the force found themselves facing hostility and often career oblivion following their rotation from Vietnam.[81]

It is very difficult to methodically categorize the brown-water Navy's contribution to the war effort. Officially the effort was regarded as, at best, a noble failure in that very few caches of arms were actually interdicted flowing from North to South. Whether this is due to an operational failure on the part of the forces or the fact that the North far preferred shipping arms over land routes is a debatable point.[82] In terms of combat power, the effect these forces had on insurgents is also difficult to quantify, as results were not readily apparent in the irregular war and those methods that were used at the time to determine success ("body count") have largely been discredited.[83] There were, however, some notable successes. During the TET offensive in 1968, it was only the rapid deployment of surface power that prevented the overrun of the southern delta, a fact later credited to the force by the commander of U.S. forces in Vietnam, General

Westmoreland.[84] Moreover, the river force itself was engaged in "irregular" missions such as support to indigenous forces, training, supply, etc., that had no appreciable measure for success or failure. Had the United States prevailed in Vietnam, the ultimate assessment of these forces probably would have been far more positive.

The experience in Vietnam had wide-ranging impact on the Navy. There was very little that was positive that came out of the conflict. The use of airpower in the conflict had been controversial during the war and became more so in the aftermath.[85] Operating in a model very similar to that exercised in Korea, carriers conducted wide operations against the North—but at considerable losses in aircraft and personnel.[86] Like the Koreans, the North Vietnamese never sought to challenge U.S. dominance at sea, rather developing an extensive anti-air network that came close to neutralizing the offensive effort.[87] Publicly, the Navy's air war showed little impact on the North and was pursued at great cost. The impact was felt not just in direct losses of aircraft and men. A vast amount of money had been spent on operations; enlistments were down; drug problems that began with the anti-war movement spread to the fleet; and race relations were at an all-time low. Moreover, the nation was tired of war; even the specter of a rising Soviet Navy did not bring with it renewed emphasis on shipbuilding or funding for the development of new naval technologies.

Internally the Navy acted as if the operations in Vietnam had never occurred, a period that was best forgotten. There were many lessons that were learned in Vietnam on the operational level, lessons that were absorbed with various degrees of success by the other services.[88] Unlike the other services, however, the Navy largely marginalized on these lessons. Vietnam—and the concept of irregular war that it introduced—were mainly viewed as an aberration. Smaller units that were designed for irregular warfare, such as the brown-water units, were disbanded, their doctrine purged from the service.[89] What is ironic regarding the Navy's irregular warfare effort is that throughout the 1960s and 1970s, the Navy found itself increasingly involved in more irregular conflicts that fell just short of combat but that demanded adaptability from the fleet even while it continued to focus on the Soviet-NATO confrontation. These included noncombatant evacuations in Greece, the Lebanon reinforcement, and Mediterranean operations in support of insurgencies. It is true that response in many of these operations involved little more than a traditional show of naval force, the raison d'être for capital ships. But it is also true that deployment of capital ships in these roles often did not offer alternatives beyond the application of firepower, which did little. Perhaps most importantly, the Navy was beginning to become the victim of its own success in pursuing its emphasis on capital ships.

Addressing all Missions: High-Low

In the aftermath of the Vietnam War, the Navy tried to recover its roots in the public eye, emphasizing the Soviet war at sea scenario. It had its carriers—15 large-deck carriers by the early 1970s—but had put so much emphasis into their construction that there was little funding available for anything else. The Soviets were apparently on the move worldwide, encouraging insurgencies and unrest in various "hot spots" around the world, the frequency and variety of which challenged the Navy's response. It now became a game of numbers; the Navy simply didn't have enough ships to be everywhere at once, and many of its commitments in crisis were clearly not appropriate for a full demonstration of capital power.[90]

This was conceptually recognized at the most senior levels of the Navy. The rising cost of ships and peacetime budget cuts (exacerbated by public backlash against the Vietnam War) made it apparent that fleets composed entirely of capital ships could only go so far in terms of meeting overseas commitments. The fleet was not "balanced" to meet a wide range of threats even during a conventional conflict—this was especially true in the surface fleet, where the construction of smaller combatants had been sacrificed to build capital ships (both carriers and nuclear submarines).[91] In 1970 the newly appointed CNO, Admiral Elmo Zumwalt, took two important steps to address this issue. The first was to commission a Pentagon study group (Project 60) to examine the problem and provide recommendations for the balanced fleet of the future. The second was to engage (for the first time) academics and professionals at the Naval War College to address the issue of a balanced fleet fighting the Soviets. The results were illuminating.

Zumwalt was no stranger to the problem of a balanced fleet. In 1962 he had advanced the idea in an article for USNI *Proceedings* recommending the continued development of capital ship power ("high" in the sense that these ships were top of the line, expensive, possessing the most advanced weapons systems) while simultaneously building a fleet of "low" ships (moderate-cost, moderate-performance vessels) that could be turned out in numbers.[92] This fleet in its entirety could be used to simultaneously conduct sea control missions while having enough numbers to deploy worldwide for a wide range of contingencies.[93] As CNO, Zumwalt was able to put this plan into action through the auspices of Project 60. Ultimately, Project 60 recommended four new classes of "low" ships, all designed for sea control and contingency response. These included a PHM hydrofoil of 170 tons, a fast, flexible combatant heavily armed with a 76mm gun and six harpoon missiles; a new type of patrol frigate of 3400 tons that was moderately capable of performing in all surface missions (AAW, ASW, and ASUW); a large surface effect ship (SES) of 4,000 tons that could rapidly deploy combat power, including several small strike aircraft (in effect a small, specialized aircraft carrier), and finally a 17,000-ton sea control ship flying vertically launched (VSTOL) aircraft. Although the most expensive, the sea control ship was the most versatile in terms of its ability to respond to contingencies that were inappropriate for deployment of a large-deck carrier. Conversely, it was also the greatest challenge to the "unions" and theorists who saw carriers as the only means to deploy strike power.[94]

Zumwalt's ideas for "High-Low" were considered radical at the time and resisted by those committed to capital ship theory. Diversification for the fleet was fine—on paper. But committing funding to new classes of ships would inevitably detract from that dedicated to capital ships, a fact that was unacceptable to the theorists. The CNO certainly had an enormous degree of influence on the course of the Navy, but his tenure was only four years; in the best of times, ship construction from plans to final launching was far more lengthy, even with complete support. Ultimately the material impact was not nearly what Zumwalt had intended. The patrol frigate was built in numbers (the Oliver Hazard Perry class) but was often marginalized in fleet operations. Six patrol hydrofoils were built but were decommissioned in the 1980s as a cost-savings measure.[95] The Navy experimented with VSTOL aircraft but ultimately decided to give the technology to the Marines for use in tactical air support. The surface effect carrier, despite promising tests, was abandoned with Zumwalt's retirement.

In the long term, Zumwalt's legacy was far more lasting on the academic front. In 1975 the Navy publicly released its "Missions of the U.S. Navy" in the *Naval War College Review*. The document was unique in a number of respects. As an attempt to institutionalize Zumwalt-era thinking, it provided (for the first time) a public explanation of the Navy's role in grand strategy.[96] It defined four main missions for the Navy (strategic deterrence, power projection, sea control, and presence) and subdivided these missions into appropriate tactics for the fleet. It called for naval officers to think about their profession in these terms and was widely circulated both in the defense establishment and academia, resulting in a minor renaissance in strategic thinking regarding the global use of sea power.

Five. Theory and the Challenge of Irregular Warfare, 1950–1980 91

The release of "Missions of the U.S. Navy" was important in a number of respects. It was a public relations coup. The author, VADM Stansfield Turner, was widely regarded as a leading intellectual, not only in the service but also in academia. This enabled the Navy, effectively for the first time, to make a reasoned and logical argument for its fleet that was available to all levels of society, both military and academic. Its underlying message (despite the support for the "High-Low" concept in the document) was that capital ship power was a valuable contribution toward national security both in peace and in a projected war against the Soviets. The document filled a conceptual void, its ideas widely debated throughout the service and in the public sphere. Unlike the other services, whose missions had become more singularly focused (and who had not issued a public explanation of service strategy), the Navy argued for flexibility across its strategic missions—and demonstrated that capital ships could provide that flexibility.

"Missions of the U.S. Navy" was the start of an important trend within the Navy: that of exploring strategic concepts throughout the service. Strategic thought was encouraged, both at the Naval War College (which became once again the center for strategic theory) and the Pentagon. In rapid succession the Navy released a number of strategic concept papers to expand on "Missions"; these included Naval Warfare Publication 1, *The Strategic Concepts of the U.S. Navy* (1978) and "The Future of U.S. Sea Power" in USNI *Proceedings*. These documents served to further refine capital ship theory vis-a-vis war with the Soviets, advertise the Navy as a truly global force, and rationalize increasing Navy budgets for improved ships and weapons systems.[97]

In the 1980s the Navy was making a solid attempt to redefine itself in its traditional role as a global force, redirecting its efforts solely toward a potential conflict with the Soviet Union. Despite three decades of active combat in regional and irregular wars, lessons from these conflicts were marginalized or forgotten as the Navy (like the other services and population writ large) sought to distance itself from the humiliation of Vietnam. Global war with the Soviets, no matter how likely, remained the basis for the Navy's core theory for the use of capital ships and so was given priority in planning and subsequent construction of vessels. Had the national political landscape remained the same, it is questionable whether the Navy's efforts toward rebuilding its fleet for this war could have succeeded. But things were about to change in the political sphere, and with its efforts toward public strategic rationalization, the Navy was in an excellent position to capitalize on this new movement.

Six

Theoretical Renaissance
The Maritime Strategy, 1980–1990

The 1980s represented a period of theoretical renaissance, not just for the Navy but for all U.S. military services. The election of Ronald Reagan and his promised new emphasis on rebuilding a military degraded by Vietnam provided the impetus for the Navy to move to the forefront of the defense establishment with a comprehensive strategy based on classical principles and a massively expanded budget plan to fulfill it.[1] It is significant that the only major force increases projected by Reagan's first budget amendments in 1981 were for the Navy.[2] In 1984, the Navy became a leader in this renaissance with the publication of the "Maritime Strategy," its blueprint for global operations.[3] A logical consolidation of classical theoretical concepts with proposed use of new technology, it was a remarkable document, serving for the first time to publicly explain the Navy's strategic viewpoint while rationalizing the continued development of a large capital ship fleet. In these dual roles the strategy was completely successful, bringing classical theory once again to the fore of public debate regarding the role of the Navy as the primary representative of a global superpower.

The release of the Maritime Strategy had enormous impact not only on the future course of the Navy but also on the formulation of strategic thought within the defense establishment. As a direct result of its publication, the Navy moved to the forefront of strategic planning and became a key player in deriving national and military strategy for confronting the Soviets.[4] Through the Maritime Strategy, the Navy was able to logically and coherently justify not only its capital ship theory but also argue successfully for massive expansion; the term "the 600-ship Navy" became a publicly rationalized objective for ultimate success in the naval Cold War.[5] While it is true that the 1980s saw considerable expansion in all services and the development of new, sophisticated weapons (famous examples include the MX missile, B-1 bomber, and stealth), ultimately it was the Navy that was the most aggressive in pursuing this expansion and arguably the most successful in terms of building and maintaining strategic power.[6] This was possible through its extensive marketing of a strategy that seemed to justify its continued emphasis on the capital ship and Mahanian principles tailored for modern combat against a traditional land power.

Timing was critically important for the success of the Maritime Strategy. By focusing on global strategy with a logical maritime component, the Navy aligned perfectly with the vision of the Reagan administration.[7] The Maritime Strategy was popular with navalists because it stressed classical roots. Although many of its tenets seemed radically new to non-navalists, it was in fact solidly based in traditional theory that emphasized the capital ship and Mahanian principles—albeit principles modified by the zealots of the Sims era that stressed forward operations and decisive battle.[8] This traditional and historical rationale—although one modified considerably to fit a modern scenario—served to provide an excellent basis for its successful reception both publicly and in a defense establishment eager to devise a consolidated Cold War strategy that emphasized a return to conventional principles after the irregular warfare experience of Vietnam. The Maritime Strategy was great power strategy with lofty aims, a return to the bold naval vision of a vanished era. Unlike operations in the ugly irregular wars of the recent past, it did not diffuse carrier power in secondary support missions for forces ashore as had been conducted in Korea and Vietnam; rather, it consolidated capital ship fleet power as a force integral to grand strategy, emphasizing the vital role of sea power in global conflict.[9] It was a popular image for navalists who saw it not only as a return to classical principles but also as a blueprint for the potential naval expansion that the demands of the strategy represented.

The path to acceptance and implementation of the strategy, however, was not a foregone conclusion even in the pro-military Reagan era. This was apparent both within and outside the Navy. After years of alternate operations and bureaucratic infighting, the Navy was not unified in a desire for a global strategy that was so focused on one particular type of power. Reforms within the Navy begun in the 1970s were starting to take hold, and the various "unions" (air, surface, and submarine) were vying for influence.[10] The strategy was a huge commitment for the Navy as a whole and a challenge to the status quo, requiring that a tired service be revitalized. Outside the service, a defense establishment steeped in land and air warfare had to be convinced of the value of the strategy if monetary support was to be guaranteed. The potential war against the Soviets was still a land war, and the Navy's position that while the Soviets could win without the sea, the Allies could not seemed to be a clever manipulation to those who questioned the new emphasis on sea power.[11] Although the fiscal environment was increasingly benign, the Navy still had to sell its strategy first to doubters within the service and then to the defense establishment—and ultimately to the public who would fund it.

There were a number of inherent difficulties in this task, most notably that the Maritime Strategy was risky in its singular focus. Although the Navy had always argued that it was a multi-mission force, its primary mission was defeat of the Soviets—a logical course of action, given the times and the course of the Cold War.[12] In focusing on the defeat of the Soviets through the use of classical forward fleet operations, the Maritime Strategy not only was extremely aggressive but also arguably marginalized the irregular component of sea power. Vast numbers of ships were committed to the tenets of the strategy that emphasized conventional fleet engagement. This not only required significant redirection of procurement priorities toward building high-tech, singularly focused assets but also a significant doctrinal shift to de-emphasize other missions. The Maritime Strategy represented full commitment to one overriding goal at the expense of all others. It worked—so long as there was an enemy that possessed the capabilities that were worthy of such a commitment.

What is ironic about this singularity is that the 1980s was a decade of irregular warfare in terms of deployment of forces and actual combat. The decade did not begin auspiciously with the debacle at Desert One; further operations in Lebanon, Grenada, Panama, Libya, and the Persian Gulf all met with marginal degrees of success in terms of demonstrating the supposed flexibility of modern naval power. Regardless of the course of these operations, the irregular component would not be the driving emphasis for the decade—but rather a strategy based on traditional themes.

The Path to the Maritime Strategy

The Maritime Strategy did not appear overnight but was rather a result of a deliberate progression toward devising a naval strategy drawing upon classical roots. As noted in Chapter Five, groups at the Naval War College had been studying the problem academically under the formal direction of Admiral Stansfield Turner throughout the late 1970s. This effort resulted in a precursor to the Maritime Strategy, Sea Plan 2000, a Mahanian-based theoretical plan that called for the aggressive use of carriers forward in a conventional war.[13] The plan was largely an academic exercise, as there was little support in the Carter administration for an aggressive and offensive use of naval power against the Soviets. For a forward strategy to work, two things were required: an identifiable threat that could be effectively targeted and a significant change in the political landscape.

Several factors made the Maritime Strategy possible in the early 1980s. The first and arguably most influential element in the successful development of the Maritime Strategy was a political one. In 1981, Ronald Reagan came to office with a very clear agenda regarding the Soviets and economic recovery, both of which fueled a vigorous arms buildup that favored the Navy. Whether this was aggressive or not was a matter of interpretation. Reagan and his supporters believed the Soviets had become more aggressive, emboldened by the perceived U.S post–Vietnam and Carter's weakness. Carter's approach toward the Soviets had been one of détente, a program that Reagan viewed as (at best) a waste of time.[14] Negotiations with the Soviets could continue, but only from a position of strength. This strength was represented not only in direct arms procurement, but also an extremely aggressive emphasis on new technologies specifically directed toward fighting and winning a global war with the Soviets. Both of these factors were significant in dovetailing with Reagan's plan for economic recovery. Under the auspices of "supply-side economics," government money spent on military programs gave a significant boost to the private sector through a boon of employment opportunities in science and industry. By focusing on a global war scenario, in effect, Reagan created a wartime economy without an actual war.[15]

Defense rearmament was popular with the Republicans and a core issue in the presidential race of 1980. Reagan had stressed the necessity for maritime superiority in a major campaign speech that (perhaps inadvertently) defined the underpinnings of the Maritime Strategy—a large force of capital ships that could match the Soviet naval threat.[16] Subsequently the concept of a 600-ship Navy became a specific plank in the Republican platform. Rebuilding the military was not just a popular theme with Republicans but also with voters writ large, who were disillusioned by the perceived foreign policy failures of the Carter administration in Iran and Afghanistan. Patriotism and the potential economic benefits of the expansion were major factors that swept Reagan into office. Immediately the Republicans launched their aggressive plan for military expansion. Significantly, this expansion was institutional as well as material. Reagan's programs bought new weapons, but new weapons systems required new thought as to how these systems could be used. This began to lead to new directions in strategic thought and intense debate on new strategic concepts that were beneficial to the military branches, intent on focusing on global conflict.

The nature of this strategic renaissance in concepts and theory for this global conflict went far beyond the use of new systems. It took on a perceived subtle philosophical shift away from the traditional U.S. reliance on nuclear weapons and retaliation scenarios when considering global conflict, moving from deterrence to war fighting. Although the Reagan program committed significant assets to upgrading the U.S. nuclear force, there was also a growing realization that a strategic nuclear exchange was not an acceptable option in a global war. Reagan personally abhorred nuclear weapons, declaring with increasing frequency that their use was an immoral act.[17] At the same time, there was no doubt that war was a very real possibility and nuclear weapons an integral part of U.S. strategy, creating an interesting contradiction. Nuclear weapons remained, but the strategic systems that were a major focus of the Reagan administration (including Trident, Pershing II, MX, and the infamous "Star Wars,") were subsequently billed as deterrent systems intended on making nuclear war far less likely or impossible. Conversely, this raised the specter of conventional conflict, a return to the classic NATO scenario of Soviet invasion. To meet this scenario required not only a new way of thinking (essentially a modified flexible response) but also new platforms to execute the strategy. Officially strategists in the defense infrastructure began to speak of the "long war" scenario, a war that—although relying to some extent on tactical nuclear weapons (in the short term)—was primarily a conventional conflict. This was an inherent benefit to the Navy. Although the Navy had stressed its nuclear role in the past to remain competitive with the other services and was certainly part of the "nuclear triad," at heart it remained primarily a conventional force.

The timing of Reagan's rearmament program could not have been better for the Navy in terms not only of providing a significant boost to the aging fleet but also of enabling its strategic renaissance. The program started by Zumwalt at the Naval War College was well established in drafting and promulgating strategy; although it would be Secretary Lehman that brought the Maritime Strategy to fruition, the War College's work was waiting for a budgetary windfall as well as political will to come to fruition. Reagan's plan provided this, benefiting not only the Navy but also important political elements outside of the service. On the political front, the economic benefits of ship construction were a major factor in political support on the Hill, a fact that remained historically consistent with previous efforts to build capital ships.[18] New ships that had been on the theoretical drawing board were now possible. Moreover, the Navy could look to the numbers required for a theoretical global conflict as actually attainable. Under the auspices of the Reagan buildup, the Navy was able to speak of the "600-ship Navy" as a potential reality with widespread support among influential congressmen.[19] The Navy moved quickly to consolidate the work done prior to this sudden budgetary windfall, publicly releasing its new Maritime Strategy in 1984.

What Was the Maritime Strategy?

The Maritime Strategy was unique in a number of respects. It was, first and foremost, a global strategy designed to engage the Soviets directly in a large-scale conventional offensive, not in the peripheral or proxy irregular wars of the previous decades. The strategy emphasized tradition while espousing modern weapons systems, returning to classic naval roots by stressing power projection forward to engage the enemy in decisive battle, an action that Mahan would have recognized and approved.[20] Like previous power-projection strategies, the ultimate purpose was to ensure sea control through the destruction of the enemy fleet at the source. Added to this traditional mission was the relatively modern role of power projection through deep strike, both at military targets engaged with land forces but also against long-range targets within the enemy homeland. These strikes were intended to provoke an offensive reaction of enemy naval and air power that would be lured out and subsequently destroyed in a new Jutland. It was a combination of the old and the new, and it was bold on both fronts.

Strategically the Maritime Strategy emphasized three roles that were closely linked.[21] First, it was a carrier strategy, emphasizing operations similar to those conducted by fast carrier groups during the Second World War. These operations were replicated by an aggressive forward deployment of concentrated carrier battle groups into the North Sea (with smaller concentrations in the Pacific and Mediterranean) to conduct strike operations against the "flanks" of a Soviet land offensive or against targets in the Soviet Union proper. This forward deployment of carrier group concentrations was the centerpiece of the strategy and by far the most controversial and debated in terms of both provocation and risk to the fleet.[22] In support of this deployment, the submarine fleet was also to deploy forward in aggressive ASW operations against Soviet attack and ballistic missile submarines in their protected northern "bastions" while supporting carriers with their own strike capability using the newly developed Tomahawk cruise missile. Finally, the strategy called for the use of a strong amphibious component to deploy Marine expeditionary forces along the northern flank of the Soviet offensive, conducting operations in Norway and other areas to blunt any Soviet attacks. These three elements were integrated to ensure not only that Soviet offensive naval power was destroyed "at the source," but also to present a credible threat to the Soviet land mass that required response, pulling (in theory) significant Soviet power away from the main battle area, where it could be engaged and destroyed.[23]

It must be emphasized that these core elements of the Maritime Strategy, while a return to classical offensive theory in many respects, were a significant departure from the operational mindset that the Navy had been pursuing since the mid-1960s. By far the most the radical element was the concentration of carrier forces forward. The Navy of the Cold War would have had difficulties in executing such an operation; during the 1950s and 1960s, "dispersion" had been doctrinally accepted as a means by which to protect the larger ships against the threat of nuclear attack.[24] Despite their size, carriers were notoriously vulnerable to damage that could prevent them from launching aircraft, requiring an extensive layered defense using ships and aircraft for protection.[25] In adopting a counter-dispersion doctrine, the Navy seemed not only to be abandoning its own core concepts of defense but also taking an enormous risk with both its core assets and the overall course of the war itself. The Navy answered this critique by espousing the new technology that allowed for such a deployment, stressing the successful development of a number of technical systems designed specifically to protect carriers while maximizing offensive power. These were points that the Navy was quite public in stressing in order to provide a rationale for its proposed operations[26]—so long as the Navy had the ships to execute the strategy.

Ships were a vital part of the Maritime Strategy; without a concentrated force composed primarily of capital power, the strategy was largely theory. Ships became available with the increase of funding to the defense establishment. But increased funding did not just result in increased shipbuilding (although this expanded massively under the Reagan administration, moving the Navy upward toward 15 full carrier battle groups), but also the development of new technologies that made the more forward offensive elements of the Maritime Strategy possible.[27] By the 1980s, new strike technology that had begun development during the Carter era was nearing completion and was rushed into deployment. This included the introduction into the fleet of the Tomahawk, an extremely accurate long-range cruise missile that could be fired from a wide variety of air and surface platforms. Possessing both conventional and nuclear capability, the missile extended and considerably increased naval strike power. Defensively, the Aegis radar system, designed specifically to target large formations of bombers and strike aircraft, was perfected and deployed, providing considerable AAW defensive capability to the fleet—a definitive requirement for carriers operating far forward near the enemy. The Close-In Weapons System (CIWS) promised to protect surface ships against enemy missile attack, while the anti-ship missile Harpoon allowed for effective counterattack against enemy surface combatants. New submarine classes were developed to operate in forward areas, especially under the ice pack and forward against protected Soviet ballistic missile submarine bastions. All of these weapons were enablers for one thing: the ability for the Navy to operate offensively against a hostile, conventional blue-water opponent. The development of weapons for any other role—such as operating in an irregular environment—lagged far behind.[28]

The concentration of carriers was a return to a classical Mahanian principle made possible (in theory) not only by the increased survivability of the larger ships but also their vastly greater capability to employ defensive power.[29] Carriers carried new and powerful air interceptors (both the F-14 and F-18 were originally designed for this role), and were supported by cruisers outfitted with the new Aegis radar system, designed specifically to defeat the Soviet air threat against carriers themselves. The strategy also employed a new defensive concept, using land-based defense to support ships operating in protected bastions. Citing lessons learned from the Falklands, carrier operating areas (the deep fjords of Norway) were to be supplemented with land missile batteries surrounding them that would cause heavy attrition in any Soviet attack before it got within immediate striking range of the ships.[30] Despite the large concentration of air power available to the Soviets, advocates for the Maritime Strategy argued that Soviet air attack against such tempting concentrations of force was in fact an advantage, as it would serve not only to draw considerable enemy air power away from main battle areas but also would allow for their decisive destruction by the concentrated carrier group AAW power.[31] Once this was accomplished, the carriers would be free to conduct tactical strikes directly against the Soviet land mass, attacks that (proponents argued) would be decisive, denying the Soviets a single theater of operations where they held the advantage—Central Europe.

The rationalization of capital ship theory using new advanced technology was a familiar theme; it had been used in the interwar period to argue the invulnerability of battleships to aircraft and to dismiss the submarine threat. This time, however, the argument was far more strategic, citing a combination of systems (rather than one, such as the introduction of sonar to justify defense against submarines) that could be combined toward the one unifying objective of forward operations. The technological rationalization for risky forward deployment of carriers took this farther by focusing on the strategic elements. Modern technology did not just make carriers more defensible; when combined with the offensive element against forward threats, it would make them invulnerable by taking the attack directly to the enemy. This was accomplished through strike from the air and under the sea.

Strike was a main component of the Maritime Strategy, strike intended both to support NATO land operations and to inflict enough damage on the enemy that it would force enemy response and engagement in the subsequent decisive naval battle. Enemy targets were of two distinct varieties. The first was land-based: enemy installations, military formations, and infrastructure. The second was linked to the concept of expanding sea control against the submarine threat. Soviet submarines had always been the primary naval threat to NATO and any resupply operation necessary for sustained operations on the continent; as we have seen, the defeat of these submarines had been given a great deal of thought in both U.S. and NATO naval planning.[32] The Maritime Strategy returned to a classical idea—the defeat of the threat forward, before it could be used against the main sea lines of communication. Again, the idea was not new—forward offensive operations against submarines had been tried with various degrees of success during both the First and Second World Wars.[33] These efforts, however, had largely been conducted through the use of air or surface strike. The Maritime Strategy was different in that it used submarines forward in an ASW role to attack enemy submarines trying to reach operational areas. Again this relied on a technological solution. Submarines had come into their own as weapons against other submarines only with the development of nuclear power. Since the 1960s, they had played an extensive "cat and mouse" game tracking enemy submarines both in the open ocean and under the Arctic ice cap.[34] But this forward deployment was different, using new submarines specifically designed for extended operations in this role.[35] Strategically, the U.S. submarine fleet was aided in this both by geography (the path to the Atlantic was relatively narrow) and the development of new submarine tracking technology such as passive arrays (SOSUSS) designed to hem enemy submarines into specific attack areas. The forward deployment of submarines called for a coordinated undersea campaign rather than pure interdiction, something that had not been attempted since the Second World War.

Technology, it was argued, allowed for the effective defense of forwardly deployed carriers and provided the ability to strike at the enemy, but it did not guarantee that classical battle would result. This led to one of the most debated elements of the strategy as a whole: planning assumptions regarding the actions of the Soviet Navy. The success of the Maritime Strategy was heavily reliant on the predictability of Soviet behavior in the event of an aggressive forward deployment of U.S. naval power. The strategy openly assumed that the Soviets would surge their naval power out to meet the advancing U.S. Navy, a move that on the surface would seem akin to suicide. Rhetoric concerning advanced Soviet capability aside, there was little doubt that in a concentrated sea battle the U.S. Navy would emerge victorious. Moreover, the tenets of the Maritime Strategy were openly advertised; the Soviets were well aware that they would be sailing into a comprehensive layered defense designed specifically to defeat their force in detail. So why come out at all?

Proponents of the Maritime Strategy argued that there were a number of factors that made Soviet actions, perceived by the Strategy, inevitable. The first was intensely cultural. U.S. naval theory held that navies were first and foremost offensive weapons to be used in that role; the idea that any Navy would lie in wait or act defensively was openly scoffed at by naval officers raised in the tradition of the offensive. Given that Soviet ships possessed a large degree of offensive weaponry, logic (at least Western logic) assumed that these ships would be used for this purpose.[36] Other reasons were more specific to the strategy. Carriers operating far forward were well within striking range not only of Soviet military operations on the northern flank of NATO but also of the Soviet Union itself; the danger of these strikes (some of which potentially involved the use of tactical nuclear weapons) would not go unchecked by the Soviets—they would demand a response. Strategically, the forward carriers offered far too tempting "bait" to be ignored; as had often been noted by NATO strategists, while the Soviets could win a war without the use of the sea, NATO would most certainly lose with the loss of sea control.[37] Carriers operating far forward guaranteed that control: as a successful attack against them could be potentially "war winning" for the Soviets, they were a target that could not be ignored. Finally, in the political realm, proponents argued that the rigid structure of the Soviet system did not allow for the flexibility to adapt to alternatives.[38] Soviet naval doctrine called for defense of the homeland, so sorties, no matter what the cost, could not be avoided, no matter what waited in the open ocean. In sum, in all of these arguments, "the enemy did not get a vote"—a remarkably idealistic assumption.

Selling the Strategy: Resistance

The Navy did an exceptional job in its public release of the Maritime Strategy, successfully arguing the case for expansion and integration into the new evolving global war plan. But the rhetoric soon ran into a number of significant obstacles. This was an inevitable consequence given the sudden and radical changes the Navy proposed regarding its force structure and role in national strategy. A number of these obstacles were traditional ones, long part of the inherent rivalries within the defense infrastructure. But others were new and specific to the various components that were the centerpiece of the Maritime Strategy. Each of these had to be addressed in turn by the strategy's proponents if it was going to be successful.

The first of these was the inevitable and constantly present service rivalry, especially as applied to the classic NATO scenario. The Navy had always been a significant part of the NATO alliance, but its mission had been regarded by the defense establishment as distinctly secondary. Despite the commitment of European naval forces to the alliance, the U.S. viewpoint of a potential defense of NATO during a Soviet attack focused almost exclusively on land and air power.[39] Traditionally the Navy was relegated to a resupply role, and then only after the first 30 days of conflict (which, in a nuclear exchange scenario, would be largely irrelevant). Offensive operations forward against Soviet land or sea space such as those envisioned by the new Maritime Strategy had been viewed as unnecessarily provocative and a diversion of resources from the central mission of defense of the resupply routes. To accomplish this task, the Navy was set as an overall force of 450 ships and 12 aircraft carriers, with no new upgrades or carrier construction set for the near future.[40] This obviously allowed the other services—specifically the Army and Air Force—to enjoy the lion's share of the budget committed to the defense of NATO. The Maritime Strategy altered this calculus considerably, making the Navy a focal point of northern NATO operations—and requiring a significant increase in funding to do so.

In ordinary budget times the expansion of the Navy called for by the Maritime Strategy would have met with a tremendous degree of resistance

Six. Theoretical Renaissance

by the other services and their allies in Congress and the defense industrial base. This was offset to a large degree by the Reagan program of massive expansion for all the services—a bureaucratic spreading of the wealth.[41] The other services found that their major weapons systems, which ordinarily would have been subject to a competitive decision process, were now fully funded, so there was far less need to enter into conflict with the other services. Whereas in the past, the construction of a new carrier would be in direct conflict for funding with another system (such as a bomber, as played out during the infamous "revolt of the admirals" noted in Chapter Four), now there was little need. This did not prevent the other services from challenging many of the premises of the Maritime Strategy, but this criticism was largely limited to professional journals written by mid-grade officers and did not appear in the halls of Congress, as had been evident in the past.[42]

A significant philosophical shift among the services also kept conflict and objections to a minimum. "Jointness," both operationally in the field and strategically among planning elements, was now a priority at the Pentagon, more so because it had been mandated by Congress and passed officially into law under the Goldwater-Nichols Act.[43] The Maritime Strategy passed congressional muster in this requirement. Although sometimes criticized as a singular strategy (a natural resistance, given its emphasis on sea power as a main war-fighting component), the drafters of the Maritime Strategy took pains to be "joint" in integration with the land battle ashore, a point the Navy repeatedly illustrated in public and in testimony.[44] Whether or not the Strategy met Congressional mandate in reality is an interesting point; after all, the units executing it were solely within the Department of the Navy's purview. The drafters had stressed "integration" and "coordination" more than "jointness," arguing that the support provided other services was "joint" in the strategic sense.[45] Somewhat surprisingly this argument was accepted by the other services with little resistance. This is perhaps due to the fact that in its own subtle way, the Maritime Strategy ensured acceptance in the joint world by indirectly supporting the expansion of the other services—openly acknowledging the importance of the main battle theater on land. The accepted theme was that there would be a protracted conventional conflict in Europe—good for the force structure of the Army and Air Force. If the Navy was going to invest so much in seeing that this battle was a success, logically the other services had to expand as well to meet the threat. For the first time, there seemed to be funding to make this expansion a reality.

While the other services accepted the Maritime Strategy as part of the overall expansion fostered and encouraged by the Reagan administration, there were other shifts and pockets of resistance that had to be overcome to ensure full acceptance. The first was philosophical, argued among both longtime supporters of naval power and senior officers. The tenets of this argument were primarily over the idea of the core naval missions required by the strategy itself. As noted in Title 10 of U.S. Code, the Navy was to be organized, trained, and equipped for combat at sea—primarily in the missions of naval reconnaissance, anti-submarine warfare, and the protection of shipping.[46] Missions such as forward projection with carriers were not only not mentioned in U.S. Code but also potentially violated the Key West agreements that established the Department of Defense in 1947. Moreover, the requirement of protecting aircraft carriers from Soviet submarines (as opposed to the protection of shipping) could potentially be seen as an abandonment of NATO, to which the primary threat was Soviet submarines.[47] The arguments against forward projection were not new (even Zumwalt had envisioned open-ocean conflict rather than projecting power so directly against the Soviets) and were more or less swept aside in favor of the improved capability of the strike fleet; as to submarines, the essence of the Maritime Strategy was the defeat of this threat at the source, which seemed to negate the requirement for escorts to be dedicated to any form of merchant or surface ship protection.[48]

Second, there was resistance to the Strategy within the Navy itself. The reasons for this were largely bureaucratic. To some degree the Navy—long used to compete against other services in the continuous budget battles in Washington and fearful of having its funding challenged—had maintained its image of superiority versus the Soviets throughout the 1970s. Maintenance had been the key, with training focused on fighting the classic NATO scenario. As previously discussed, Zumwalt had challenged this maintenance by arguing that the Soviets were in fact a superior force, testimony that had been given mixed reviews by the Carter administration. Zumwalt succeeded in getting additional funding and had many of his reforms passed (although as we have seen, his non-traditional ship designs for IW, including "high-low," were not accepted within the service and were ended with his administration).[49] Some of these were potentially challenged by the provisions of the Maritime Strategy, giving many in the service pause. What ultimately convinced the bulk of the service was the new threat analysis offered by the administration that not only accepted Zumwalt's position but embellished it.[50] The funding associated with this served to quiet voices that were questioning the operational wisdom of deploying the bulk of the carrier fleet in harm's way.

Additional objections from outside the defense structure were far more challenging. Primary concerns were from the NATO allies regarding what was perceived as a major shift in U.S. war-fighting policy and from the broad-based community of military personnel and academics who focused on various elements of nuclear strategy. While NATO had concerns in both regards, the most immediate was what was perceived as a shift of focus. The scenario of a Soviet invasion of Europe had not fundamentally changed despite the new technology and tactics being advocated by the United States. NATO planners still regarded this as first a conflict to be deterred (largely through the nuclear force) and, if necessary, fought with the traditional defense strategy.[51] As noted, seaborne resupply was crucial to this scenario, as was engagement with Soviet maritime power. The Maritime Strategy stressed these elements but did so not only from a very aggressive posture (seen by many as unnecessarily provocative), but also from a global perspective—many of the naval forces that had heretofore been committed to the European theater were now allocated to operations against Soviet naval power in the Pacific.[52] The Navy took pains to address these concerns, arguing that even given the traditional scenario, a forward deployment would eliminate the threat to the mid–Atlantic supply operation far more expeditiously than the previously envisioned open ocean ASW war. This seemed to have impact among senior planners in the alliance, as most of the subsequent official policy was pro-Navy in its stance.[53] In terms of global operations, the force increase provided by the Reagan administration would more than address any perceived weakening of NATO and could act as even more of a deterrent against any Soviet adventurism.

Operations against Soviet strategic forces, however, remained far more problematic in terms of gaining widespread acceptance of the Strategy. As noted, Reagan's program significantly modernized the nuclear force while taking pains to argue that the actions were in fact to create a more effective deterrent force, allowing for the significant expansion of conventional forces in all services. This argument of deterrence, however, did not fit with classical theory. Many systems, such as the short-range MX missile, had the potential to be offensive in nature. Although that was subject to some debate, there was no debate regarding the Navy's plan to directly target Soviet SSBNs in their protected bastions.[54] This counterforce targeting was the first time the United States had openly admitted that nuclear forces would be actually hit in a conventional conflict, and as such it was inherently de-stabilizing, according to accepted nuclear theory.[55] This point was made not only by peace groups that were opposed to the Reagan administration on anti-militaristic grounds but also by academics who specialized in nuclear theory: something of an odd combination of allies.[56]

The Navy was never completely successful in addressing the issue of targeting Soviet SSBNs directly, but the issue was soon overtaken by others within the Reagan administration. Nuclear strategy, long the exclusive realms of academics, moved into the public sphere, where targeting one system was but a small part of a larger debate. The upgrade of the Air Force, the use of stealth, development of new missiles, and a growing movement of glasnost took attention away from the Navy's SSBN plan, which admittedly required war in order to actually be implemented. Regardless of this issue, the Navy moved forward in acquiring the assets and training for implementation of the new Strategy in a series of exercises in the North Sea to demonstrate its viability.

In the rush to implement the Strategy, many of the traditional components of IW fell by the wayside. The use of naval power in addressing local contingencies, presence, or operations short of war were not a priority in the effort to develop the new, grander elements of the Maritime Strategy. Interestingly, however, in focusing on conventional global war, the Maritime Strategy gave birth to a new form of irregular naval warfare that hadn't been seriously addressed since the early days of World War II—the need for some form of protection of the homeland. How the Navy met this challenge is illustrative of the tendency to give emphasis to a specific element of IW that seems relevant to the broader needs of the service but to quickly de-emphasize it once the immediacy of the crisis has changed and to return to traditional elements.

Irregular Components of the Maritime Strategy

In 1984, arguably for the first time since the Second World War, the Navy began to look at the problem of coastal defense in the strategic sense. This was the result of the strategic debate that had been opened with the publication of the Maritime Strategy. The theoretical renaissance started by the Reagan buildup was not limited to forward operations and weapons procurement; the Navy's reliance on classical principles had "opened the door" to a widespread study of not only the philosophers of war (in the land and political dimensions, Clausewitz and Jomini enjoyed their own respective rebirths in military academia, as did Mahan and Colbert) but also potential "strategic" problems that had formally been ignored. The most significant of these from a maritime perspective was a "what if" scenario of an attack against the U.S. coastline from undersea or special operations forces, particularly against strategic outload ports. Submarines were a particular problem in this regard. While there was never any official doubt that the vast bulk of the Soviet submarine fleet would be contained (and defeated) by the forward operating force, the fact that a few submarines could "escape" (or be deployed in advance of hostilities) was troubling, especially with regard to potential threat to munitions outload vital to NATO.

The vulnerability of the "western tier" of the Atlantic bridge was a particularly sore point for maritime planners. Historically the threat had been well illustrated; in December 1941, a handful of German U-boats were unleashed on the east coast in operation "Drumbeat," which left the United States reeling. The U-boats were spectacularly successful, sinking over 400 merchantmen in a matter of months and seriously threatening the overall war effort.[57] Traditional naval ASW tactics proved difficult in shallow waters—the submarines were ultimately defeated through an innovative mixture of convoying, coastal command organization, and intelligence. The potential to repeat history was very much on the minds of planners who theorized that a similar scenario could be in the making if a small number of Soviet submarines was loose in the Atlantic. Although technology had certainly altered undersea warfare, modern ASW was largely focused on an open-ocean scenario using passive listening gear—gear that was very fickle in shallow water. Moreover, whereas in the past submarines primarily targeted vessels, now a greater opportunity lay in closing a port through mining or special operations attack, methods against which the Navy had no real doctrine of defense.[58] The outload of munitions from the United States required to fight a conventional war in Europe was staggering, flowing from 23 strategic ports along the eastern seaboard in accordance with a complex logistics plan.[59] The problem was not the outload itself but the vulnerability of the source. U.S. ports are commercial enterprises, not fortresses, and even a cursory analysis demonstrated that they were vulnerable to attack. As the closure of any one strategic outload port could have significant impact on operations overseas, this was a singularly unique irregular problem that had to be addressed. This was accomplished through the creation of a combined coastal defense command, the Maritime Defense Zone (MDZ).

The MDZ was unique in a number of respects. The two MDZs (one Atlantic and one Pacific) were third-tier Navy commands composed of assets from both the Navy and Coast Guard, operating together in one unified structure with the primary purpose of coastal defense against irregular threats.[60] To accomplish this, the commands were organized with a large number of assets that were themselves irregular, units that did not "fit" into the aggressive forward component of the Maritime Strategy. These included older Navy frigates, Coast Guard cutters of various sizes and capabilities, mobile inshore undersea warfare (MIUW) units, explosive ordnance disposal (EOD) teams, and other specialized units dedicated to port security.[61] The MDZ was organized into various "sectors" that were geographic areas of defense centered on strategic outload ports. Established in 1986 by Coast Guard Commandant Paul Yost, the MDZ represented a significant shift for the traditionally law enforcement-centric Coast Guard to a wartime/combative posture, while moving irregular assets away from traditional Navy missions to a new focus on coastal defense in the continental United States.

The Maritime Defense Zone would have two significant impacts, one strategic and one political. Strategically, there was a certain degree of sense in providing some form of defense against threats that were considered "irregular," such as mining or special operations. As the MDZ was never tested against an enemy, the results were difficult to ascertain.[62] Although the Maritime Defense Zone conducted a number of significant fleet exercises to test the concept in the joint community, there is considerable debate as to how seriously the Navy regarded the threat. Actual Navy assets assigned to the MDZ were either decidedly second-tier (the Oliver Hazard Perry class frigates were older models with limited use forward in execution of the Maritime Strategy) or irregular units that needed a "home" in the grand operational scheme.[63] The MDZ did, however, serve its purpose as an official command-and-control organization that addressed the potential problem of coastal defense. Whether that was ever seriously acknowledged by the Navy as an actual problem was another matter.

Politically, MDZ provided the Navy with a rational argument to fully commit to its forward operations and remain wedded to its established theory. The argument that the coastline was "defended" freed up significant assets that otherwise might have been committed to a rear defense, an idea anathema to theorists and those steeped in naval tradition. Accordingly, the Navy worked hard to integrate various "breakout" operations in fleet exercises designed to demonstrate the viability of a coastal defense organization.[64] In theory, these exercises publicly validated several important concepts that were critical to addressing critiques of the Maritime Strategy. This included demonstrating the ability to rapidly deploy naval power unmolested from the coast of the United States and provide a means to protect the critical resupply effort. These operations continued throughout the Reagan era; in the latter days, MDZ became very much a Coast Guard operation, which committed assets to it diligently until the collapse of the Berlin Wall, whereupon modern concepts of coastal defense effectively disappeared. The Navy was quick to point out that as the Soviets were no longer a threat to the U.S., there was no need for this irregular component to the strategy, and the Coast Guard moved on to other traditional (and funded) missions. No one could foresee that 20 years later the threat to the homeland would return, in a far more irregular form.

The Reality of Irregular Warfare

The 1980s were not only a decade of theoretical renaissance, they were also a decade in which sea power was applied a number of times in a very wide range of irregular-style conflicts. These conflicts were conducted almost exclusively through the use of capital ship power—but had very mixed results. As there was no established IW theory in the 1980s for the use of sea power, the forces at hand were forced to adapt—forces that were trained and equipped for a very different mission. The decade began with a massive application of naval power in a conventional operation that illustrated the difficulty of achieving multi-service cooperation, and it ended with a new definition of "jointness"—and a Navy firmly committed to its own strategy. In between there were a number of smaller-scale operations and contingencies ranging in form from new to traditional—but all of them possessed an irregular character. For ease of discussion these operations will be divided into three groups: invasions, retaliation and response, and traditional-style operations.

THE INVASION: URGENT FURY

On 14 October 1983, the deputy prime minister of Grenada led a coup against the established government, resulting in the prime minister's overthrow (and subsequent murder). The government of Grenada had long been eyed with suspicion by the United States, which subsequently used the coup as a catalyst to invade, citing the danger to American nationals on the island as the immediate cause. Strategically, the Grenadian government's revolutionary leftist character, its long association with the Soviet Union and Cuba (both of whom had stationed advisors in the country), and its development of an airstrip capable of supporting Soviet bombers were all viewed as a threat to U.S. and regional security. The invasion, dubbed Operation Urgent Fury, was launched on 25 October. With overwhelming force, the island was subdued in two days.

From the naval perspective, Operation Urgent Fury involved a complete Marine Expeditionary Unit (MEU) of 1200 men with heavy equipment and a large battle group to support it. In theory this should have been enough; indeed, given that Grenada was an island, it would seem that the operation fell exclusively in the purview of the Navy. This was not the case. As the first real test of the new conventional power developed as part of the Reagan defense buildup, all the services insisted on a role and provided significant forces for the invasion.[65] Ultimately it was a success in that the coup was defeated. But in terms of the application of conventional power in an irregular environment, the operation was widely regarded as less than perfect.[66] The United States employed overwhelming combat power with very limited coordination against approximately 700 Cuban troops and Grenadians—almost none of whom were professional soldiers, let alone in possession of modern weapons that could resist the firepower deployed from sea and air. Regardless, the United States suffered a disproportionate number of casualties from friendly fire, poor coordination between service components unfamiliar with each other's procedures, and a lack of intelligence.

What is telling from a Navy perspective is the amount of force dedicated to this comparatively small operation and how it was employed. Urgent Fury employed two aircraft carriers (USS *Independence* and USS *America*), four large amphibious ships, six capital ships (cruisers and destroyers), six smaller escorts, and two submarines.[67] While the need for this amount of force is certainly debatable given that there was no seaborne enemy to fight (as the first naval operation since Vietnam, it could be argued with some justification that the military force dedicated to Grenada was a political consideration), there was little for these ships to do besides provide strike support—support that, against an irregular opponent, was of dubious effectiveness, as it did a great deal of damage to the island but not to the dispersed enemy.[68] Despite the enemy being clearly irregular, the invasion was planned by Navy planners as a conventional operation completely aligned with traditional theory, including the establishment of invasion beachheads with dedicated strike components in the fashion of Normandy.[69] Special operations forces designated to take key objectives were used poorly; a lightly armed SEAL detachment, assigned a mission with no support, was almost wiped out attempting to rescue the British ambassador, while others retreated from a failed mission to rescue political prisoners at the island's center.

Six. Theoretical Renaissance

Although largely condemned internationally, Urgent Fury was widely hailed as a success in the United States. Operationally, the analysis clearly illustrated the problems in applying conventional power to an irregular conflict. The threat in Grenada was diverse and not well defined by pre-invasion intelligence, nor were there identifiable "centers of gravity" that could easily be targeted, as is usual in conventional operations.[70] In such a scenario, the classic form of attack is through a "coup de main"-style operation of decisive surgical attack directly against the few military forces opposing the invasion.[71] There was very little that was specialized or "surgical" about the assault on the island, which was conducted with the classical overtones of a prolonged campaign against a conventional opponent. Even without the coordination problems, the massive commitment of naval power to this operation was politically sensitive—given the expense (and the limited opposition), there had to be better uses for the fleet.

THE RETALIATION AND RESPONSE OPERATIONS

In September 1982, U.S. naval forces deployed to Lebanon as part of a multinational force designed to provide a buffer between warring factions of Shiite and Druze militias in Beirut. Poor command decisions, a misunderstanding of the threat, and restrictive rules of engagement proved disastrous. On October 23, 1983, the marine barracks in Beirut was attacked by a suicide bomber, killing 241 marines in one of the most horrific attacks on U.S. forces in decades. Following additional attacks against aircraft, naval forces were used to retaliate.

This was accomplished in two ways. The more traditional was through the use of the battleship *New Jersey* in its classic role—providing gunfire support for friendly forces and punitive fire against enemies far ashore. At first glance, the battleship seemed to be the perfect choice. Reconstituted from mothballs specifically for "presence" in cases like Lebanon, there seemed to be little doubt that the impressive fire from 16-inch guns—well within sight of land—would serve not only to intimidate but also to provide devastating and punishing fire to any who opposed the peacekeeping mission. But despite a spectacular round of salvos, the battleship's results against the Shiites and Druze were never analyzed; the one noted success occurred in February, when 30 rounds of the 288 fired hit a Syrian command post, killing the senior general in Lebanon.

The second reprisal was conducted using naval air striking from the carrier USS *Kennedy*, far off shore. Although the targets were within range of the *New Jersey*'s guns, naval air was chosen as the means of attack, a rationale that has never been properly explained.[72] Striking at Syrian positions in the Beqaa valley, the raid resulted in no significant damage to the enemy and two aircraft shot down, proving to be an operational failure and a diplomatic embarrassment over negotiations for the return of a captured aviator.[73] In the aftermath, the general consensus was that excessive micromanagement from the chain of command (how high was never determined) resulted in critical operational details being changed, including moving up the time of attack, resulting in improper ordnance being placed on the aircraft (one was launched empty) and the planes attacking at the worst possible time, with ample warning for the enemy.

The operations in Lebanon were a low point in the use of naval power, but they were overshadowed by other events. In the missions of presence and response to crisis, the Navy had a number of successes using capital ship power. This included Navy response to Gaddafi's attempt to close the Gulf of Sidra, the interception of terrorists attempting to escape the hijacking of the *Achille Lauro* and the murder of an American citizen, and noncombatant evacuation (NEO) operations in Liberia and Sierra Leone. Significantly, these operations relied on carriers operating continuously on forward station to respond to these types of contingencies—a tactic that was fairly new but that would become standard in the future.

Traditional Operations

Arguably the most successful irregular-style operation of the 1980s was one that emulated classic evolutions of the past. In 1987, the Navy sent ships into the Persian Gulf to escort tankers sailing from oil outload ports in Operation Earnest Will, designed to protect neutral ships from Iranian attack. The tankers had at first been threatened and then attacked by gunfire and missiles from Iranian patrol craft then engaged in a prolonged war with Iraq. Although escorting the tankers was a classic operation for combatants (harking back in some ways to the early days of convoying), the unique element of this evolution was the "re-flagging" of the tankers as U.S. vessels, thus rationalizing the use of escorts. The operation was completely successful in ensuring that oil continued to flow from the Gulf (although carriers did not enter the gulf, other capital ships—such as cruisers—did to provide support for the operation).[74] It was not, however, without cost. In 1987 the USS *Stark* was struck by an Iraqi missile (the pilot mis-identified the ship, an act for which Iraq apologized), and in 1988 the USS *Vincennes* mistakenly fired on an Iranian civilian Airbus, killing all aboard.[75] Operating in an irregular environment, especially in the presence of another conflict and civilian activity, had its risks: a lesson that the Navy would learn again in the future.

It should be noted that by the invasion of Panama in 1989 (Operation Just Cause), the Navy and DOD had incorporated many of the lessons of the decade, including assigning and streamlining appropriate service forces for operations. In the aftermath of Goldwater-Nichols, operations in Panama were almost exclusively conducted by land components (Army and Marine) with Air Force and special forces support; Navy involvement was limited to one major combatant and several smaller units providing special warfare support. Given that the Panama plan was almost exclusively land-based, the Navy did not push to provide forces to support it—and, with its Maritime Strategy well developed and being supported by exercises in the far north, it was busy with other things.

Conclusions: Did It Work?

Publicly, the Maritime Strategy had all the appearance of a radical departure from traditional Navy operations. But the reality is that the Maritime Strategy was a return to the Mahanian principles advocated by the zealots of the age of Roosevelt and Sims. The Maritime Strategy offered modern navalists an opportunity to fully give voice to their theories that were now supported by both money, technology, and a political will. It was a powerful combination that the Navy took advantage of both materially and intellectually.

Materially there was no doubt that the Maritime Strategy was enormously successful for the Navy in the short term. The strategy successfully rationalized a massively increased budget for ships that were built according to capital ship theory, including new aircraft carriers, cruisers, and large ships designed specifically to fight a blue-ocean, equally capable threat. The building of these ships and public explanation of their use in the context of the strategy was an enormous public relations coup for the Navy, so much so that in many respects the Navy became the face of Reagan plans to combat the Soviets. Intellectually the Maritime Strategy caused a resurgence in strategic thought. There was no doubt that Mahan enjoyed a renaissance along with the strategy, as elements of his philosophy were publicly cited as rationale (much like the Army's citation of Clausewitz for their air-land battle concept).

The operational reality for the Navy, however, was quite different from the theory presented by the Maritime Strategy. Secretary of the Navy Lehman was quite clear on his view of operations outside the conventional fight with the Soviets, stating, "Maritime superiority does not mean that we seek to be omnipresent on all oceans, nor act as the world's maritime policeman. It means only that in those areas of our vital interests, that we can prevail if challenged by the combined military might of our adversaries" (in this case, the Soviets).[76] But real-world operations during the Reagan era were far more "traditional" than those envisioned by Lehman and the Strategy. When interventionist actions were actually authorized by Reagan, he relied on limited covert operations or displays of force rather than conventional commitment.[77] Reagan's ultimate goal had been to deter the Soviets through a show of strength: détente with the flavor of force rather than negotiation, an approach that arguably was successful (and one that remains hotly debated). The Navy's Maritime Strategy fit in nicely with this approach.[78] It is significant to note, however, that the Soviets were remarkably silent regarding the Navy's publicly stated intent to go on the offensive. Whether this was due to a different naval focus from that predicted by the Strategy, whether it served to feed their paranoia or even apathy, is a question that remains unanswered.

In the grander scheme there is some debate as to whether the Maritime Strategy was successful. For all its publicity, the Maritime Strategy was never part of a grand national strategy, a strategy that eventually morphed into one of Reagan-style détente in the era of glasnost. As a service and military strategy, the Maritime Strategy was not a political one; with its sole focus on the Soviet Union, the Strategy had a difficult time adapting to political change. This was an interesting ahistorical contradiction—the Navy, traditionally the most flexible service in terms of its political savvy, was locked in a strategy that fully committed it to a Cold War vision. Without the Cold War, that vision became increasingly irrelevant. The Cold War had ended as a result of negotiation, not confrontation. This would be critically important to an isolated Navy whose strategy had relied so much on having a traditional enemy—a service that found itself suddenly adrift in an age without a classical Mahanian enemy, where irregular warfare was becoming increasingly the norm.

Seven

Strategy Adrift, 1990–2001

The end of the Cold War heralded the end of an era both politically and militarily for the United States. The sudden collapse of the Soviet Union, while an enormous victory for the West, also brought tremendous uncertainty within political and military establishments. Almost overnight the threat that Cold War militaries had been designed to defeat was gone, bringing into question the need for such large (and expensive) forces in a world that now seemed far safer.[1] While this proved to be an illusion—war was still very much alive and well, as Saddam Hussein's invasion of Kuwait demonstrated—the small wars of the 1990s were not mass global conflicts against a monolithic Soviet threat but were rather complex, messy affairs for which U.S. conventional forces were neither trained nor designed.[2] The new era challenged conventional military forces at the very core, questioning not only the composition of armies and fleets but also the validity of traditional strategic concepts such as using overwhelming force. The ending of the bi-polar world opened up the door to a form of conflict that was distinctly irregular in nature, a phenomenon that would soon spread throughout the globe as nations emerged from the umbrella of the previously overarching East-West conflict.

Perhaps no other service was so challenged by the new paradigm of war than the Navy. While it was true that wide-scale conventional war was the primary focus for the other military services in the U.S. during the Cold War, each had also maintained a distinct irregular component that could be re-emphasized in the new era. This was not the case for the Navy, with its focus on the Mahanian legacy. Ships that could function effectively in an irregular environment, such as smaller or more diverse combatants, had been sacrificed to the Mahanian vision of a capital ship fleet that culminated in the Maritime Strategy.[3] The end of the Cold War nullified not only the Strategy but also threatened the force structure of capital ships designed to support it. Historically, capital ships do not adapt well to missions for which they are not designed; this was (and is) especially true of modern, high-tech combatants. Despite Navy claims of flexibility, the force was designed primarily (and almost exclusively) for traditional open-ocean, blue-water combat against a foe similarly armed and trained.[4] In the era of the "peace dividend" and calls for rapid demilitarization, the Navy had to move quickly to justify not only its fleet but also the core principles about which that fleet was designed if it was to remain relevant in the new era.

The Navy attempted to accomplish this task with the approach that had been so successful during the Cold War, through the vigorous promulgation of strategy in the public and professional arenas. The Maritime Strategy had been singularly successful in not only telling the Navy's story but also in justifying its force expansion; this model could work again. Prior to the 1980s, the Navy had issued few if any of these types of documents; now they began to flow from higher authority. The Navy attempted to explain its position through a series of strategies that emphasized the potential adaptability of capabilities developed for execution of the Maritime Strategy while simultaneously appearing to explore irregular mission areas that had been heretofore regarded as being outside the established norm. This was not completely successful, for regardless of rhetoric concerning change, at the core of this reinvention remained components of traditional theory that emphasized capital ship power. The Navy's attempt to reinvent itself while still clinging to its Mahanian mindset proved to a significant challenge; in the ten years between the fall of the Berlin Wall and the new millennium, the Navy published eight successive strategies, each striving to adapt to a rapidly altering political and military environment while maintaining the legacy of a core theoretical focus on a Mahanian-style fleet. An examination of these strategies is illuminating in terms of demonstrating this desire to remain wedded to theory despite an increasing irrelevance in the "new world order" for the relics of the Cold War Maritime Strategy. The Navy would match its rhetoric with a building program centered on capital ship power, including new carriers and high-tech combatants centered around the Aegis combat system, specifically designed to defeat a Soviet-style air attack in a conventional war. This development of capital ship power would be present and emphasized in each of the successive strategies of the 1990s.

What was remarkable about the Navy's effort to maintain its theoretical base was that the demand for U.S. forces throughout the decade was for involvement in increasingly irregular conflicts, ranging from wars between emerging states and ethnic conflicts to a wide diversity of humanitarian crises.[5] Despite the rhetoric of Navy strategies purporting (and promoting) change, the reality of fleet construction and employment of operational assets in training and remained focused on a Cold War-style threat.[6] The Navy noted the increasing importance of irregular-style operations but continued to train for another mission entirely, both in doctrine and in practice. This had predictable results. On the eve of 9/11 the service was adrift, a conventional force attempting to fulfill missions for which it was not designed and facing almost certain budget cuts and overt bureaucratic and institutional challenges to its very existence. Ironically, it would take a form of irregular attack at the end of the decade to bring the Navy back to strategic relevance—and only then a relevance that was carefully managed to allow for its continued reliance on capital ship power.

Prelude of an Uncertain Future: Desert Storm

It is difficult to overstate the rapidity or the degree of change that occurred in the aftermath of the sudden end of the Cold War in terms of military strategy and planning. The Navy was not the only service (or organization) to be taken by surprise by the collapse of the Soviet Union and the speed of events that were precipitated by this event. The change that followed Berlin was global in scope; in rapid succession, Germany united, many of the members of the former Soviet Bloc moved quickly to establish democratic governments, apartheid ended in South Africa, and peace agreements were reached in long-standing conflicts in El Salvador and Nicaragua.[7] These events moved so rapidly that the new G. W. Bush administration effectively had no long-term strategy to deal with them; arguably it would have been difficult to devise one that would have remained relevant. Indications that the world was moving toward mass democratization put the administration in a reactive mode, which quite wisely let events play their course, advising but not intervening so as not to alienate new friends and potential allies.[8] The sole exception to this policy of "wait and see" was the rapid U.S. response to the sudden invasion of Kuwait by the forces of Saddam Hussein.

The decade that would bring so much confusion and potential change within the traditional Navy theoretical mindset did not begin with the allocation of the much vaunted peace dividend, but rather in conflict that was distinctly conventional. On August 2, 1990, the Iraqi Army of Saddam Hussein invaded neighboring Kuwait, rationalizing the attack with a long-standing claim to territory but immediately bringing international condemnation.[9] The details of the conflict are well known. Following a six-month buildup in the desert of Saudi Arabia (Desert Shield), the U.S. and its coalition allies launched a brilliant conventional offensive (Desert Storm) that completely annihilated the enemy, liberating Kuwait and forcing Iraqi withdrawal. Although a "joint" operation in every regard, Desert Storm was a land conflict with primary focus on modern offensive air power (the distinct "winner" of the war in terms of news coverage of its effect) and a reaffirmation that the mechanized Army the United States had built to deal with the Soviets could in fact have other uses. This was a war in which the Navy played a part; although most of the postwar analysis focused on the Air Force's role in strike, one third of the air strikes launched during the war came from carriers operating in the Persian Gulf or were composed of Tomahawk missiles from ships and submarines.[10] But given the expense associated with Tomahawk missiles (each cost over a million dollars) and operating ships, it was argued by some that in terms of pure application of power the contribution of the Navy was not nearly what it could have been or—by implication—worth the investment.

This critical position is not entirely fair, as strategically the success of the war was due in large part to the effective use of sea power in a number of areas that reinforced traditional concepts. The first and probably most important was that the United States exercised complete control of sea, which enabled the coalition to bring a massive amount of supplies directly into the theater to pre-position for both the defensive buildup in Saudi Arabia and ultimately the offensive into Iraq. The value of the sea in this case is undeniable; 90 percent of forces and supplies were moved by the Military Sealift Command (MSC), a mixed Navy-civilian contract organization responsible for this mission.[11] Navy operations were not limited to guaranteeing that land forces were supplied. In addition to direct combat operations, the fleet also conducted maritime interception operations against oil carriers, significantly reducing Iraq's economic ability and indirectly affecting Hussein's ability to wage war.[12]

Prior to the deployment of land power, the first American forces on the scene consisted of ships from the standing Mediterranean force (including one aircraft carrier, soon bolstered to six) whose deterrent effect on stopping the dictator from continuing a feared offensive into Saudi Arabia will never be known. Amphibious ships positioned off shore, threatening the Iraqi left flank, forced units of the Iraqi Army to remain out of the fighting to guard for a possible offensive "end run" from the sea,[13] and as noted, strike from the sea using air power and cruise missiles was aggressive and consistent throughout the conflict. What was different

Seven. Strategy Adrift, 1990–2001

about these operations from previous wars (or theory) is that they were carried out without any real threat outside the battle zone. High-value assets usually needed to obtain command of the sea were being used to project power ashore; this was not the most efficient use of force, as much of the naval power deployed was dedicated to protecting the power-projection assets (smaller combatants in the carrier battle group surrounded the carrier to defend against attack, a standard conventional tactic), against which there was no threat. Navalists could argue that this was due to the overpowering force represented by the Navy (an excellent long-term investment in this view), while pessimists noted (correctly) that Iraq possessed little naval threat to begin with, so the bulk of the fleet was chronically unemployed.[14]

Officially, the Navy was quick to point out the benefits of these operations and sea power to the overall success of the campaign. The public, however, was occupied with other aspects of the war presented in far clearer terms.[15] The small Iraqi Navy was neutralized almost immediately in the conflict, giving voice to the argument that "sea control" existed with or without the presence of the six carriers ultimately deployed for the conflict. The fact that the main threat came from a distinctly irregular source—mines, which seriously damaged several combatants—was marginalized by the Navy in proposing future operations.[16] Deterrent results against Iraq were debatable points that could never be conclusively proven.[17] Strike operations during the war were certainly effective, but naval power was only a part of this remarkably successful campaign, a part that was arguably far more expensive than that conducted from quickly established land bases. The fact that naval airpower was usually far more flexible in deployment than its land component was lost in the public relations blitz conducted during and after the war. It was here that the Navy demonstrated a noticeable weakness, a remarkable fact given its known sensitivity regarding relevancy. Desert Storm represented the first media "24/7" war, images (and ongoing analysis) being broadcast live into living rooms from the fledgling CNN network. Very few of these images focused on the Navy, which conducted a lackluster public relations effort. While there was a number of standard shots of aircraft being launched from carriers, there were no media briefings held afloat, and Navy admirals were noticeably marginalized at the podium during the famous CENT-COM briefings held by Generals Powell, Schwarzkopf, and others.[18] Ordinarily this would not be a driving concern in operations, but the Navy soon learned that the perception of the war was solely in the here and now of the new 24/7 news cycle, a phenomenon that was ignored at the service's peril. This was especially true in an environment with a public and government increasingly concerned with growing costs and making budget cuts. The Navy won the test of combat but lost the public relations war.

The New Decade and the Rush for Justification

Despite successful operations in Desert Shield and Desert Storm, it was painfully obvious to Navy planners and strategists that the fundamental strategy that had been so successful in the 1980s—and on which so much had been based in both training and force structure—had to be rewritten, and rewritten quickly, in the face of the fall of the Berlin Wall and the sudden evaporation of the Soviet threat.[19] As noted, the Maritime Strategy was not only the primary source for war-fighting policy and doctrine for the Navy but also served as the main justification for the massive shipbuilding effort sponsored by the Reagan administration. Although the Republicans remained in power with the election of George Bush and the military as a whole was enjoying renewed popularity in the wake of Desert Storm, the Navy was painfully aware (as were their opponents) that without a conventional blue-water threat, the structure of the fleet—the carriers and capital ships—was at risk. The Navy's gamble in adopting the Maritime Strategy had paid off so long as there was a conventional opponent to fight; without one, capital ship theory once again faced a significant challenge to its relevance.

The relevance of capital ship theory would have special importance in terms of force procurement. Prior to the collapse of the Soviet Union, the Navy had argued for (and was achieving) its goal of 15 aircraft carriers to support the Maritime Strategy, several of which were nearing the ends of their regular service lives.[20] Without funding, modernization for these ships was at risk. But carriers were not the only concern. During the 1980s, the Navy had moved away from its model of naval platform diversity (the "high-low" concept articulated by Zumwalt) and moved to adopt a "mid-high" model in its combatants by replacing lower end vessels (frigates, hydrofoils, and smaller combatant craft) with the new Arleigh Burke Destroyer (DDG-51), a capital platform intended to be the mainstay of the surface fleet.[21] A large Aegis-based strike platform, the vessel was designed specifically as a high-tech blue-water combatant tailor-made for forward strike operations against the Soviets. It was distinctly non-irregular; early models (or "flights") could not even maintain a helicopter,

Seven. Strategy Adrift, 1990–2001

a fact that was addressed in later models in the face of rising criticism, including from within Navy ranks.[22] Even with this weakness addressed, however, it was difficult to argue that the expensive new mainstay of surface power was a "new" way of thinking, especially when challenged by budget-minded politicians who noted the enormous cost of even one ship of the class while openly questioning the ship's purpose.[23]

The challenge from the political sphere was not long in coming. In April 1990, Senator Sam Nunn, chairman of the Senate Armed Services Committee, openly called for a new mission analysis, stating that "forces should be reduced consistent with changes to the threat."[24] This was followed by a rash of additional proposals, including open questioning of 15 carrier battle groups, new calls for reunification of common mission areas among the services, use of common platforms (such as attack aircraft) between the services, and even a suggestion that competition among the services be encouraged as being beneficial to the formulation of strategy.[25] The Navy was not prepared to meet this onrush of proposals. While it is true that prior to retirement the CNO (Admiral Carlyle Trost) had written in USNI Proceedings a "Maritime Strategy for the 1990s,"[26] there was little in the document that was overtly new, nor did it address these new challenges. It was obvious that immediate formal and decisive action had to be taken.

The Navy's plan to address this challenge was to immediately issue a new strategy, appropriated titled The Way Ahead, that recognized the "new world order" as characterized by President Bush while also reclaiming its need to maintain a large fleet.[27] Given how long it took to research, draft, and promulgate the Maritime Strategy, the speed with which this new document was released is illustrative of the recognition by the Navy of the potential challenges of the new decade. The Way Ahead was released in 1991 as a public document published in the Naval Institute Proceedings[28] that served as a salvo against critics lining up to attack the Navy's Cold War budget and shipbuilding program. There were two singularly unique elements to the document. The first was philosophical. For the first time, the Navy publicly departed from its traditional themes and acknowledged the potential primacy of missions other than the traditional blue-water, forward combat emphasized by the Maritime Strategy (and by extension its Mahanian roots). Although forward operations were clearly stressed, the document openly stated that in light of the changing security environment, new missions such as "presence, humanitarian assistance, nation building, security assistance, peacekeeping, counter narcotics, counterterrorist, counterinsurgency, and crisis response operations will receive new emphasis."[29] This was a remarkable philosophical—and public—break with the classical Mahanian legacy and most certainly reflected the tenor of the times. It should be noted, however, that while this strategic posture was extraordinarily forward-leaning for the traditional Navy, the statement was not backed by any substantial shift away from shipbuilding or a notable change in operational doctrine, which still very much reflected forward strike missions with capital ships.[30]

This was not immediately apparent in the rhetoric surrounding the second unique point of the strategy, which openly acknowledged—and attempted to justify—a standing force of 450 ships. Arguably this appeared as a significant reduction, as the stated goal for execution of the Maritime Strategy had been the much-touted 600-ship Navy and as such it appeared that the Navy was acknowledging the need for a smaller force in light of the changing world situation. The reality was far more subtle; even during the Reagan years, the goal of 600 ships was declared fiscally unobtainable by the administration (Navy Secretary James Webb had resigned over this point),[31] and given the ongoing construction efforts left over from that era, the number 450 would ensure that building efforts would continue unabated. It should be noted that this apparent redirection of effort did not alter the focus of the shipbuilding program, which continued to emphasize capital ships, a point that would soon be noted by the growing chorus of critics.[32] The Navy effectively preserved its core activities, which were carriers and capital ships.

The theory presented in The Way Ahead was conceptually ahead of its time in proposing missions that would become increasingly the norm for not only the Navy but also for the U.S. military writ large in the coming decade. But as a strategy it had little impact either within or outside the service. Funding, shipbuilding, training cycles—all took time to change, and the suddenness of the collapse of the Soviet Union and the end of the Cold War did not seem to have immediate impact on these long-term elements.[33] Moreover, while the philosophical shift may have appeared radical to navalists, it was not as apparent to critics. The strategy openly stated that "many of our fundamental interests remain unchanged," leading observers to point out the numerous repeat clichés regarding naval forces and sea control throughout the document.[34] Politically, the timing could not have been worse. Outside the Navy, the public was far more focused on social issues and problems than any plans for alternative strategies. The "Tailhook" scandal that had erupted in 1991 was now center stage, not just for the Navy but also as part of the national dialogue regarding gender integration in the U.S. military.[35] On the Navy's part, an incompe-

Seven. Strategy Adrift, 1990–2001   123

tent investigation coupled with a remarkably glib public relations strategy served not only to severely undermine senior leadership but also to stain the reputation of the entire naval officer corps, making any focus on strategy problematic.[36] The public—and, increasingly, influential congressmen—were far more interested in plans for integration than any ideas about fighting new enemies in the era of the "peace dividend." The pro-defense, bipartisan Congress was beginning to break down.[37]

External politics aside, there was a recognition within senior leadership in the Navy that additional guidance had to be provided to the service regarding missions that would have priority in the future that went beyond the broad direction of The Way Ahead. While the Cold War mindset would never completely fade (and, as we shall see, will remain a constant theme of various degrees of influence for navalists), there was clearly a need for direction to deal with the new reality of the era following the Cold War. In 1992, the Navy published *The Navy Policy Book*, a work that served not so much as a strategy but rather a set of "principles" that were an extension of the broad strategic concepts described in The Way Ahead, intended to guide the Navy in the coming years. Drafted by the OPNAV staff at the personal direction of CNO Frank Kelso, the *Policy Book* was both an internal document intended to provide a common "worksheet" for the Navy while also serving as a reaffirmation of core principles for readers within and outside the Navy.[38] These principles were not solely strategic, nor were they focused solely on war fighting, but rather addressed all levels throughout the service. In addition to a professional reading list and explanation of the new Total Quality Leadership (TQL) program being employed for management, the *Policy Book* focused on three familiar strategic themes for the future of the Navy: deterrence, forward presence, and force projection. This last element was particularly emphasized throughout the work as a primary area of focus for the Navy in the new era. This was reflective of a growing trend that was demonstrated during the Gulf War: the ability to strike flexibly with rapid and effective power from the sea using capital ships (such as the new cruisers) outside the traditional carrier model.

Despite a somewhat unique approach in formulating strategy by addressing both an internal and external audience in an attempt to provide a common picture of the Navy, the *Policy Book* made little impact either within or outside the service. "Tailhook" remained an ongoing scandal, and TQL, despite much fanfare, was unpopular within the service and widely viewed as simply another management fad.[39] The strategic issues that the book addressed were largely ignored, overshadowed by disagreements within the ranks over these two issues. In retrospect, by attempting to address a way ahead at all levels, the *Policy Book* was unable to single out strategic themes and thus generated little interest, especially among those making budget decisions on the Hill. There was a lesson here that the Navy quickly learned: strategies had to be public, dynamic, and introduced with a solid backing of unified leadership.

This was accomplished to some extent by the next attempt: *From the Sea*. Published in 1992, *From the Sea* was billed as an express attempt to prepare the Navy for operations in the 21st century. "Change" was the theme throughout, not only as recognition of a new world order but also to illustrate to the public at large that the Navy was capable of adapting to new strategic challenges.[40] Continuing scandal as well as a clear lack of mission had created the perception that the Navy was by far the most traditional and hidebound of the services—and therefore potentially the least relevant outside of the Cold War context and vulnerable in the ongoing budget debate. This was a familiar theme. *From the Sea* attempted to attack this problem head on by stressing not only change but also alignment in a number of core mission areas with other services. The strategy was rolled out with considerable fanfare by senior Navy leadership as a clear and concise methodology not only to address new threats, but also to serve as a unifying document with other services meeting similar challenges.[41] Although not nearly as effective as the Maritime Strategy in terms of a public relations coup or impact on other services' strategies, it did hold the potential to meet the Navy's needs in explaining relevance in the context of the new world order—at least for a time.

At the heart of the new strategy were core missions that seemed to indicate a new approach while simultaneously pleasing the traditionalists. As the title implied, *From the Sea* was a forward strategy, relying on traditional concepts of forward operations and the relatively new mission of deep strike using high-tech weaponry—elements that implicitly demonstrated the need for carrier and capital ship power. But strike was not the only component of this strategy. As the title implied, force was to come "from" the sea to land proper. This required a strong expeditionary component that could respond flexibly to a wide variety of scenarios, in this case a role for which the Marine Corps was well suited. The marines had always been part of the Department of the Navy, but in the aftermath of the Cold War, the argument had once again been made that the Corps could potentially form a separate department or, conversely, be disestablished and melded into the Army, a familiar argument that received little attention, largely due to the marines' well established public relations program.[42] Regardless of the logic of these proposals, both scenarios put the Marine Corps at risk in the ongoing budget battle prior to the release of the new strategy.[43] *From the Sea* served to negate these arguments, presenting an image of the Navy as one unified force that would be the "first" to be called on in event of crisis, as it now possessed the ability for rapid strike, significant power projection, and sustainability in crisis in all dimensions. This was a solid argument based on the traditional mobility advantages of sea power—and seemed to provide ample justification for continued use of capital ship power in this role. The Marine Corps thus became wedded to the strongest part of the Navy; its capital ship force.

In the "joint" world, *From the Sea* took pains to stress the continued relevance of sea power to contingencies and crises involving other services. The strategy stressed "joint" operations even more than the previous Maritime Strategy in a much more tenable way for the other services. Naval power was no longer the sole focus but was rather an enabler for joint operations in contingencies.[44] This appealed to the joint community and was also in keeping with the tenor of the times that stressed consolidation as a matter of budgetary and operational efficiency. Joint operations in contingencies, however, were varied and covered a wide range of possibilities. As there was effectively no longer a traditional blue-water opponent, the Navy altered its focus to a geographic area, as opposed to a specific enemy. In this regard, the strategy stressed the importance of the littoral in modern contingency operations, an element that was relatively new for the Navy (and one it had been criticized for minimizing in the past).[45] The strategy noted that most of the world's littorals—especially areas of conflict that had heretofore been ignored in focusing on the Soviets—were well within strike range of the new modernized fleet, emphasizing Navy versatility to contribute to "forward" contingencies in these regions. To stress this point, operations were envisioned using various "force packages" of fleet power that could be tailored to operate in various types of conflict supporting the other services.[46]

The forward operations prescribed in *From the Sea* were generally popular with a Navy that was becoming increasingly focused on strike warfare in the aftermath of the practical operations of Desert Storm and the theoretical change represented by the Maritime Strategy. In terms of force structure, this mission was completely aligned with capital ship theory; both carrier air wings and the new DDGs were designed primarily for strike against both open-ocean and land targets. But forward strike missions were emphasized at a cost, most notably in a radical change in traditional sea control concepts. This was especially true in anti-submarine warfare, which was reduced from a primary mission to secondary status throughout the fleet in favor of offensive strike theory. This was largely the result of a strategic and cultural trap that the Navy, with its reliance on capital ship theory and high end platforms, found itself locked into.

Strategically, ASW was a primary mission against the Soviet Union and its large, modern fleet of submarines; this had been used for years as a justification for larger ships and especially high-tech nuclear submarines.[47] Throughout the period, other types of submarines (such as diesels) or other potential enemies with smaller fleets had been marginalized. As the Soviets were no longer a threat, this mission did not require the emphasis it had in the past. Moreover, any open-ocean threat would certainly be minimized as the vast majority of world naval powers did not possess the modern (nuclear) submarines of the Soviet fleet—and U.S. ASW theory held that if a submarine was not nuclear, it was not a significant threat.[48] Following this engrained logic, it seemed that ASW was no longer required given the low regard held for non-nuclear alternatives. This allowed the Navy to re-allocate funds from ASW (and smaller ASW ships, which were decommissioned in increasing numbers) into newer, larger combatants that emphasized strike.

In this regard, however, the Navy found itself in a rather unique theoretical trap. Forward operations implied that sea control in the open ocean was a fait accompli given U.S. overwhelming capital ship power that would theoretically eliminate any threats (which it had during Desert Storm). But the other navies of the world were not Iraq. This assumption ignored the growing numbers of submarines that were being acquired by smaller navies worldwide, submarines that (while diesel) were extremely capable platforms. The Navy's culture under the Rickover regime had been to ignore these submarines as not worthy of their U.S. nuclear counterparts or the ASW capability of the surface fleet—a fact that might be true in the mid–Atlantic (and the point was debatable) but was certainly questionable in the forward operating areas of the littoral, where diesel submarines operate in their element.[49] The Navy's culture insisted these smaller platforms were not worthy threats, at best an irregular adversary that could be defeated by conventional power. This logic did not stop with submarines. Simply put, capital ship power would sweep away any irregular threats, including mines, shore-based missiles, smaller craft hiding in the clutter of the littoral, aircraft, or any other threat that the enemy was foolish enough to deploy. This was, in many ways, a remarkable argument, as it was completely dismissive of any type of irregular threat. The Navy's vulnerability to mines, demonstrated several times in Persian Gulf operations, was largely ignored, as was vulnerability to any type of small vessel threat. Moreover, the peculiarities of operating in the littoral—such as identifying enemy targets hiding among normal coastal traffic and activity—were not addressed, nor were the various environmental elements that proved to be challenging for capital ships. Given the growing technical capability of smaller navies worldwide in these areas, these were interesting assumptions.[50] Littoral operations were stressed in *From the Sea* (which would seem natural, given the forward-offensive nature of the strategy), but the force structure designed to operate in the littoral was based on a very traditionalist rationale. Blunt power seemed to be the answer. The strategy emphasized the means—but not the how.

Despite these operational misgivings, *From the Sea* was far more successful than its predecessor.[51] The strategy not only seemed to address a changing world but also struck the right chord with many in the defense establishment in its efforts to modify its way of thinking. The Navy used the strategy in an organized public relations campaign stressing its relevance and flexibility, an effort that seemed to pay dividends. Unfortunately, the world continued to change rapidly, presenting the Navy with new challenges not only on the international stage but also domestically.

Clinton and the Era of Reinventing Government

In 1993, Bill Clinton succeeded George H. W. Bush as president, marking the end of twelve years of Republican occupancy of the White House and control of the defense infrastructure. Part of the stated Clinton agenda was a re-examination of government budgeting processes, formally established as the National Performance Review (NPR). As a coordinated program to end government waste, the NPR set an immediate goal of a 10 percent reduction in all government agencies for operating costs.[52] To some extent the Navy had anticipated a significant force reduction in the aftermath of Desert Storm; despite the success of that operation for DOD, it was clear that without a global Soviet threat, there would be cuts. The Navy had attempted to be forward-leaning in issuing its strategies describing its relevance in the new era. But, as noted, there was still the tinge of the Cold War in these documents, and the fleet was still being constructed in accordance with the fundamental premise that capital ship theory would remain the mainstay of future operations. The funding and emphasis the Navy dedicated toward that end remained significant.

The Clinton administration's agenda presented two immediate challenges to this mindset. The first was the size of the proposed cuts. Capital ships and their operating costs were clearly the most expensive items in the fleet and inevitably would be targeted for cutbacks. The second was the operating philosophy of the new administration. Clinton was initially concerned with building the international financial structure required for the new concept of emerging globalization, and his policies reflected this approach.[53] Early interventions in Somalia and Haiti (the Haitian intervention relying heavily on naval power to conduct migrant rescue and interdiction operations, as well as a forced blockade) did not ensure democracy as intended, ultimately making the administration hesitant to commit forces overseas.[54] Ongoing conflict in Bosnia and continued operations against Saddam Hussein required military force—but these were diverse conflicts that required very specialized application. Arguably ensuring the free flow of oil from the Persian Gulf was a naval mission (and one that was given high priority by the administration, given its emphasis on economic issues), but this was a mission that did not require the full force of the Navy. In terms of rationalizing a large strike fleet, capital ship power was once again in jeopardy.

The response from the Navy was to once again update its strategy with a public release of a new posture statement, "Forward ... from the Sea." Written in 1994, "Forward ... from the Sea" took pains to recognize the early conflicts of the Clinton era as evidence of "the new way" of conducting operations regardless of how much naval power was actually used. This approach was far more specific than the wide-ranging conflicts noted in *From the Sea* (which generally examined a broader set of contingencies); emphasis now was on regional conflict, specifically in known hot-spot areas. Politically the strategy attempted to align itself with the goal of the administration, directly citing policy regarding contingencies and the use of military force.[55] It did not abandon the fundamental premise of forward operations espoused in *From the Sea*; rather, it enhanced these concepts in light of new international developments. The strategy was more specific to sea control concepts in the littoral and made a specific link to the ongoing budget decisions being made within government. Emphasis on forward operations stressed combat capability of naval forces in the joint arena, again emphasizing strike and the link to the Marine Corps.

As with *From the Sea*, the Navy employed an aggressive public relations strategy in presenting its new document. The new strategy became an official capstone document cited in a blitz of public speaking opportunities by Navy admirals and officials and was frequently cited in a rash of official and semi-official articles promoting it in USNI *Proceedings*.[56]

Seven. Strategy Adrift, 1990–2001

Although billed as a new strategy, there were some familiar themes in the new document. Once again, capital ship power was noted as the "basic building block" of naval strategy.[57] There was some variation in this theme. In addition to carriers, amphibious ready groups (ARGs) were given almost equal billing with traditional capital ships, acting on one hand as a means to stress unity with the Marine Corps while on the other simultaneously stressing forward strike operations. It should be noted, however, that significant funding was not diverted to the maintenance of the amphibious force, which was beginning to show its age. While new ships were planned for the amphibious fleet, it would be years before these plans began to come to fruition.[58] The existing building program for strike cruisers and continuous modification of carrier air wings continued unabated.

"Forward ... from the Sea" was successful in that it solidified the Navy around its strike mission. Both publicly and within the service, strike was now clearly the priority for naval operations, adjusted to meet contingencies requiring a combat presence. To reinforce this point, the Navy issued the Naval Operational Concept (NOC) in 1997. The NOC was written due to concerns that simple forward presence had grown somewhat stale in light of new technological developments (especially new concepts in net-centric warfare, which were beginning to dominate military literature); new technologies needed new thinking around the familiar theme.[59] As its title implied, the NOC stressed an operational concept of maneuver warfare for forces engaged in contingencies and also stressed operations in transitional periods from peace to crisis to war. While these were important themes, the NOC had little impact within the service, primarily due to its excessive emphasis on net-centric warfare, which was still a new and largely misunderstood concept within the ranks.

The final attempt of the decade to appeal to congressional and public opinion was the release of "Anywhere, Anytime" in late 1997. Like previous strategies, it was released as an article in the well-respected and widely read Naval Institute journal *Proceedings* by the chief of naval operations. The strategy was in many respects an attempt to crystallize familiar themes: forward operations, direct strike ashore, and the need for capital ship power. Emphasis in "Anywhere, Anytime" was not only on precision strike (a capability that had increased exponentially with newer and cheaper versions of the Tomahawk, which had become the main strike weapon for the fleet outside carrier power) and the ability of the forwardly deployed Navy to decisively impact events ashore.[60] In many ways the strategy was even more forward than "Forward ... from the Sea" in that it emphasized the "shock and awe" elements of naval power—and that it could reach much farther than in the past, thus becoming a decisive element in determining the course of events ashore. Initially this public posture statement seemed to have some success as it became (like previous strategies) a key element of the Navy's public relations program. But like strategies in the past, it suffered from a general lack of interest; without a commonly perceived threat that could be specifically targeted, it seemed like more of the same rhetoric. A lack of emphasis from future CNOs on the strategy condemned it to the fate of others written during the decade—just another document that enjoyed brief commentary before fading into obscurity.

Reality vs. Theory: Irregular Warfare in the 1990s

Although the Cold War had ended, the 1990s were far from a peaceful decade. It is perhaps ironic that while the world avoided the mass conflagration that plans called for in a U.S.-Soviet conflict, the end of the traditional rivalry did not foster increased peace throughout the world but rather an explosion of conflict and combat among smaller and new and emerging powers. The decade following the collapse of the Soviet Union will likely be remembered in history as the era of irregular warfare. Without the common binding framework of the East-West conflict (and subsequent alignment with one power or another), causes and movements that had been heretofore suppressed gained new freedom in their ability to wage war; irregular wars and smaller internal conflicts, both internal and between emerging states, became the norm rather than the exception.[61]

But these were "wars of choice" outside the national interest, and as such, many of these wars, especially smaller "brushfire" conflicts in Africa, were largely ignored by the West—some, such as the genocide in Rwanda, with tragic results. But others created the need for deployment of NATO or U.S. military power either as a show of force or as direct participants in conflict. Even though many of these conflicts involved the use of naval power, there was no political pressure for the Navy to adapt to this type of war, so any lessons that were gained in execution were marginalized in the continued quest for capital ship dominance. This does not imply that the Navy did not respond; the need to demonstrate relevance led to a philosophical change in the use of capital ships as first responders for a wide range of contingencies, but there was little regard as to whether the type of strike power they represented was appropriate for the requirements of

Seven. Strategy Adrift, 1990–2001

irregular warfare. The Navy operated with the tools at hand—in this case, capital ships—with little consideration as to whether irregular war would become a threat to the United States in the future.

Capital ship power underwent two changes that were significant for contingency-style operations. The first was a change in deployment philosophy that was more closely aligned with the Navy's views on forward operations. Whereas in the past carriers had surged from home ports in the U.S. for various contingencies, they now rotated on station in crisis operating areas in a form of "mini-containment" to provide strike airpower as required.[62] This new operational tactic resulted in carrier power being employed briefly in Somalia and more extensively in the Adriatic in support of NATO operations in Bosnia and in the Persian Gulf, enforcing "no-fly" sanctions against Iraq. The long-term effect of this was to make such operations routine for Navy personnel; actual contribution to combat operations, however, is difficult to measure. This is due to the second change, a more deliberate shift toward the actual use (as opposed to Cold War threat) of strike power. The Tomahawk, which was now carried by most capital ships, was a low-risk/high-yield option and was becoming increasingly the weapon of choice in the political sphere for crises that required a rapid show of combat power.

The use of the Tomahawk fundamentally altered the calculus of the traditional "naval show of force" mission so important to the "big gun club" of a bygone era; whereas in the past the mere presence of such a vessel within sight of a hostile shore could be a potential diplomatic game changer simply by implying power would be used, now it was the actual use of strike power launched far from land. Carriers and capital ships were strategic assets and far too valuable to risk close to enemy littoral threats and thus operated far off shore and were virtually unseen, limiting any form of visual or "presence" deterrent. Who or what delivered that strike was now largely a mystery to an unsuspecting opponent. While it is true that carriers maintained a versatile air wing that could deliver a number of strike options (although this was becoming increasingly specialized with the move to one universal airframe, the F-18[63]), the future for this mission seemed to belong to missiles. The difficulty this presented, despite the efficiency and accuracy of the new ordnance, was that it actually had to be used to be a deterrent. Capital ship power had become far more lethal—but was also limited in its traditional mission of deterrence.

This is not to imply, however, that naval power was not employed in irregular crisis operations. While carriers were operating off shore with increasingly specialized air wings, other types of combatants were responding to a wide range of diverse and irregular threats. These operations can be categorized in three respective areas: "contingency" operations (such as the Haitian blockade during Operation Uphold Democracy and the Haitian/Cuban boatlifts), non-combatant evacuation (NEO) operations of U.S. citizens from crisis areas, and humanitarian/disaster relief operations. The primary naval component for these operations were amphibious ready groups (ARGs) composed of a wide range of ships, from larger helicopter carriers to smaller vessels capable of deploying in a littoral environment. These types of ships dominated responses to contingency operations throughout the decade, demonstrating a high degree of versatility in irregular environments that was lacking in the carriers.[64] Carriers were deployed for five contingency operations in the 1990s, while amphibious ships were deployed for 27. This is controversial; a Center for Navy Analyses (CNA) study notes that while ARGs deployed more in numbers, the station-keeping strategy of keeping carriers on scene actually indicated that carrier power was equal to amphibious response in the long term. The point is debatable.[65] In Somalia an ARG was fully engaged both in landing forces ashore and acting as an offshore supply base; two CVBGs that were sent to the region as a "show of force" had no impact on the conflict.[66] Haiti was "blockaded" by the Navy in 1994 in an effort to force regime change, but the primary target of this operation were small Haitian "yolas" (sailboats) that hardly merited the commitment of significant surface power (a number of the new Arleigh Burkes and much carrier-based airpower were dedicated to the operation, with limited effect). The mass migrations that occurred during the period (from both Haiti and Cuba) were handled by Navy amphibious ships and cutters from the Coast Guard.[67] Carriers contributed strike power to the NATO response in Bosnia/Herzegovina in two separate strike operations (Allied Force and Noble Anvil) as part of a coalition force, so it is difficult to distinguish between the effectiveness of sea-based and land-based airpower out of Aviano Italy, both of which was used in abundance.[68] Continued economic sanctions against Saddam Hussein in enforcement of the "no-fly" zone over Iraq also employed combined land/sea air power, carriers operating continuously on station in the Persian Gulf contributing to the multinational force. How effective these operations were is often contested, especially given subsequent U.S. actions against Iraq after September 11, 2001.[69]

But while amphibious power and smaller combatants seemed to be the platforms of choice in contingencies and irregular responses—and certainly cost less—in terms of funding and shipbuilding, the amphibious community took a distinctly second tier below the carrier fleet; moreover, although these types of operations were described in the number of strategies the Navy produced (as noted above), associated doctrine in support of irregular-style operations was not forthcoming. These ships may have been the workhorses of the reality of irregular warfare, but they were not the darlings of theory.

Conclusions

The 1990s were a pivotal time for the Navy as it clung to its theory despite a clear need for change—and a very practical challenge in the form of continued irregular wars. The Navy attempted to adapt to the uncertainty of the era through repeatedly issuing strategies that recognized "change" but ultimately rationalized theory that did not escape the Mahanian legacy. When examined together, the strategies of the 1990s illustrate a number of important trends. The first is a certain desperation within Navy senior leadership to illustrate relevance in a rapidly changing strategic environment; navies were now being used, but not for the core missions supported by theory and tradition. Each of the strategies purported to be an agent of "change" within the fleet, recognizing (correctly) the new and varied threats faced by the United States in the aftermath of the end of the Cold War. But while the strategies were quite direct in emphasizing "new" types of conflicts, the answer inevitably rested on the bedrock of capital ship power, which continued to be built and planned by the Navy in the form of new carriers and strike cruisers. Types of ships called for in strategic execution remained distinctly traditional; with the exception of calls to operate farther "forward" (itself a traditional concept) there were few new ideas offered by the plethora of strategies released by the service. Moreover, clear operational direction and rationalization of forces—key selling points of the Maritime Strategy—were lacking. Calls for the "need" to change were answered with extremely vague platitudes as to the "how" this was to be done, beyond stating the continued requirement for a strong striking force. As such, the strategies as a group could be regarded as a restatement of the traditional Navy concept of large fleets and capital ship power. The legacy of Mahan and the spirit of Sims were alive and well but ultimately failed to rationalize the need for a large fleet in an increasingly hostile government bureaucracy. Had the world not encountered a new threat at the decade's turn, the ultimate fate of the capital ship fleet might have been very different.

Eight

The New Challenge
9/11 and the Use of Naval Power in Irregular Warfare

The United States was attacked by Al Qaeda on September 11, 2001. It was in every respect a turning point in history. The 1990s in the U.S. and the West had been an era of rising prosperity and peace; 9/11 ended the "end of history."[1] The world's only superpower was suddenly and unexpectedly attacked by an asymmetric and irregular enemy that effectively bypassed a huge and well-established conventional force structure to strike directly at the centers of American economic and political power, deliberately targeting civilians to cause mass casualties. The attack has been well documented and endless commentary made on virtually every element of the event. But what was the impact on established military theory? It would seem that given both the nature of the attacks and the new asymmetric enemy, there could be no greater indication that the war of the future was to be an irregular one; even the U.S. counterattack into Afghanistan to strike at the core of Al Qaeda and its Taliban supporters was directed against an irregular opponent with limited conventional power. Because the United States had been attacked directly by an enemy that was not a nation-state and that operated in the shadows, irregular warfare was no longer confined to small overseas theaters. For the U.S., it was now a global war to be fought on two fronts: the homeland and abroad. The strategic priority that the U.S. military and the Navy in particular had largely ignored for years was now the national military priority.

But as a predominantly conventional force, the U.S. military (and the nation) faced a number of unique challenges in the new era. One of the most significant impacts of the 9/11 attacks was a very dramatic and public shift of opinion regarding war and its effects. The apparent vulnerability of the nation called into question some elements of operating forward, generating a need for the creation of a system of homeland defense. For the first time in modern memory the U.S. had been attacked; moreover, the target had not been a military one but rather was chosen deliberately to maximize civilian casualties using WMD employed by a terrorist organization rather than nation-state.

This had two immediate impacts on public perception of war. The first was a huge public desire for offensive action, which resulted in very rapid operations against Al Qaeda in Afghanistan by overwhelming military force in what would be characterized as the first phase in the "global war on terror" (GWOT).[2] The second reaction was far more long-term— and not as subject to principles of military logic. This was the immediate creation of a far greater national concern regarding defense of the homeland against future attacks. There is little doubt that the events of 9/11 radically altered the American psyche on a number of levels, perhaps none more so than in the perception of threat. On September 10, the average citizen's perception of threat, both national and local, could be characterized as relatively benign or esoteric; as the world's only superpower, external threats seemed to be confined to economic affairs or environmental concerns.[3] On September 12, Americans faced a new shadowy enemy, an enemy that seemed to be everywhere and capable of striking anything. It is often said that "everything changed" after 9/11; whether or not this is true in terms of practical military operations in the United States, it was certainly true in terms of the perception that there was a new threat that could strike at any time with catastrophic effects.[4] This perception manifested itself in a passion for the protection of the homeland, resulting in a national defense effort the size of which had not been seen since the Second World War.[5]

There were many positive results of this passion for defense, including the creation of the Department of Homeland Security, which consolidated the effort of the large number of very different government agencies responsible for some element of security in their own right prior to 9/11. But this new paradigm also presented certain challenges for established military organizations, not only in how to apply traditional military concepts to the idea of "homeland defense" but also in determining the true nature of the potential threat. For the sea services, this was critical, as the threat would have significant impact on the effective application of sea power in new and very different environments. Because the concept of defense and irregular threat were almost foreign to established naval theory, these elements presented the most significant challenge to theory in decades. Unlike the budget battles of the 1990s, the challenge now was real war—but a war that was not suited to traditional operational methods. This appeared to put the Navy in a huge dilemma between determining how to fight a non-traditional war while attempting to maintain its core theoretical concepts—or being forced to change.

How well did the Navy, especially a Navy based on Mahanian theory, adapt to this new challenge of irregular warfare, not only overseas but also in the homeland? The answer is complex. Irregular warfare was "new" only inasmuch as it had now been used directly against the United States and thus could not be marginalized or ignored. As a global force dedicated to the security of the seas as well as the defense of the homeland, this new threat had to be addressed. But at the same time it was unlikely that the Navy was about to give up on its well-crafted rationale for large strike fleets, especially as the actual threat facing the nation was a mystery, a factor not just for the sea services but for all forms of military power. Before a proper strategy could be devised, the new paradigm had to be defined. This began with threat analysis.

Threat: The New Paradigm

Properly defining threat in irregular warfare has always been, at best, problematic. As noted in Chapter One, the very nature of the irregular warfare "combatant" often defies conventional definition. This can be an advantage to IW practitioners who employ methods such as sabotage or terrorism to provoke an overwhelming response from conventional enemies that can widen the conflict or place sympathy with the irregular force. As discussed, this is even more problematic in modern times when "irregular" forces can act in asymmetric or hybrid conflicts utilizing modern technology that make them virtually indistinguishable from non-combatants.[6] September 11 emphasized these asymmetric elements not only by exporting a religious conflict that had been ignored by most Americans into a global war zone but also by maximizing the effect of fear in areas (the United States) that were heretofore invulnerable.[7] This created a "perfect storm" in terms of creating a threat mythos. Before examining the Navy's application of sea power in the post-9/11 environment, it is critical to examine this new perception and the impact of the irregular threat on the United States to determine its effect on established military theory.

Perhaps no other factor associated with the attacks on 9/11 was as dramatic as a complete reversal in the United States regarding the perception of threat. During the Cold War the threat to the nation, while potentially catastrophic (and generally thought to be unlikely), was relatively clear and responsibility for meeting it generally confined to the military and intelligence services.[8] The attacks on 9/11 muddied that picture considerably. Anything could be a potential threat in the asymmetric world; in a sense, this was a classic example of the power of irregular threat, just on a much broader scale. This perception has not only affected the public mindset, but also radically altered the established process for planning military forces and devising national strategy. For many years, threat analysis was conducted using an established analytical process based on assessment of conventional military force. The asymmetric threat of terrorism challenged this process, but more importantly in the aftermath of 9/11, threat analysis became subject to undue influences outside the normal scope of traditional methods. Thus 9/11 was an emotional event that demonstrated what terrorists are capable of given the tools and opportunity. In terms of threat analysis, this has had the unfortunate effect of creating a number of popular scenarios that were based more on emotion than logical, reasoned analysis. This in turn created the potential for misdirection of scarce resources toward defending against an unlikely threat (at one point, for example, White House attorneys rationalized the military taking over many elements of domestic law enforcement to deal with the terrorist threat—an action that did not come to pass, although federal government power in law enforcement did increase substantially with the approval of the PATRIOT act).[9] Thus perception of threat, rather than logical analysis, drove the strategic planning process.[10]

In the aftermath of 9/11, there was a great deal of speculation regarding the form future attacks could take, ranging from the catastrophic (use of a weapon of mass destruction, be it nuclear, chemical, or biological) to economic, such as an attack on critical infrastructure or industry.[11] In short, suddenly everything was potentially vulnerable, and it was hard to foresee and defend against a possibly nationally catastrophic strike. Many of these scenarios were not only highly speculative but also extremely unlikely, a logical outcome of the highly irregular and unusual form of the attacks of 9/11.[12] This had the unfortunate effect of creating something of a cottage industry in the military-industrial complex, ready to design various defensive systems to deal with more esoteric "threats," including defending coastal cities against terrorist cruise missiles and Al Qaeda attacks against the smallest towns of middle America.[13] However unlikely (or in some cases, simply silly) these threats might appear now, they did have significant impact on the national dialogue regarding the terrorist threat, especially as each had to be answered—and answered quickly—by a conventionally based military now tasked with direct defense of the homeland.[14] The added elements of national fear and urgency led to increased political pressure, factors that made any honest evaluation of threats extremely problematic, all the more so because of the inherent conventional weakness in IW threat analysis.[15]

The military is, of course, no stranger to planning based on threat. During time of war analysis of threat is fairly straightforward; in peacetime, it is more problematic. Threat analysis is important because it drives the national strategy and subsequent force procurement designed to meet the perceived threat.[16] In conducting threat analysis, military planning traditionally focuses on two areas: capabilities and intentions. "Capabilities" are a combination of weapon strength, numbers, ability to deploy weapons, and various effectiveness factors such as overall training, force integration, etc. "Intentions" are based on an intelligence assessment of geopolitical factors, history, interpretation of enemy doctrine and tactics, and other intelligence factors. Of the two, capabilities are far easier to measure, as this assessment is weighted heavily toward acquired hardware. Capabilities-based assessment is generally considered the cornerstone for force structure design.[17] Although overly simplistic, it is fair to say that forces are designed to match (or exceed) enemy capability in quantity and/or quality. But capabilities are only part of the picture; potential enemy actions with these capabilities must also be surmised. In determining these "intentions," planners often err on the side of caution by assuming that if the enemy could employ weapons in the "worst case" scenario with some chance of success, then the enemy would do so.[18] This "could" is far more nebulous an assessment, as it is based on an interpretation of intelligence that can be subject to individual, group, or political bias (the "falling domino" theory being one widely discredited example of perceived enemy intentions).

The Cold War provides a classic case study in this regard. Although the capabilities of Soviet weapons systems were generally known, how and under what circumstances the Soviets were going to employ them remained a mystery. As we have seen, strategies during the Cold War were based on a combination of speculation and analysis, usually centered on a worst case in terms of mass conventional war followed by nuclear exchange. Since it was known that the Soviets possessed both a large nuclear and conventional capability, it was assumed that this force would be used offensively to promote communist ideals if there was a reasonable chance of success (and survival). This analysis led to the development of nuclear strategies such as Mutual Assured Destruction (MAD) vs. Nuclear Utilization Target Selection (NUTS), and a conventional strategy designed to inflict maximum attrition against an anticipated Soviet offensive into Europe.[19] It should be noted that in hindsight, Cold War threat analysis was not perfect. Soviet capabilities in retrospect were not as robust as many analysts claimed, leading to charges that the threat had been exaggerated to bolster various defense budgets.[20] While not without weaknesses, the military model for threat assessment was a logical, straightforward, and fairly reliable method to drive U.S. strategy and subsequent force procurement to meet a relatively clear threat.[21] But this model of "threat equals capabilities plus intentions" changes in an IW model when it attempts to consider asymmetric capabilities and intentions about which there is little agreement.

In classic threat analysis, asymmetric capabilities are less defined and thus more difficult to measure using this established methodology.[22] It is not hard to see why. Weapons such as improvised explosives, suicide and car bombs, or even forms of improvised WMD are tremendously difficult to quantify. This problem was not unknown prior to 9/11, where threat analysis resulted in a slightly different methodology. When applied to terrorist groups, the model relied on historical behavioralist trends, terrorist motivations, and an estimate of capability acquisition to determine threat.[23] In general the application of this type of rationale resulted in a view that terrorists were usually localized with a specific cause, did not use violence except for a very specific reason against selectively targeted groups, and usually did not strive for mass indiscriminate casualties.[24] The uniqueness of the September 11 attacks challenged all of these assumptions as well as the model that predicted them. Because 9/11 was a completely unforeseen event, the "shock and awe" of the attack led to a growing trend in asymmetric threat where capabilities assessment was based on worst-case speculation rather than historical examples.

Changes in the basic analytical methodology of capabilities and intentions led to a very diverse interpretation of the threat that lacked a solid analytical basis.[25] This is especially true in a number of popular scenarios that influenced public perception of threat. In reviewing these scenarios, a very common theme emerged where a relatively low-probability event became the focus of national attention. This included nuclear, biological, and chemical threats—none of which were based on actual evidence of terrorists possessing these capabilities, but rather what would happen if they did acquire them, no matter how unlikely this event might be.[26] This "what if" was a radical departure from established capabilities-based planning that was a direct challenge to traditional theory, especially in naval theory that prescribed forward operations against any enemy.

The most obvious manifestation of this trend was an obsession with an exotic worst-case scenario. This did not fit in well with theoretical examinations of terrorists prior to 9/11. Historically terrorists have almost universally relied on relatively simple means to strike their targets with the idea of creating selective fear or making a statement through inflicting casualties on non-combatants.[27] The attacks on 9/11 were designed to create mass casualties (relatively rare in terrorist cases), so popular post–9/11 threat scenarios took this to the next logical step in the public's eyes, focusing on WMD in the form of nuclear, biological, or chemical attack.[28] Oddly, this created public awareness of WMD that far eclipsed that felt during the Cold War when, it could be argued, the likelihood of being attacked by nuclear weapons was far greater.[29] But the WMD in the case of Al Qaeda were far more exotic and a very different threat than that posed by the Soviets in that there apparently was no classic nuclear or deterrence theory that applied. Rather, terrorist WMD had a tinge of irrationality. In addition to the assumption that if ALQ had these weapons they would be used (a radical departure from the Cold War threat analysis that assumed WMD would only be used if an enemy had a significant chance of victory), it was also assumed that terrorists would ignore any retaliation against such use, the most common description of terrorists groups being that "they were simply crazy" and willing to face total annihilation.[30] The highly technical nature of WMD and the delivery systems for these weapons also became a casualty to the popular image, as this was now regarded in light of potential asymmetric delivery methods that were "common" and almost impossible to stop—making the de-facto argument that WMD could be literally anywhere.[31] For a seaborne threat, these methods include shipping containers, merchant vessels, general cargo delivery vehicles, and, in one of the more bizarre scenarios, SCUD missiles fitted with nuclear weapons and fired from the sea.[32] The subtlety was that WMD could strike anywhere and any time in areas that were previously regarded as safe. Technical limitations of these types of weapons were generally not a factor in the public eye; threats such as the "briefcase nuke" (a technical impossibility) became all the rage in mass media and popular techno-thrillers.[33]

In general, the services were not keen to adapt to the new asymmetric threat, especially one that was driven by influences outside the normal threat-planning process. For the sea services, the national paranoia resulting from the attacks of 9/11 created a mindset that was directly counter to established naval theory. The hue and cry was now for defense of the "homeland" (the term itself had been used sparingly in the years prior to

9/11 but was now coined in the immediate aftermath of the attacks)[34] against any threat or (worse) any perception of threat, which as we've seen were quite diverse. This was equally true on land or sea. The attacks on 9/11 had not come from the sea nor were they associated with maritime power, but even a cursory glance at the empty sea by new homeland security experts seemed to indicate vulnerability. With 95,000 miles of coastline on two coasts, it was argued that the U.S. was in fact vulnerable to attack from the sea; if this were indeed the case, defense of some kind (hopefully a visual one in the minds of many) was the obvious answer.[35] But the tradition of the U.S. on the sea is the offensive; as we have seen in our examination of the evolution and continued influence of the Mahanian legacy, defense is at best anathema to navalists. In the U.S. navalist tradition, "defense" is conducted through forward offense to destroy the enemy fleet or forces. But in an irregular conflict—and the GWOT was nothing if not irregular—how could sea power logically be employed in this role?

The Navy approached this problem in three ways, each of which was deeply embedded in its strategic culture. First, traditional forward operations in support of conventional strikes began almost immediately in support of military operations in Afghanistan and later Iraq. As in the past, this carrier-centric effort dominated the bulk of Navy attention and time. Second, the threat to the homeland was addressed—but only in conjunction with other agencies in a form that gradually relieved the Navy of much of the responsibility for homeland defense duties near the coastline of the United States in favor of forward operations. Finally, in operations reminiscent of Vietnam, irregular warfare units were begrudgingly formed to meet the need as the overseas wars dragged on and strategic emphasis moved from conventional strike operations to irregular warfare—a pattern that was achingly familiar.[36]

First Shots in the GWOT

The United States did not remain an isolated fortress for long. With no immediate direct threat from the sea, the Navy began to plan for its role in the upcoming offensive campaign against Afghanistan. When it became apparent that ALQ had been backed (or at least housed) by the Taliban, there was no doubt that military action was forthcoming. The president's speech to the nation on 14 September made this clear. After a brief diplomatic overture to the Taliban to turn over responsible elements of Al Qaeda and disband its terrorist training facilities (which was refused), offensive operations began against Afghanistan on 7 October 2001. In a stunningly successful campaign, within a month the government of Afghanistan was effectively smashed, its conventional strength completely nullified.

In the post-operations analysis following initial American operations in Afghanistan, it seemed that carriers and forward operating theory were completely vindicated by the rapid success enabled by naval power.[37] At the outset, the United States had very limited capability to strike at Afghanistan; with no nearby land bases, the alternatives consisted of long-range bombers flying from extreme distances (in some cases, directly from the United States) or the use of naval strike power. Carriers were the obvious answer, especially given the Navy's policy of maintaining carrier battle groups on station in the Middle East. Within days of the attack, carriers were within striking range of Taliban and Al Qaeda targets. Operation Enduring Freedom began on October 7, 2001, with air attacks against targets in Kabul and Kandahar, including Taliban airfields, air defense positions, command and control nodes, and known ALQ training camps.[38] Throughout the first week of the operation, naval aircraft conducted multiple missions from a distance of 600 miles, flying from three carriers operating on station in the North Arabian Sea.[39] These attacks were remarkably precise, employing new Joint Precision Guided Munitions (JDAMs) that significantly enhanced the effective firepower of the carrier air wing. As the war gradually changed to a land conflict against a dispersed enemy, the nature of these strike operations changed as well, from deliberate attacks against infrastructure and known targets to attacks against targets of opportunity directed by overhead Air Force command and control assets and special forces (SOF) operating on the ground.[40] The SOF link was especially important as the main ground effort was conducted by these forces in the earliest phases of the war. Naval power supported this effort in a very unique role; in addition to traditional logistic support, the carrier *Kitty Hawk* was used as a deployable SOF platform for SEAL and Ranger helicopters performing special operations missions in the early phase of the war, removing part of its attached F-18 air wing to make room for the special operations helicopters.[41]

The lessons from the initial phases of Enduring Freedom seemed obvious. Navalists had argued for years that the great advantage of carrier striking power was the ability to rapidly deploy and strike at areas where land-based air was restricted; Afghanistan was the very definition of this argument. The power of the carrier air wing had been decisively proven through the rapid destruction of the Taliban's and Al Qaeda's infrastruc-

Eight. The New Challenge

ture. Moreover, SOF operations from the *Kitty Hawk* demonstrated that carriers were flexible components of power clearly not wedded to one specific mission set as critics claimed. There seemed to be little doubt that the investment in the modern carrier fleet had paid off and that the forward theory designed to around these carriers was sound.

But strategically, cracks appeared in this argument. Carriers had provided rapid strike power—but they had not operated with as much independence as had appeared. F-18 strike aircraft, the mainstay of the strike fleet, were never designed for long-range missions and reached their targets only through an elaborate tanking scheme that relied heavily on Air Force support from tankers based throughout the Middle East.[42] As organic tanking capability was severely curtailed in favor of the F-18 development, without the support of these huge tankers it is debatable whether the sea-based planes could have reached their targets.[43] These targets were strategically controversial. Taliban and Al Qaeda infrastructure had indeed been destroyed and the government had collapsed—but the Taliban was at best a third-rate conventional opponent with extremely limited capability to fight back against a modern power employing strike (although they would soon prove to be a superior and experienced insurgent force). After a month the planes literally had nothing left to bomb, due certainly to their efficiency of operations but also due to the fact that there was little to bomb in the first place.[44] The demonstrated "flexibility" argument used in the case of the *Kitty Hawk* being modified for special forces operations was an interesting one; this had been proposed in the era of the "peace dividend" of the 1990s, where it was quickly shouted down by navalists as a waste of a capital asset.[45] The sudden agreement in this case to employ a carrier in this role may not have signified a change in theory so much as the fact that there was a dire need for this requirement—and the *Kitty Hawk* was the oldest carrier in the fleet, whose strike power, given the availability of other carriers, could be modified with little strategic loss.

Perhaps the greatest criticism of the perceived success of the conventional strike campaign was that no matter how successful the strike portion of Operation Enduring Freedom appeared, it did not in fact end the war in Afghanistan, which quickly became a prolonged conflict fought along distinctly tribal and cultural lines. The Taliban was well versed in the art of irregular warfare that had been practiced in Afghanistan for centuries, and it was to this type of conflict that its fighters rapidly returned. In the face of overwhelming conventional power, the Taliban faded into the mountains and commenced fighting the irregular war to which it was accustomed—a type of war in which strike power, unless carefully coordinated, had very limited effects unless the enemy made himself vulnerable. This occurred during the first major ground offensive against the Taliban, Operation Anaconda, a poorly planned campaign whose ultimate success (or in critics' eyes, the prevention of a disaster) relied on the calling in of massive air support. Both sides learned—the U.S. would continue to rely on strike power, while the Taliban would never again make itself the target for massed attacks. Air power was employed in a tactical capacity that was "on call," orbiting the country until required for battlefield engagement as determined by an increasingly centralized and restrictive CENTCOM targeting center sensitive to collateral damage—a key factor on the irregular warfare battlefield.[46] Eventually naval strike support was whittled down to one carrier as the ground war moved on.

The first phase of the bombing ended on December 18; in two months, 6,000 combat sorties were flown, 4,500 of which were naval aircraft.[47] Ten thousand air-launched or dropped munitions had been employed, 60 percent of which were "smart" weapons of remarkable precision.[48] Ultimately 8 of 12 active carriers in the fleet would participate.[49] Conventional Taliban power was destroyed, the government toppled, and U.S. troops were on the ground supporting a government that was friendly to their aims. But despite rosy reports of progress, the war was far from over; in fact, it was only beginning. In an analogy eerily similar to Vietnam, "victory" against conventional forces was in fact an illusion as the war moved into its next phase—an irregular conflict in which naval power, despite its continued presence, command of the sea, and ability to provide support, contributed very little. Theory of sea and air dominance had been trumped by the reality of modern irregular war.

Strategic Interlude: Sea Power 21 and the Fleet Response Plan

In 2002, the Navy released "Sea Power 21," a vision, as opposed to a proper strategy, for global naval operations in the war on terror. "Sea Power 21" was composed of three core elements: sea shield, sea strike, and sea basing.[50] Although billed as a response to the GWOT, in reality the concepts described in SP21 had been in development for some time as part of the ongoing "transformation" initiative at the Pentagon that relied heavily on high-tech and networked operations.[51] This was especially true in the case of Sea Strike, the offensive arm of the strategy. Sea Strike presented a traditional concept for carrier and surface strike operations reflective of DOD emphasis on precision strike and joint network integration. Offensive power in this regard was to be directed at military, economic, and political vulnerabilities. The force structure to execute these forms of offensive operations was to be composed of high-tech, large combatants, emphasizing the maintenance of twelve carrier battle groups.[52]

Sea basing was an extension of the global stationing concepts developed in the 1990s, expanded to include new crisis spots for the GWOT. SP21 called for carrier battle groups to maintain station in these areas, supplied by an expanded force of support ships that would operate in various stations as mobile depots.[53] This required improved maritime sea lift forces as well as increased development of heavy lift capability, items that had been in the works prior to 9/11. Additionally, the concept required sustained coordination and operations on a much broader scale than had been practiced by Navy forces. Although solid in theory (some form of "sea basing" was traditional in the Navy as part of sustained amphibious assault) the cost and technology required to maintain large sea bases quickly became prohibitive.[54]

The newest part of the vision, "Sea Shield," was in direct response to the requirement for homeland defense, but it quickly took on global overtones. Originally designed as part of the "layered defense" of the homeland, where naval power would act in specific offshore areas based on capability to detect and intercept inbound threats to the United States (much like that adopted during the days of MDZ, but this time a concept that remained in its definition despite the expansion to global emphasis), Sea Shield adopted principles of defense against land-launched threats in forward areas, the littoral seas where the USN expected to contribute to the GWOT.[55] It was highly dependent on advanced technology, moving "beyond" task forces and into net-centric warfare with assets and agencies ashore. Sea shield was intended to be intensely interagency in sea approaches and coastal areas of the United States, while focusing on defense of the deployed assets on the sea and forward, including (for the first time) moving into the field of ballistic missile defense, an area that would become increasingly a mission for capital cruisers in the next decade. To quote the VCNO directly, "Sea Shield will project defense beyond what any Navy has been able to accomplish—i.e., deep inland against cruise and ballistic missiles" using an array of cruisers, upgraded AEGIS, and the new DD(x) destroyer.[56]

As a vision, SP21 demanded more "high" end ships, in contrast to those that had been advocated by Zumwalt thirty years before, that were large, capable of strike, and extremely technical. The projected number for this fleet was presented as 375 hulls, the majority of which were carriers, cruisers, and destroyers. These ships would be clustered into the 12 traditional carrier battle groups, supplemented by 12 "Expeditionary Strike Groups," primarily composed of cruisers and other Tomahawk-equipped ships with an amphibious component as required. But despite these specifics, SP21 was not presented as a strategy—rather, it was an expansion of the CNO's "goals" to reflect world changes in the GWOT. The practical application of SP21 was the implementation of the Fleet Response Plan (FRP). The FRP was a theoretical deployment plan for global contingencies that streamlined naval operations in order to provide for the ability to deploy (often rapidly) six carrier battle groups simultaneously. Given the maintenance and training levels require to continuously deploy forces of this magnitude—not to mention the increased funding requested to make the plan a reality—there were skeptics, especially in Congress.[57]

The overriding message of SP21 was that for the USN, even homeland "defense" was to be forward. In the event an enemy got through this defense, assets in the U.S. would be able to respond according to the mandate of the FRP. Whether or not forces in the U.S. could have responded to a sudden maritime event in the homeland is debatable given the new overseas requirements of SP21 and the FRP.[58] The FRP did, however, significantly increase training and readiness cycles for traditional strike operations in the joint environment, a factor that would have significant effect in the next phase of the GWOT.

The War on Terror Expands: Iraq

As the war in Afghanistan began winding down (at least in appearance), the Bush administration set its sights on regime change in Iraq. Officially Iraq was drawn into the GWOT nexus due to its failure to cooperate with U.N. WMD inspectors, a fact that had been noted by the administration as early as November 2001.[59] Planning for war began at CENTCOM in early 2002.[60] A number of factors were immediately apparent in the preparations for this new campaign. First, the war that was planned in 2002 could not be a repeat of 1991. In the global viewpoint the case for war was thin; this time, international support for actions against Saddam Hussein were lacking, so much so that former allies refused not only basing but also overflight rights for strike aircraft and missiles.[61] Carrier airpower had been used in Gulf One but had been largely overshadowed by the Air Force. This time, the lack of basing rights made the Navy's participation more critical. But if Afghanistan did not present much of a conventional threat to carrier-based strike power, the same could not be said of Iraq. Although wounded in Desert Shield/Desert Storm, the Iraqi forces had been rebuilt and presented a potentially significant conventional challenge to the military forces poised to invade. Iraq possessed a modern military with well-established command and control nodes and intelligence capability and thus represented a far more extensive conventional target than the Taliban.

The campaign conducted in Operation Iraqi Freedom (OIF) was the most "joint" ever executed by the U.S. military. Once again, carriers and naval strike power seemed to be the perfect instrument to fill a critically empty gap. Strike power from the sea came from four carriers on station (the number would grow to six) and a large number of surface combatants firing Tomahawk missiles at infrastructure targets. The "shock and awe" campaign was twofold: a very brief air campaign of 96 hours against critical infrastructure targets to disrupt communications followed by a shift to attacks against conventional forces in the field acted as a precursor to land attack.[62] Once again, the effort was completely successful; within ten days the allies reported complete air supremacy; soon after, air planners reported that they were running out of targets.[63] The campaign on the ground was so successful that the biggest problem faced by the strike aircraft was coordination with conventional armored forces that quickly overran pre-planned strike targets, reducing aircraft to providing strike of opportunity capability.[64]

The actual Navy participation in OIF went far beyond its carrier force. In sum, six carrier battle groups were the core of a larger U.S. naval presence in the war zone that included three amphibious ready groups and two amphibious task forces totaling nearly 180 U.S. and allied ships, 80,800 sailors, and another 15,500 marines. Navy and Marine Corps aircraft flying from carriers and large-deck amphibious ships flew nearly 5,600 combat sorties.[65] These aircraft contributed significantly not only to the destruction of the command and control infrastructure of the Hussein regime but also aided in the almost total destruction of the Iraqi Republican Guard, which lost over 700 tanks to the air effort.[66]

Again, there is no doubting the efficiency of the air campaign against Iraq, nor the fact that forward based naval strike power played a key role in a remarkably successful campaign. But the campaign, no matter how successful, was not "war winning" in any regard. Despite the infamous claims of "mission accomplished," Iraq quickly devolved into irregular war, a war that was, however, much different from that being fought in Afghanistan.[67] Rather than taking advantage of mountainous terrain and fighting a classic guerrilla conflict, Iraq plunged into sectarian violence and ultimately civil war against which no form of conventional power could guarantee success. Like Afghanistan, the conventional phase did not lead to victory but rather evolved into irregular war.[68] While the streets of Fallujah and the sectarian civil war were not the mountains of Afghanistan, the war in Iraq was still an irregular one, one that naval power was ill equipped to handle. Air support continued in the ongoing campaign of SOF forces, providing fire on demand services—but there was nothing uniquely naval about this mission, nor, in the long-term analysis, was it particularly effective.[69]

In the grander scheme of the GWOT, one of the stated strategic purposes of the offensive operations in both Afghanistan and Iraq was the new concept of "preventative war"—eliminating the threat overseas before it could be exported to the homeland.[70] Given that the bulk of the enemy in both Afghanistan and Iraq were not associated with Al Qaeda, in hindsight this is very much a matter of debate. But from a maritime perspective, these operations did not in themselves eliminate the threat to the homeland given the size of the global commons and the vast amount of potential activity on the sea that could ultimately be a threat to the United States. The war on terror was envisioned as a global effort, and overseas wars were only part of the security equation. The new threat to the homeland—a threat that, given the nature of the GWOT, was distinctly irregular—had to be addressed.

Protection of the Homeland: Irregular Threat and Response

If there was a threat on and from the sea, it would seem that the answer to defeating it would be obvious. The U.S. Navy, despite its capital ship focus, was still the largest in the world and could in theory provide an unbreakable shield of maritime power around the United States. But a number of factors, including culture, asset specialization, and above all forward theory complicated this solution. These complications were immediately apparent when examining the new theory of irregular threat.

What was the threat to the homeland from the sea? In the public eye, like other types of asymmetric scenarios, threat was initially viewed with an eye toward the worst case. Although there were many variations and themes, maritime threat post-9/11 focused on two broad areas. The first was a direct attack from the sea, generally viewed in several forms. This could be accomplished through the use of vessels as weapons that could be detonated in American ports or somewhere along the coastline against civilian targets or critical infrastructure. The means of detonation included smuggled WMDs or the use of naturally dangerous or explosive cargoes (such as Liquefied Natural Gas [LNG] carriers), which could theoretically be detonated in ports, causing critical damage or inflicting mass casualties.[71] While the availability of practical means to employ an explosive attack could be questioned, there was no doubt that the effect would have considerable impact on the economic infrastructure of the U.S. and present the opportunity for thousands of casualties. The element of catastrophic consequence had an equally disruptive effect on logical threat planning for sea events as it did on land; in addition to scenarios involving LNG tankers or WMD in ports, other esoteric scenarios also had to be considered (and usually dismissed) by defense planners, including the use of ships as suicide rams against infrastructure or, in one of the more bizarre scenarios, as launch platforms for terrorist cruise missiles.[72]

While ships may make poor platforms for direct attack, they were (and are) superior assets for clandestine transport in the global commons. One of the public surprises concerning sea power in the aftermath of 9/11 is that much of the global ocean commons was completely invisible to the common eye.[73] There was no international "tracking" system beyond limited theater systems maintained by various militaries for their own national purposes and those operated by commercial entities for their own merchant fleets; the role of international organizations (such as the IMO) were largely regulatory.[74] Fictional thrillers aside, there was no system of maritime air traffic control that guided ships' movements on the world's oceans; not only was such a system viewed by most nations as prohibitively expensive, but it could also be viewed as a violation of the free use of the seas—a principle that has always been fundamental to U.S. interests. This lack of regulation or tracking seemed to indicate that terrorist organizations were free to use the sea to transport weapons, personnel, or both into the United States. This was a "hot button" political issue given the large amount of maritime trade (much of which was containerized) that passed through U.S. ports, especially in regards to the potential for the smuggling of WMD, which could then be transported anywhere into the United States.[75] While this threat may have been subject to undue speculation, it was certainly true that free terrorist use of the maritime domain was a distinct possibility.[76]

The sea could also be used as a means of transport within U.S. waters for internal attack, especially in the ports in a *"Cole"*-style attack against vessels or infrastructure. As noted during Cold War planning for the Maritime Defense Zone, ports in the United States are commercial enterprises, not fortresses; even ports that host large naval bases and other military presence share facilities with civilian operations. The critical infrastructure of these facilities was vulnerable, and there was the potential to cause mass casualties by targeting tourist areas. The memories of the bombing of the USS *Cole* were very much in the mind of maritime defensive planners after 9/11.[77] Small-boat attack or transport of explosives into these areas by smaller commercial vessels was a very real concern to officials in both DHS and DOD given that both military and civilian agencies shared facilities in many large commercial ports.[78]

This assessment of threat is obviously quite broad, covering a wide range of potential terrorist actions—all of which, in the post-9/11 environment, had to be addressed. The classic approach in dealing with these threats was the establishment of some form of sea control. If there was indeed a threat from the sea to the continental United States, it would seem that the obvious answer to defeating that threat would be to surround the coastline with naval power. This did not occur. Although some Navy combatants did supplement the Coast Guard in enhanced patrol duties in the immediate aftermath of 9/11, as no immediate threat was apparent, USN support for homeland security (in terms of assets and combatants) quickly evaporated as soon as the GWOT got under way and evolved into a longer-term solution that reinforced the Navy's traditional forward operational role.[79] This redirection of classic military power away from homeland defense was not an action that was limited to the sea services, but rather part of the broader national discussion of the role of the military in the defense of the homeland for the long term. How the United States defined its bureaucratic response to the attacks of 9/11 was to have direct impact on the role of sea power in the years that followed.

With the establishment of the Department of Homeland Security, the "defense" of the homeland began to evolve into two separate yet linked mission areas, that of "homeland security" and "homeland defense." This was as much a cultural as bureaucratic separation. While historically the military has always had a role in defending the homeland, these actions have generated deeply rooted concerns about the use of military force on U.S. soil.[80] The Posse Comitatus Act restricting domestic use of the military was written to reflect this viewpoint.[81] Although the military has been used in active defense during wartime, this has traditionally been against a direct and specific military threat (such as the U-boat attacks

Eight. The New Challenge

during the Second World War). This role has occasionally been modified based on need or policy; during the 1990s, for example, the military moved beyond some traditional roles by supplementing certain "lower-intensity" law-enforcement-style operations by providing surveillance and intercept capability in the drug war and countering illegal immigration. Regardless of the success or increasing frequency of these operations, the military— and especially the Navy—moved cautiously, especially as time used for non-traditional operations detracted from training required for conventional missions.[82]

This cultural mindset changed after the 9/11 attacks for the U.S. population as a whole.[83] While it is true that Posse Comitatus remained unchanged, the direct attack on the United States vastly expanded the military in both size and mission scope. Although there was some argument that a "war on terror" was a misnomer, the attacks demanded a military response.[84] The logic for the offensive operations in the GWOT was ultimately protection of the homeland, but given the nature of the irregular threat, the potential existed for another catastrophic attack of the United States regardless of operational success overseas. Al Qaeda's demonstrated ability and willingness to cause mass casualties demanded that the military have a strong role in "defense" that potentially went beyond traditional law enforcement's ability to counter domestic terrorism events. But simultaneously, the ability of terrorists to act covertly in the United States placed many of their acts solidly in the realm of law enforcement, which possessed the investigative capability (and legal authority) to counter their actions. The problem this presented for a comprehensive defense was that there were two distinct communities to deal with one threat.

This problem was addressed through a unique bureaucratic solution that attempted to satisfy cultural tradition and legal concerns while effectively designing a defense against the terrorist threat. Rather than viewing the defense of the homeland as one unifying mission, it was divided into two separate and distinct missions: "homeland security," defined as "a concentrated national effort to prevent terrorist attacks within the United States, reduce America's vulnerability to terrorism, and minimize the damage and recover from attacks that do occur" (the responsibility of the newly formed Department of Homeland Security)[85] and "homeland defense," defined as "the protection of U.S. sovereignty, territory, domestic population, and critical defense infrastructure against external threats and aggression"[86] (the responsibility of DOD). In effect, "homeland security" relieved heavily on law enforcement agencies with support by military forces as required, while "homeland defense" was DOD-centric, with law enforcement playing a supporting role. The two missions did not officially separate the organizations per se, but rather assigned primary responsibility to each depending on a number of factors, including level of threat, location, and requirement for specific resources.[87]

The intent in creating separate mission areas was twofold. In defining separate missions, the U.S. cultural tradition of separation of civil and military authorities was adhered to, while simultaneously categorizing threats for appropriate action. In theory this placed agencies in their respective "boxes" where they could apply their individual capabilities and expertise in the most efficient manner. The separation of missions into HLS and HLD allowed for considerable law enforcement assets (and perhaps more importantly, expertise) to be brought to bear on a security problem where a strict application of military force was not appropriate (and might in fact be counter-productive).[88] Similarly, a clearly military threat requiring a military response (such as terrorist use of aircraft or threat of WMD that needed to be destroyed inbound to the U.S.) could be classified using military methods and dealt with using firepower as appropriate. At least in theory.

Within the continental United States, this concept was relatively clear—after all, despite the use of National Guard units for security at some airports and critical facilities, in general, U.S. citizens are extremely wary of having armed military visible in their streets (except when help is needed in overwhelming circumstances, such as natural disasters).[89] The ocean was another matter. Areas of responsibility for operational purposes on the sea had always been nebulous for U.S. forces; although areas "near" the coast were traditionally the responsibility of the U.S. Coast Guard, that service also considered itself a worldwide deployer,[90] while the Navy often conducted training operations well within the coastal zones. Who was responsible for what in terms of "defense," especially given the separation of responsibility under homeland security/homeland defense, was extremely ambiguous, complicated by the uncertain status of vessels as potential threats on the high seas.[91] Dealing with the new irregular threat and sorting out respective areas of responsibility in the complex maritime environment obviously required detailed planning, especially with regard to the detection and classification of threats operating on the seas close to the United States. Although the Coast Guard had authority in this area, the Navy clearly had superior technical assets for surveillance and interdiction—but was firmly wedded to its forward theory, more so now that there was a war to fight overseas. Who was to search, detect, and interdict threats on the scale required for effective defense was an enormously complex question. This dichotomy was addressed by the first major maritime initiative to consider surveillance after 9/11, an interagency effort known as Maritime Domain Awareness.

The Invisible Ocean: Maritime Domain Awareness, the Thousand Ship Navy, and PSI

The attacks of 9/11 were cited as ultimately a failure of intelligence, resulting in a complete overhaul and reorganization of the U.S. intelligence system.[92] Part of this reorganization process was a government-wide assessment of perceived weaknesses and potential areas of enemy attack. Attention was immediately directed toward the maritime domain; as noted, the United States possessed over 95,000 miles of coastline that had little or no surveillance dedicated to it.[93] While it is true that this number is somewhat inflated in terms of real threat—not all of the coast could be effectively accessed from the sea—there was still a significant portion of it that was vulnerable, including multiple ports where an enemy could strike.[94] This problem of surveillance was not limited to the coastline of the United States. The ocean was a vast, mostly unregulated, and largely invisible global commons where potential threats could operate with impunity. In the era of the GWOT, this was unacceptable. This problem was addressed by the creation of an entirely new concept, Maritime Domain Awareness (MDA). For the United States, this was a new name for an old idea—the use of navies to be aware of who and what was approaching the coastline, a practice that foreign navies not focused on power projection had been practicing for generations.

The Maritime Domain Awareness initiative was one of the largest strategic security measures enacted by the U.S. government following the 9/11 attacks.[95] MDA was simple in concept: the creation of an information system to monitor activity in the global ocean commons. The idea itself was not new; prior to 9/11, the U.S. Coast Guard had experimented with various vessel-tracking initiatives to determine location and movement of "special interest vessels" (SIVs) approaching the U.S. mainland.[96] The definition of these vessels varied; prior to 9/11, it included vessels from hostile nations (Communist Bloc), vessels carrying particularly hazardous cargoes, or vessels that were potentially an environmental hazard.[97] After 9/11, this definition expanded considerably. Given the new asymmetric threat, most if not all unsearched vessels approaching the U.S. now fit into this category, resulting in a massive expansion of the previous effort under the auspices of the new MDA initiative. This new interest was not limited to vessels operating in the proximity of the U.S. coastline. As identifying and ultimately defeating potential threats began with knowledge of who (or what) was operating in the maritime domain, MDA was an attempt to gain global knowledge of all actions that could affect the security of the United States.[98] It was not tracking per se, but rather a combination of global intelligence, passive and active tracking efforts, and analysis to determine threat.

MDA was driven by the asymmetric nature of the GWOT and was quite different from the surveillance required in conventional fleet operations. As noted, in conventional naval war, the enemy is relatively well defined and almost universally a combatant. MDA recognized that in the post–9/11 environment, any vessel could be a potential enemy or weapon carrier or any maritime event could have an impact on the security of the United States. This demanded a much higher level of awareness than normally exercised in conventional naval conflict. This was recognized by the formal definition of MDA, which stated:

> [MDA is] the effective understanding of anything associated with the global maritime environment that could impact the security, safety, economy or environment of the United States. This is accomplished through the integration of intelligence, surveillance, observation, and navigation systems into one common operating picture (COP) that is accessible throughout the U.S. Government.[99]

There are several key points in this definition that bear close examination. Unlike traditional naval operations, it is apparent that the goal of MDA was far more than simply looking for potential enemy targets. "Anything associated" with the maritime environment that can impact (not necessarily threaten) the security, safety, economy, or environment goes far beyond what many would envision as a classic maritime threat. This included smuggling of people or dangerous cargoes, piracy, proliferation of weapons of mass destruction, identification and protection of critical maritime infrastructure, oil spills, weather, and environmental concerns, among other events. These elements and a host of others were lumped together in an effort to determine an overall comprehensive picture.[100] To some extent this expanded emphasis was reflective of the large number of agencies that were contributing to the new effort, each of which specialized in a particular area in the maritime domain which now could be classified as representing an asymmetric threat. But there was strategic disagreement among the agencies as to what should be emphasized in the surveillance effort. Classic naval principles were not ignored in deriving

Eight. The New Challenge 155

the concept; the Navy was particularly insistent that MDA focus on "forward" threats wherever possible, an insistence that was mandated in presidential policy.[101] In terms of an intelligence problem, this global outlook expanded the demand for information enormously; because of the potential impact to homeland security, activities occurring overseas and in foreign ports were very much a part of MDA. For example, if a cargo was loaded in Singapore and its ultimate destination was the United States (via several other international ports), the loading, transport, security, and all matters associated with that container would be part of MDA. Given the extent of cargo bound for the United States (the port of Los Angeles alone routinely handles 18,000 cargo containers daily),[102] this was clearly an enormous undertaking. How it was to be accomplished presented a significant challenge—especially in terms of actual assets dedicated to surveillance.

Early in the concept development process, Coast Guard leadership formed a strong partnership with the Navy in planning the core elements of what would become the MDA strategy. During an "MDA summit" held at the secretary level in May 2004, Mr. Paul McHale (Assistant Secretary of Defense, Homeland Defense) and Admiral James Loy (Deputy Secretary Homeland Security), with the concurrence of Secretary Rumsfeld and Secretary Ridge, brought together senior members of 16 respective departments and agencies involved to some degree with the maritime domain.[103] The ultimate goal was to devise a plan for these agencies to work together for both implementation and continued execution of MDA, coordinating a compilation of diverse information into one common, usable format that could be accessed by all the agencies. Conceptually, the result was to agree on the way ahead to formulate a unified strategy. But theory and service rivalry soon intervened, especially over the use of assets. In a world where terrorists could be anywhere, assets were limited—and strictly controlled by agencies according to their own agendas, especially in the maritime domain.

This was apparent in the conflict that rose over the actual task of surveillance. The key to MDA was surveillance and processing of intelligence for which a number of options were available. Surveillance of the global commons could most certainly be conducted by national assets (satellites), but redirection of this capability inevitably resulted in loss in another mission area—which, for DOD, represented activities forward in potential battle areas. In lieu of satellites, the best form of surveillance was performed by assets on scene—in this case, ships and aircraft. As the main force provider for these assets, the Navy faced the uncomfortable reality that dedication to the MDA mission would require allocating ships to patrol and surveil areas outside its traditional operating areas, mainly along the coastline of the United States (rather than operating forward).[104] This was unacceptable to the Navy given its theory and wartime requirements overseas. Interestingly, the Coast Guard also balked at this idea of Navy operations along the coastline, viewing that operational area as its traditional "turf."[105] The resistance was not only over assets but also over authority. In traditional U.S. maritime operations, the search and boarding of potential threats was regarded as a function of law enforcement (in contrast to strictly military) operations as clarified by U.S. law (U.S. Code Title 14). Terrorists might be an asymmetric threat that was best handled by military power, but finding them involved tactics and techniques that were best addressed in the law enforcement arena. As noted, this argument had been made by land components in both DOD and DHS regarding military operations in the United States (where it was solved rather quickly), but the wide area of the ocean commons, conflicting authorities, and scarcity of assets made it a unique problem on the ocean where there was no clear "dividing line" between the various agencies.

In terms of coastal operations this was "solved" through some unique bureaucratic wrangling between the sea services. The homeland security/homeland defense mission separation conceptually applied, as the Coast Guard was a member of DHS and the Navy, DOD; the Navy and Coast Guard worked to apply this to the global commons. The Navy, using its established fleet and doctrine, would operate "forward" in execution of its traditional missions while conducting MDA overseas, while the Coast Guard would operate within its traditional areas (generally within 500 nautical miles of the coastline).[106] As neither service was comfortable with being assigned to "boxes" that were viewed as operationally (and doctrinally) restrictive, there was a sharing of areas where both were comfortable operating, such as the "approaches" (mid-ocean), where operations would be coordinated. Coordination would between the two would be through the establishment of one common operating picture managed by a yet-to-be-determined agency.

This plan worked—in theory—and seemed to satisfy the core theoretical components of both maritime services. On paper it appeared that the Navy and Coast Guard in conjunction had formed an impressive "layered defense" on the ocean that could effectively keep out all threats. But appearances were deceiving, especially regarding the allocation of actual assets from both services that were available to perform this mission. And it was not without its critics. Assistant Secretary of Homeland Defense

Eight. The New Challenge

Paul McHale was particularly vocal in despairing that few or no Navy assets were actually available for homeland defense duties as the Navy continued sending assets forward.[107]

The Department of Defense had noted the priority for homeland defense by establishing a new combatant commander (COCOM) dedicated to the mission—Northern Command, or NORTHCOM—but there were very few Navy assets actually contributed to surveillance in the homeland or the "approaches" region.[108] The Navy's insistence that surveillance could be conducted "virtually" came under fire from no less than future chief of naval operations Admiral Mike Mullen, who stated, "virtual presence is actual absence."[109] The Navy and Coast Guard did create a common operational picture—of sorts, based on shared technology that had been used prior to 9/11—but the strategic coordination to determine global threat was slow. Today the effort is still ongoing.[110]

Given the requirements for global surveillance demanded by MDA, it was imperative that the Navy come up with additional means to provide effectively capability—or potentially risk pulling combatants away from their core mission of forward operations. One of the more creative solutions to this problem was the concept of the "Thousand Ship Navy" first proposed in 2005.[111] Loosely based on previous coalitions such as the NATO maritime alliance, the Thousand Ship Navy envisioned a global cooperation of naval forces that would focus on irregular threats, reporting such events (ideally) in one common operational picture to the mutual benefit of all. Recognition of the commonality of the goals of the GWOT was essential in this regard: a stateless enemy was as much a threat to one participating nation as to all.[112] As the concept developed, it was expanded beyond surveillance to include cooperation in missions that were distinctly irregular or outside the norm of traditional fleet operations, including mutual response to natural disasters, common operations against pirates, and providing humanitarian assistance. Although the idea prompted a great deal of discussion among navies and generated considerable academic and professional commentary, in terms of practical application, its effects were limited. The sharing of information in the maritime realm proved to be difficult, not only from a technical standpoint but also conceptually. Until 9/11 the United States had always been a primary proponent of the concept of "freedom of the seas"; it seemed that the concept was subject to modification if the security of the United States was involved.[113] For commercial purposes, the sea had always been regarded as strictly laissez-faire; so long as overtly illegal acts did not occur (smuggling, environmental violations, etc.), commercial interactions were largely unchecked. Sharing potentially sensitive commercial information with governments smacked of regulation—or worse, direct control by one nation.[114] Diplomatically, this proved difficult. Moreover, gaining the cooperation of the private sector was difficult, as there was mistrust commercially as to how national information could be used by potential competitors, especially in the tracking of various commodities that had little or no apparent relation to the GWOT.[115]

This is not to imply, however, that efforts to create MDA and surveillance cooperation in support of the GWOT were a failure. One of the more notable successes in the aftermath of 9/11 was the formulation of the Proliferation Security Initiative (PSI) as a corollary of MDA. Proposed in 2003 as an international consortium with the unified goal of tracking and interdicting the global shipment of weapons of mass destruction, the agreement eventually brought together 21 nations as signatories with another 77 agreeing to the concept in principle.[116] Although PSI had a land component, the vast amount of its activity occurred at sea, and interdictions were of a number of high-profile weapons shipments, including nations with a history of support of terrorism.[117] A similar agreement, the Container Security Initiative (CSI), implemented a global tracking system of inter-modal containers in both U.S. and participating ports overseas, making significant inroads toward tracking illegal shipments of weapons and improving security of the system as a whole.[118] The goal of global surveillance received a considerable boost in 2004 when the International Maritime Organization (IMO) mandated that all vessels over 300 gross tons be equipped with the new Automated Identification System (AIS), a tracking transceiver that provided location data for search and rescue purposes—but that also could be used by nations to effectively track activity off their coastline, most notably those participating in PSI and MDA.[119] This information was used to track vessels in newly developed Coast Guard and Navy joint command centers and the development of joint intelligence databases to be shared between the services for strategic planning and operational response.[120]

The Coastal Challenge Overseas and Abroad

Surveillance of the ocean was an important step in dealing with potential threats, but the reality was that threats were more dangerous (and prevalent) in the littorals, both overseas and in the homeland. For a threat to be directly engaged, smaller assets that could operate in the littoral were a necessity. In this regard the Navy was forced to return once again to its pre–Mahanian roots of irregular warfare in designing not only assets but also procedures to deal with a diverse littoral enemy. This was complicated not only by the unique situation in Iraq, but also by the threat to the homeland, which, as we have seen, was challenged not only by bureaucratic and cultural hurdles but also by the extremely diverse (and potentially catastrophic—in perception if not reality) threat. The answer to problems in both of these theaters of operation was distinctly cultural.

Despite successful strike operations from the sea in both Afghanistan and Iraq, neither conflict was an "ocean war." Even in the case of Iraq, bordering the Persian Gulf, any naval threat was eliminated within hours of the initial attack, once again giving the United States complete command of the sea. But while Afghanistan had no link to the ocean or navigable waterways per se (future Navy involvement in the country, apart from considerable investment of special forces troops, was limited to the "individual augmentee" (IA) program that provided sailors in second-echelon support roles),[121] the same was not true of Iraq. As the conflict moved from the conventional phase to prolonged irregular war, there arose a need in Iraq for small coastal combatants and riverine forces to deal with insurgents who had free rein in these waterways. The Navy responded much as it did in Vietnam: by creating these forces from scratch—and relearning the lessons that had been shelved away decades before.

Riverine forces were formed in October 2005 under the new Naval Expeditionary Combat Command (NECC), a unit designed specifically to engage the irregular threat.[122] Like similar units in Vietnam, it was a mixture of various communities and specialties within the small Navy irregular warfare community, including special boat units, emergency ordnance disposal teams (EOD), divers, special warfare, and psychological warfare experts. From the first, the unit was a source of controversy. Although created with much fanfare as an answer to the growing irregular threat in Iraq, it initially received no extra funding from the service; money came from internal sources—in Washington, D.C., terms, not a priority. Moreover, the unit was not designed as a direct combat unit, but rather a support unit, half of which was composed of reserve forces.[123] This was remedied after the issue received congressional attention, allowing the command to procure a number of new special warfare craft specifically designed for the rivers and coastal regions of Iraq.[124] Operating in conjunction with Coast Guard boarding teams, the NECC first deployed combat units to the theater in 2007, where they met with some success, notably in conducting defense of oil rigs in the Persian Gulf against small-boat attack and in supporting ground forces operating inland along rivers.[125] After redeployment from Iraq, however, the fate of the NECC remains unclear.

In the homeland, the Navy addressed the potential IW threat to ports and its facilities by partnering with the Coast Guard in the formation of Joint Harbor Operations Centers (JHOCs), command and control facilities designed for multi-agency surveillance and coordination of law enforcement and defense assets. JHOCs were far more than a merging of traditional CG roles and responsibilities with USN security procedures. Coast Guard and Navy cooperation is neither new nor particularly unique. Since the earliest days of each organization, both used similar equipment and procedures in order to effectively operate together during time of war. But despite overseas operations in the GWOT, U.S. ports were not on a war footing. Rather, for financial reasons, commerce and port operations continued at the normal pace, albeit under increased security procedures. Recognizing the number of agencies that operate in ports and the vast information requirements to obtain true MDA, an effort was made to make JHOCs truly inter-agency by providing linkage to other maritime agencies, including the establishment of formal liaison positions and data sharing protocol, with the goal to merge regulation, law enforcement, and anti-terrorist force protection data and procedures.[126]

The first experimental JHOCs were constructed and successfully tested in San Diego and Norfolk, ports that represented high strategic interest due to major Navy presence and the volume of overseas commercial traffic. The JHOC's multi-agency design was based on relationships the Coast Guard had previously established during its normal operations within each port. As part of the JHOC operational procedures, merchant vessel regulation focusing on maritime security was "pushed" far off shore, with the establishment of a layered defense.[127] The new threat also affected other agencies with maritime security concerns. Ports with high Navy interest such as Navy bases, research facilities, critical infrastructure, and outload responsibilities augmented traditional security with extensive anti-terrorist force protection (ATFP) procedures to prevent, among other things, a USS *Cole*-style attack on potentially vulnerable warships. U.S. Customs immediately implemented increased forms of container and cargo security measures that were completely lacking prior to 9/11. These new multi-agency security requirements demanded revamping the traditional dual-track and somewhat laissez-faire command system exercised in U.S. ports prior to 9/11. The JHOC structure fit in well with the MDA initiative in providing tactical information to both Navy and Coast Guard high-level commands.

Originally the JHOC Memorandum of Understanding (MOU) signed by the Navy and Coast Guard called for the creation of six JHOCs, with the possibility for a total of twenty along both coasts in strategic ports.[128] Time and events, however, overtook this plan. As the Coast Guard consolidated its operations under the new sector construct, the Navy ceded operational authority and reduced asset support to the coastal mission[129] Unless the IW threat was directed against a naval facility, it was solidly delegated to the Coast Guard and DHS. Given that the majority of practical missions conducted by the *JHOCs* (later renamed Sector Command Centers, Joint, or SSC-Js) were focused on law-enforcement actions such as tracking and boarding civilian vessels, this made a certain degree of sense. But areas of operation that were solidly in a "DOD lane," such as mine warfare or enhanced boarding procedures (using special warfare units) were either marginalized or ignored in the bureaucratic battles for assets and funding. If there was an IW threat to the homeland, the Navy's basis philosophy held strong—that it was best handled forward, with capital assets.

The Decade Ends: The Cooperative Strategy

In October 2007, with much fanfare, the chiefs of the Navy, Coast Guard and Marine Corps jointly signed the Cooperative Strategy for 21st Century Sea Power. The strategy had been billed as a unifying document, discussed in advance with "conversations" throughout the country regarding the reasons for its writing and implementation.[130] There were a number of key points and themes that dominated the public relations campaign. Key was a direct response to the idea that the Navy should be used as a defensive force surrounding the nation. Using detailed examples from history, the point was raised repeatedly regarding the offensive nature of naval force that could be used to defeat the enemy before he could become a threat to the homeland. The history focused on the use of capital ship power, enhanced by the use of modern technology that enabled instantaneous surveillance and coordination. Adaptability to flexible overseas scenarios was stressed, as was cooperation with allies and successful use of strike power in support of ongoing combat operations.[131] The strategy that followed solidly reiterated these points.

There were some familiar themes in the strategy. It listed six "strategic imperatives": limit regional conflicts through forward deployment, be a decisive maritime power, deter wars, win the nation's wars, contribute to homeland defense in depth, foster and sustain cooperative relationships with international powers, and prevent or contain local disruptions.[132] These were to be accomplished through mostly traditional means: forward presence, deterrence, sea control, power projection. Non-traditional means included maritime security and humanitarian assistance/disaster response (HADR). Cooperation between the services was stressed, particularly in the "non-traditional" areas. Even these, however, emphasized forward operations; maritime security was to be conducted under the auspices of the Global Maritime Initiative (the formalization of the thousand ship Navy concept), while examples of HADR operations focused on overseas events such as the Navy's tsunami relief operations in 2004.[133] At first glance it seemed that the strategy "hit all the right buttons" in describing the new global operating environment and the challenges of non-traditional operations; even former Secretary of the Navy John Lehman, the author of the classic Maritime Strategy of the 1980s, called it a "home run."[134]

But the strategy did not enamor all its readers. In Congress, a number of members were troubled, noting that the strategy rehashed similar themes but was short on details regarding how the Navy was actually going to change or, for that matter, effectively engage an irregular enemy.[135] Beyond stating the need for continued maintenance of the fleet there was no programmatic plan for the development of specialized IW units.[136] Indeed, as simply a generic list of future operating conditions matched with categorized responses, there was some doubt as to whether the strategy was a strategy at all. It did not address how the services were going to win the war in which they were currently engaged (the so-called "long war" against radical extremists), nor which wars they were most interested in preventing using the application of sea power; in the words of one author, it was "old wine in new bottles."[137]

What was apparent with the new strategy, and troubling for the Navy's future engagement in irregular warfare, were references to globalization and traditional means of meeting future peer competitors on the sea—in this case, a not-so-subtle reference to the rise of China. Despite the fact that America in 2007 was still very much engaged in Afghanistan and Iraq, despite the persistent threat of Al Qaida and the threat to the homeland, the strategy provided the first real indications that the Navy was looking elsewhere for another enemy, that once again it would be falling back on its classical theory to rationalize a fleet that could meet and defeat a rival on the high seas potentially worthy of its steel. This would become increasingly apparent in the next few years as focus once again shifted to traditional battle on the high seas.

Nine

The Legacy Lives On

In December 2011, the last U.S. combat forces departed from Iraq. There were no celebrations in the United States marking the conclusion of the eight-year conflict. What was left of the naval IW mission faded without fanfare. In the meantime, the conflict in Afghanistan, the longest war in America's history, continued with no apparent end in sight. As the Afghan war evolved into increasingly irregular operations and drone strikes, the contribution of naval power to it has become a distant memory.[1] Although under a different auspice—today the war on terror is referred to as "Overseas Contingency Operations"—the GWOT continues both overseas and in the homeland even following the death of Osama bin Laden.[2] Despite the application of mass conventional power in the early part of the decade against a global enemy, the specter of irregular war is still alive and well.

Since 9/11 irregular warfare has had major impact on the American military mindset.[3] In terms of sea power this has translated into rhetoric of adaptability for the fleet. Given the experience of the past decade in active combat, it would be logical to assume that the naval lessons of the decade would be analyzed, assimilated, and applied to create a force capable of dealing with the ongoing reality of irregular war. It terms of study and analysis, there was some movement in this regard. In 2008, the Navy established a formal irregular warfare office at the Pentagon and moved to formalize the NECC budget by funding it through regular budget channels instead of the supplementary funding it had obtained for Iraq.[4] But in terms of practical applications of the lessons of a decade of irregular war, there seems to be little change in operational refocus, training, or, most importantly, the procurement of assets. This is not to imply that there was no change in Navy thinking regarding the role of sea power in the 21st century; in point of fact the Navy is on the verge of a major change in operational focus—but one away from irregular warfare. Rather, with the reduction in the use of naval power in Iraq, Afghanistan, and the GWOT, there is a shift back to a traditional focus against a potentially new conventional opponent. It is true that the irregular warfare experience in Afghanistan and Iraq did not challenge the full striking power of the fleet. But it is also true that Navy has a history of shifting away from irregular operations and back to what is preferred—large-fleet, Mahanian-style operations.

The Fading Irregular Mission: The Rhetoric and Reality

The United States has been engaged in active irregular warfare for over a decade on a global scale. As sea power has been an important element of that engagement and was employed in some form in every region of conflict, it is appropriate to provide a brief overview analysis of how effectively that sea power has been used. This is best accomplished through an examination of the theoretical element of maritime irregular warfare and the actual application of sea power in the conflicts of the post–9/11 era.

As discussed, modern irregular warfare theory is relatively new and is constantly evolving. Maritime application, however, is more solid in theory due to the fact that many of the heretofore traditional secondary missions of navies can be classified as "irregular" when considered in the context of modern conflict. Strategically there are four different mission areas for naval forces in irregular warfare. These include: maritime dominance, maritime security, maritime stability, and counter-insurgency/counter terrorism (COIN/CT) operations.[5] As we have seen, the Navy has dedicated time and effort to each of these missions since 9/11 with various degrees of success.

Maritime dominance in its simplest form is command of the sea. In accordance with classical theory, maritime dominance requires the presence and use of credible combat power. Dominance is the ability to use the sea in any way desired; this is obviously a mission area for which the modern Navy has been designed and trained. In the GWOT, there has never been a credible challenge to U.S. maritime dominance in terms of direct threat. During the irregular wars of the past decade, there was no doubt the Navy was able to exercise complete maritime dominance in its ability to use the seas freely in deployment of combat power. In the wars in Afghanistan and Iraq, this dominance allowed the Navy not only to strike rapidly but also to allow for subsequent follow-on deployment of land force unimpeded. As there was no credible maritime threat to U.S.

forces, it could be said that maritime dominance was completely achieved, at least theoretically, on the high seas.

But did achieving dominance on the high seas matter? In the context of determining outcome of the irregular war being fought on land, this dominance was almost irrelevant. As we have seen, maritime dominance allowed for the continued application of strike power from the sea, but even with the application of this traditional power, the conflicts in Iraq and Afghanistan did not end, but rather evolved into war that was even more diverse and sophisticated. The Navy had enormous combat power and the unfettered ability to use it—but against an irregular enemy it fell short because there were few conventional opponents that could be targeted. Even against known insurgents and enemy fighters, it was extremely difficult to measure any noticeable strategic result. Whether or not the Navy's dominance of the sea was even relevant to the enemy is unknown, as they made no serious attempt to wrest control or even use the sea to any great extent. Although the Navy deployed smaller irregular units to Iraq when the need became apparent, whether or not maritime dominance was ever actually achieved in an irregular sense is questionable. Navy and Coast Guard patrol boats and special warfare assets conducted multiple boarding operations in the Iraqi littoral and protected oil platforms and other infrastructure (and suffered casualties in thwarting suicide boat attacks),[6] but it is unclear as to what extent the insurgents completely stopped using the sea because of these operations.

The concept of maritime security is not a new one, but as a principle, it was significantly altered by the attacks of 9/11. It could be argued from a global perspective that prior to the attacks, maritime security was an implied goal that was generally accepted by seagoing nations; the idea of maritime security against common threats (such as piracy) has long been enshrined in international law, and over time nations have agreed to cooperate against threats that they see as universal (such as narcotics smuggling and human trafficking).[7] A fundamental purpose of navies—and the U.S. Navy in particular—was to ensure security on the seas to promote and allow for free use. But while there has always been a criminal element on the seas, this took on new dimensions with the attacks of 9/11. Hoffman's concept of "hybrid warfare" was directly applicable to potential maritime threat in the GWOT, with the potential for the seas to be used by terrorists either as a means of attack or transport of WMD.[8] This brought about an entirely new dimension to the idea of security on the seas; now irregular threats could have the ability to strike catastrophically against a wide range of targets both abroad and in the homeland. Obtaining security against these threats was addressed in a number of ways, including the establishment of the Global Maritime partnership (the so-called "thousand ship Navy"), the creation of the Proliferation Security Initiative (PSI), and the Maritime Domain Awareness (MDA) program.

In the United States, these attempts at obtaining global surveillance and security were pursued through interagency and international agreements that were intended to serve as force multipliers in achieving some sense of global stability. As the primary representative of U.S. sea power, the Navy was at the center of these initiatives. But the success of these initiatives is difficult to quantify. It is true these initiatives created a new sense of global cooperation, and it is also true that there have been no maritime attacks against the West since 9/11—but whether this is due to enhanced maritime security or simply because the enemy has not employed these methods is unknown. What is important to note in terms of the influence of traditional theory on irregular warfare operations is that these methods, extensive as they were, were secondary in terms of the actual use of fleet power. Modern surveillance of the maritime commons is often best served by the collection and coordination of intelligence, but it should be noted that modern naval assets (especially capital ships) have tremendous capability for surveillance, command and control, and coordination. The assets dedicated to surveillance operations such as MDA, security operations near the United States, or, in the case of a rising number of counter-piracy operations, were limited compared to those committed to traditional strike operations.[9] Although declared a priority by the Navy, the hulls actually performing these missions were—and are—few and far between. What impact this had on initiatives such as MDA is unknown. But there is no doubt that in terms of asset use the bulk of the fleet was employed in more traditional roles, a valid choice given no threat.

In the classic irregular warfare theory, the idea of stability is fundamental. This is generally achieved through the assistance and promotion of host nation infrastructure and economic development.[10] Achieving stability requires the execution of a number of "soft power" missions that build up a conflicted area while denying insurgents or irregular forces their legitimacy.[11] This mission has been somewhat controversial within Navy circles. In terms of sea power, stability operations have generally focused on the development of maritime infrastructure and various assistance missions.[12] Interestingly enough, the role of humanitarian assistance and direct response operations (HA/DR) are considered by some naval analysts to be outside of the normal scope of maritime stability operations, a debatable point given that such operations are often successful in winning over local populations.[13] One stated rationale for this is a fear of "mission creep," where capital assets could be assigned missions beyond their original purpose.[14] This is certainly a valid concern—the Coast Guard, for example, has long encountered "mission creep" in accepting new roles to the detriment of the material condition of its fleet, such as massive expansion of the oil response mission after the Exxon Valdez spill after 1990 and current emphasis on increased operations in the Arctic.[15] Throughout the GWOT, the Navy conducted a number of high-profile HA/DR missions, including the deployment of hospital ships to conflict zones and the often cited Philippine tsunami relief effort in 2004. Officially, however, HA/DR is not considered a standard mission in the operational lexicon but rather a target of opportunity mission to be conducted sparingly. Ships today, for example, conduct limited training in this role and are generally not equipped for it.[16]

As the main naval counterinsurgency effort was in Iraq, this study focuses on this irregular conflict. While the Navy deployed considerable special operations forces to Afghanistan, these units acted strictly in accordance with land power doctrine—a natural course of action, given that any form of maritime operations in landlocked Afghanistan was limited to strike from the sea. Counterinsurgency in Iraq was exclusively focused in littoral and riverine operations. By all accounts these met with success in providing maritime security and direct combat support for special operations and other land forces.[17] The experience in Iraq followed a historical trend. Naval COIN operations in Iraq were reminiscent of those conducted in Vietnam, using hastily constructed units composed of irregular warfare specialists (Emergency Ordnance Disposal (EOD) detachments, special warfare units, psychological operators, etc.), supplemented by newly designed, heavily armored small craft specifically built for littoral warfare in the region. The funding and emphasis given to these units, however, never approached that allocated to the traditional strike mission—a situation again very similar in many respects to Vietnam.[18]

Like all irregular warfare missions, these established maritime categories obviously represent a tremendous diversity in terms of requirements. This diversity is so great that irregular warfare threats are often not referred to as threats per se, but rather as "irregular challenges" in Navy literature.[19] These extend to blue-water missions including traditional challenges such as counter-piracy operations and new ones such as WMD interdiction. This terminology and the broader mission set it represents were first used in the Cooperative Strategy for 21st Century Sea Power, the source of some criticism, as it seemed that the strategy expanded the definition to such a degree that there was no specificity as to what exactly constituted a priority threat.[20]

Fitting the Force: Adaptability or Staying the Course?

As we have seen, the Navy's response to the irregular wars following the attacks on 9/11 was almost exclusively through the use of capital ship power operating in traditional strike roles. In the immediate aftermath of the attacks, this role was generally accepted in the United States given the desire for immediate retaliation against Al Qaida. But as time went on and overseas conflicts became more and more irregular, discussion once again began in defense circles regarding the need for smaller, more agile irregular combatants. This was especially true among pundits who for years had been arguing for a fleet of smaller, more specialized combatants.[21] The argument that the Navy required smaller combatants had been one that periodically gained voice in the press, especially with regards to aircraft carriers (where it was almost always dismissed by an aggressive PR campaign by navalists). But the new irregular war requirements gave this argument more credibility. This argument was a clear threat to capital ship theory. The repeated answer stressed the inherent adaptability of capital ships; in public statements, the Navy claimed that capital ship power represented a multipurpose capability to properly address the requirements of the four missions areas of maritime irregular warfare.[22] A number of specific cases are frequently cited to prove this point. The use of the aircraft carrier *Abraham Lincoln*, which provided tsunami relief in 2004, was once again used as a case in point for this versatility,[23] as was the use of DDG-51s in counter-piracy operations. In an interview with the Congressional Research Service, Vice Admiral Barry McCullough, the deputy Chief of Naval Operations for Integration of Resources, described these operations, stating, "That covers the spectrum of warfare" ... that's not what those ships were designed for, but it just goes to show you, the inherent flexibility of naval platforms."[24] It should be noted, however, that no training for specialization in these somewhat ad hoc missions was provided to ensure they could be performed on a regular basis at a future date.[25]

Interestingly, McCullough was not so kind in describing other IW capabilities the Navy possessed. While the Navy was very clear in stating that capital ship power was more than capable of adapting to the requirements of irregular warfare, those capabilities that had proven themselves

Nine. The Legacy Lives On

in IW missions were dismissed. The various highs and lows of the NECC have already been noted, but long before this unit was conceived, another type of irregular warfare asset was under increased criticism from within Navy ranks. This was the Navy's small fleet of special warfare patrol craft, designated PC-179s.[26] Despite a very robust IW capability, the ships were never popular with the Navy, coming under harsh criticism from the established surface warfare community. Originally designed as special warfare support craft (primarily for transport of SEALS), the vessels were disavowed by the traditional surface community as being "too small and specialized," too singularly focused and not multipurpose enough to be able to operate in a three-dimensional environment; the lack of sonar and ASW capability, for example, was cited to prove the vessel was vulnerable to submarine attack (despite its speed and ability to operate in shallow water, capabilities that inherently defeated any form of submarine threat).[27] In addition, "short range" was also cited as a weakness, despite the fact that the ships had transoceanic capability.[28] The fact that these vessels were effective in the littoral or capable of dealing directly with the IW threat did not seem to be a factor in the increasingly vehement attacks. Ultimately a number of the ships were transferred to the Coast Guard for use in the ongoing counter-narcotics effort; the ships were returned to the Navy in 2011 under considerable congressional pressure in light of the ongoing effort to fund the littoral combat capability.[29]

Why were the PCs subject to such criticism? One immediate cause was bureaucratic. PCs were not auxiliary craft but rather were commissioned warships carried on the Navy's rolls. The fleet size is ultimately designated by Congress, which sets numbers of combatants, but with the exception of aircraft carriers, the size of the ships is usually decided by the service. A PC, despite its size, was a commissioned warship—effectively equal to a larger combatant in terms of "counting" the hull according to the quantitative analysis of naval power.[30] In the simplest of bureaucratic terms, one PC was theoretically equal to a cruiser by the numbers. Moreover, the success of the PC in IW could potentially run counter to the claim that all Navy ships were effective in this role, especially in littoral operations. If the PC were an effective IW littoral platform, the specter of a fleet of PCs was a very real one. This potentially not only threatened the claim of multi-mission capability for larger combatants, but also another program the Navy had been developing: the littoral combat ship.

In conventional theory, the littoral is not a particular problem for forces operating forward; against an enemy coastline, the shallows are theoretically swept of all opponents using combinations of naval gunfire, airstrike, and amphibious operations. In practice, however, the littoral has always been problematic in conducting naval operations forward against an enemy, especially in irregular warfare. Modern conventional weapons that an enemy can use in the littoral include mines (a threat that the Navy has had enormous difficulty in countering in recent campaigns in the Persian Gulf) and shore-based cruise missiles.[31] In an irregular environment or pacification campaign, the diversity of the threat as well as the requirement to operate close to shore makes this even more of a challenge, especially in an environment where the sea is used commercially—which is true of most littorals. Small boats, dhows, fishing craft, and smaller merchant traffic utilizing coastal sea lanes all present challenges and potential hazards to capital ship movements, as events in Yemen and the Persian Gulf amply demonstrated. The most famous example of a successful smallboat attack was, of course, the *Cole*, but the problem was subject to intense analysis prior to the irregular conflicts post-9/11. The main threat in the Gulf during the Iraq War was small combatants and suicide-type attacks.[32] Capital ships, for all their size, were neither armed sufficiently nor maneuverable enough to deal with the diversity of this threat; moreover, the crippling of a capital ship would represent a significant loss to fleet power. These considerations demanded a smaller and more specialized combatant that could confront these irregular threats in the littoral.

Elements within the Navy hierarchy had been discussing the idea of a smaller combatant for some time prior to 9/11, primarily as a replacement platform for the aging Oliver Hazard Perry class of frigates designed and built during the Zumwalt era. The idea was given formal recognition—and very high-level support—in the aftermath of the September 11 attacks. The first experimental hull form for LCS ("Sea Fighter") was launched in 2003 to act as a test platform for more of the more specialized systems the final ship was to possess.[33] Although there was a great deal of speculation regarding what the final vessel would look like (and accomplish), the concept itself had a very high level of support. Chief of naval operations Vern Clark, in testifying to Congress following the attacks, stated it was a capability he needed "yesterday."[34] The original plan for the LCS was ambitious, calling for a fleet of over 50 small combatants—although it should be noted that "small" in this case was only relative to capital ships, as the LCS was envisioned as being over 400 feet long.[35] Clark proposed an aggressive program of restructuring, specifically toward redesigning the fleet with smaller combatants to meet the irregular warfare threat, including maritime and homeland security requirements.

The plan for LCS was launched with much fanfare, billed by the Navy as the "answer" to the irregular warfare challenge across a broad set of missions. The concept was innovative. Key to covering the diversity of the littoral was a modular design concept for specific mission areas fitted to a hull that could be easily adapted. These modules individually focused on anti-submarine warfare, surface operations, and mine warfare, all areas that were potential littoral challenges.[36] Yet after years of work, there appears to be little sense of urgency or movement in creating this as a fleet concept beyond the experimental stage. In 2010 the second LCS was launched, following years of development. The design of the ship had been controversial; no solid agreement existed as to what form (or capabilities) the vessel should possess, so ultimately two types of hull designs were built by competing contractors. From concept proposal to the launching of these vessels, well over ten years had passed. Despite the sense of urgency that had been purported by the Navy, key issues such as operational concept, doctrine, or even an established mission that could be linked to fleet operations was missing. Moreover, the program came increasingly under scrutiny by budget-minded oversight committees; the original concept was for a relatively cheap ($200 million) combatant, but as of 2010 the cost for each platform was close to a billion dollars, 120 percent over budget, an issue so contentious that it became a major talking point in presidential campaign politics.[37]

Whether or not the LCS will continue to be a viable program remains to be seen. Arguments have always been made against the platform, including familiar objections that the platform is too specialized, unable to adapt to multiple missions in the littoral, and of limited effectiveness in fleet or blue-water operations.[38] Funding, especially during the post–Iraq drawdown, is also a contentious issue. Enthusiasm is notably waning: after a decade of development, only a handful have been commissioned, and their visible lack of real operational commitment has led to them being branded with the derisive term "stealth ships."[39] The original argument that the cost of these ships would come down with mass production (a logical assumption) has been challenged by navalists who state that the program should be scrapped completely in favor of building more capital ships (DDG-51s), a proven hull design that could easily cover the littoral mission—effectively a repackaging of traditional capital ship theory. After years of attempting to address the new threat with an innovative platform, it seems that once again prevailing theory was the answer. This is especially evident as discussion in strategic circles moved away from the irregular environment of the littoral and toward a new, more traditional enemy.

The New Threat: The Rise of China

In 2005, the U.S. Navy published a startling photograph portraying a Chinese periscope with a U.S. aircraft carrier in the background. Although it was long known that Chinese submarines were actively tracking U.S. naval assets on maneuvers in the Sea of Japan, this was presented as dramatic evidence not only that China had a modern fleet but also by implication that the fleet was a significant threat to capital ship power and U.S. interests. A number of instances seemed to confirm that the Chinese were moving toward a path of confrontation, including the cancellation of a port visit by the carrier *Kitty Hawk* in 2007, the 2009 harassment of the survey ships *Impeccable* and *Victorious*, and severe limitations on military-military contact.[40] The emergence of China as a competitor on the high seas seemed to be confirmed in August 2011, when the first Chinese carrier, long rumored to be suffering mechanical difficulties, began sea trials.

Long before the last American unit redeployed from Iraq, Navy planners were looking East at a potential peer rival. Throughout the 1990s, China had been developing as an economic powerhouse, including rapid expansion of its fleet to include modern blue-water combatants.[41] It is true that the United States and China had been rivals and potentially faced conflict over a number of issues, including the status of Taiwan. There were always plans in DOD and the Navy for a Taiwan contingency, but the importance of these waxed and waned with the political importance of the region and relations to China. But until China began to develop its fleet, plans for potential conflict at sea with the Chinese were a relatively small (although ever-present) part of Navy planning.[42] Today the discussion of potential contingencies with China dominates the current rhetoric regarding the future of United States sea power.

The emergence of China as a sea power is seen as the arrival of a new capability and has fostered a great deal of debate within the U.S. defense establishment.[43] There are a number of important elements to this debate, the first focusing on historical analysis. One group sees the (relatively) sudden emergence of a large Chinese blue-water fleet as an act that is widely viewed as outside established cultural norms. Proponents of this view note that historically, imperial China was an inward-looking society; even as a modern state, plans to build a Navy were diverted by other interests, such as the Korean War, the Sino-Soviet split, and internal reforms.[44] It was only in the 1980s that a stabilized China was able to look outward, aided to some degree, interestingly enough, by the United States, which provided naval gas turbine and other technologies, an exchange that ended with Tiananmen Square.

The end of support from the U.S. did not, however, end China's naval expansion. Turning to India and Russia for technology and expertise, by 2006, the Chinese Navy was composed of a formidable fleet of all classes of ships, including nuclear submarines, cruisers, frigates, amphibious forces, and a sizeable air arm.[45] Moreover, China publicly expressed interest in developing aircraft carriers, first through acquisition of decommissioned carriers from the West and ultimately through the building of its own vessel.[46] Other historians dispute this claim of historical deviation, noting that Imperial China was during certain times in its history a global power on the sea, the fleet being destroyed only at the whim of the Emperor.[47] The Chinese themselves have made this point, arguing that given the established length of their recorded history, the return to the sea is not atypical at all, but rather part of an established culture.[48] While it is true that China in the modern era has been primarily a land power, much of its history has been one of internal reorganization and reunification; in their view (and in the view of some Western historians), a return to the sea is a natural course of action once this reunification is complete.[49]

Historians are not the only ones who disagree about the meaning of the rise of the Chinese Navy. Political scientists are not unanimous in their assessment. There is no doubt that in the latter 20th century, China has become an economic powerhouse, expanding into capitalist markets while maintaining a semblance of its communist structure. The rise of the Chinese Navy has often been presented as a natural part of this expansion; writing in *Modern Navy* in 2000, staff writer Niu Baocheng noted that the traditional role of protection of the coastline and EEZ was no longer sufficient if China was to continue development; rather, expansion into international trade and the development of resources at sea demanded protection of maritime rights and interests.[50] Practically, Chinese naval strategy has shifted from a coastal defense posture ("near seas" in Chinese naval parlance) to active defense ("mid-seas") and ultimately international operations ("far seas").[51] This strategy was publicly described in a Chinese White Paper published by the PLAN in 2004.[52] Many in the West do not see this as benignly or as natural as the Chinese, rather seeing it in classic realist terms of power play between nations, similar to the imperialistic developments of Europe at the end of the 19th century.[53]

In naval circles, the question regarding the motives and role of the new Chinese Navy has sparked fierce debate, a natural circumstance given that China is most obviously the only potential rival for the U.S. Navy. This began, interestingly enough, with a resurrection of Mahan. In October 2010, Toshi Yoshihara and James Holmes published *Red Star Over the Pacific*, a book examining modern China's challenge to U.S. Maritime Strategy. The main thesis of this book was that Mahan was making a comeback in the 21st century, this time in Asia through the emergence of a modern battle fleet that was being developed—and potentially employed—in accordance with the basic tenets of Mahan's theories. This contention sparked considerable debate in academic circles; noted Chinese naval experts Dr. Bud Cole and Norman Polmar vehemently disagreed with this thesis, noting both the historical and economic background for the development of the Chinese Navy and openly questioning whether a 19th-century western navalist could have such a profound effect on a very different culture. Today the debate is still ongoing—and is as contentious as ever.

For the Navy, however, there was little doubt as to what this development meant. They weren't the only ones in the DOD watching China. In September 2009, the Air Force and Navy signed a classified memo to cooperate on a new inter-service operational concept called the Air-Sea Battle. In subsequent months the details of the concept emerged as its basic underpinnings were released to the public. Although not a strategy per se, the Air-Sea Battle moved the Navy and Air Force together toward one specific objective—the containment of a rising China through conventional forward presence of combat power. Officially, there was a new power on the seas to be addressed. The public face of the Air-Sea battle began with a request. In 2010, Defense Secretary Gates asked for a study to determine methods by which sea lanes could be kept open during times of conflict—a request that, given the proliferation of anti-access technologies such as new long-range anti-ship missiles, had a definite logic to it.[54] There is some debate as to what Gates was actually asking for; anti-ship missiles were (and are) certainly a threat, but it is a threat that would normally be addressed by a tactical or technical solution. What Gates got was a strategy. In subsequent weeks, the Navy and Air Force formed an Air-Sea Battle Office (ASBO) at the Pentagon to publicly formulate a long-term solution to the problem; significantly, the Army was not invited to participate.[55] It did not take long for the ASBO to come up with a document that was reminiscent of "War Plan Orange" from the late 1930s, this time substituting China for Imperial Japan.[56]

Officially, the issue of whether the Air-Sea Battle is specifically designed to counter China is a political liability. The language regarding the concept (it was changed to a "concept" following political backlash over the idea that the Navy and Air Force were developing a strategy specifically to address China, which still remains a primary trading partner of the United States) was somewhat nebulous. The 2010 Quadrennial Defense Review (QDR) stated that the Air-Sea Battle concept would:

> [Defeat] adversaries across the range of military operations, including adversaries equipped with sophisticated anti-access and area denial capabilities. The concept will address how air and naval forces will integrate capabilities across all operational domains—air, sea, land, space, and cyberspace—to counter growing challenges to U.S. freedom of action.[57]

While no specific nations are mentioned in this guidance, the clear impetus was to counter China—and, to a lesser extent, Iran. Analysts were quick to point this out, stimulating the debate.[58] No other powers possessed the capability to act as anti-access or area denial opponents; this is especially true of China with its large fleet of nuclear submarines (a natural target for the Navy) and its space/cyber capability (solidly in the Air Force realm).

For the Navy, the Air-Sea Battle met a number of obvious requirements. In addition to solidly justifying continued investment in its capital ship fleet, it also demonstrated a certain degree of fiscal responsibility in its "joint" nature, a clear selling point to Congress.[59] The concept was not one devised by a single service, but rather a collaboration between the two most high-tech (and expensive) services, a clear fiscal advantage in an increasingly austere budget environment. Many of its stated concepts—maintaining freedom of the seas, free access, support to allies—were traditional themes that were comforting both to overseas partners threatened by the rise of China and to the Obama administration, which was attempting to end the wars in Iraq and Afghanistan.[60] In doing so there was a distinct shift away from the increasingly unpopular themes of COIN and Irregular Warfare, which had proven to be immune to easy answers for success. The Air-Sea Battle was—and is—a return to great power strategy waiting for a regional spark. To date, this follows that pattern of Navy commitment to capital ship theory. The allies remain ambivalent; the commitment and presence of capital ship power to the Pacific is certainly reassuring, but using it in conflict is another matter.

Does the Air-Sea Battle necessarily mean conflict? Considered in these terms, one must evaluate what type of threat the Chinese Navy is to the interests of the United States. Although billed as a "peer competitor," the fact remains that the Chinese Navy, despite some very impressive technical advances, is still very much a regional force. It is certainly capable of conducting an anti-access campaign in its region, and its overseas deployments have demonstrated it is capable of projecting power.[61] But how much combat power this actually represents is minimal compared to that possessed by the U.S. Navy, let alone any allies that might join the U.S. in the event of conflict.[62] Today the Chinese Navy possesses one aircraft carrier, the U.S. Navy twelve—six of which are available for rapid deployment into the PACOM area of operations. Any conflict with China is speculative (and there are many scenarios that have been discussed); these include a regional conflict that draws in other powers that, interestingly, could take on a distinctly irregular focus given the terrain and history of conflict in the region. The Navy's focus is obviously war at sea—but it has not been one that has centered on any type of smaller or irregular conflict, but rather one of access, strike power, and sea battle. Given the forces available to China, the idea of completely re-capitalizing and rebuilding a modern U.S. Navy with the rationale that it must be ready to meet China is not a logical course of action—unless it's based on theory that once again dominates U.S. Navy planning. The Navy is looking for assurance that it can operate freely—which, according to its traditional focus, means the development of capital ship power. The Navy, according to this argument, should be bigger—and more powerful.

Regardless of the logic of this argument, it would seem to hold sway. In December 2011, the president of the United States announced a new Defense Strategy that verified the conceptual underpinnings of the Air-Sea Battle concept, stressing that emphasis would be given in the future to Navy and Air Force strike and expeditionary capability, while the forces that had been engaged in irregular warfare for the past ten years (the Army) would be reduced.[63] It is true that that like all services, the size of the Navy was reduced by this strategy—a small number of cruisers were cut from the inventory—but compared to the force reductions of other services, this was minimal. And the centerpiece of Navy strategy, the carriers and their battle groups, remained untouched. For all intents and purposes, capital ship theory had returned to the forefront of U.S. defense planning.

Conclusions
The Cycles of History

As a singular case study, the Navy's return to capital ship emphasis after the irregular wars of the global war on terror could be rationalized as a logical response to the rise of a new traditional threat. But in a broader sense this action is illustrative of a historical pattern, the legacy that has repeated itself since the time of Mahan. Once core capital ship theory was established, the Navy has never seriously diverged from this path despite changes in threat, geopolitical realities, or domestic challenges. Rather, it repeatedly provides some adaptation to deal with these considerations, following which it reverts to its original model. This has occurred in every time period and conflict examined in this thesis. Despite the serious challenges of irregular warfare in its recent experience—a condition that still exists today—the Navy has never seriously wavered from its core theory. We are in a new era, but the theory remains.

In its unwavering commitment to theory, the Navy is unique. Mahan was an international phenomenon for his time and was eagerly embraced by all the major powers as a means for imperial greatness. Those powers that had established fleets—such as the British—used Mahan's rationale to make their forces stronger, while emerging maritime powers, such as Kaiser Wilhelm's Germany, saw him as the answer to meet the challenge posed by the stronger powers. The United States, emerging on the world stage, used Mahan as a rationale to develop a fleet that seemed to be the answer for its expansionist desires but ultimately as representative of its ideological posture regarding freedom on the seas. But unlike other powers that developed capital ship fleets, the U.S. Navy never lost its attraction to Mahan. While the United States did not embrace Mahan's philosophy fully—his exhortations to develop a strong merchant fleet as representative of mercantile power ultimately fell by the wayside, as did many of his other precepts, such as the idea of a balanced fleet to conduct other missions that a global power would inevitably face—the idea of a powerful fleet remained entrenched as a core theory by navalists who embraced Mahan and took his theory to an entirely new level never envisioned by the philosopher. For navalists, sea power was fleet power. This core theory has remained at the centerpiece of U.S. naval theory ever since.

It is true that for the United States, fleet power proved itself an invaluable asset itself in global conflict—the Second World War was, in the words of Samuel Eliot Morrison, a "two-ocean war" in every respect. But it also true that major regional conflict is a rarity and that capital ship power, when applied to the most common type of conflict—irregular war—has had mixed results. While other powers engaging in irregular conflict have reduced the size of their capital ship fleets or modified them to reflect this reality, the United States has held firm in its commitment to theory, consistently building a fleet that is reflective of its core beliefs.

As we have seen in this examination of U.S. naval history and strategy, this is reflective in a legacy that has repeated itself throughout the history of the Navy as a fleet power. Capital ships have been built during times of peace for future conflict, rationalized in a number of ways that are almost always reflective of the idea of matching or exceeding the strength of a peer competitor so as to engage in decisive battle to achieve command of the seas in the image of the Mahanian conflict. At times this has been obvious, such as during the naval arms races of the 1930s between the various major powers. At other times, the quest for decisive battle has been distinctly one-sided, relying on rationale that in retrospect is at best dubious. During the modern era the United States has developed its capital fleet to meet competitors whose aim in retrospect was not to engage in decisive battle at all, but rather to act as a defensive force far more in the model of Corbett than Mahan. This reality is clouded by a U.S. theoretical approach that states that the development of any offensive power by a competitor must be used in accordance within a very specific set of Mahanian-style principles; offensive force means offensive battle in the classical sense. Any other use—despite the benefit of hindsight (especially with regards to the Cold War era and the Soviet Navy)—are simple not acceptable. We see this pattern of rationale being espoused again today as navalists examine the development of the Chinese fleet.

But in the final analysis, Mahan is not enough—or rather, the modification of Mahanian theory that focus on mass firepower on the seas. The United States has exercised command of the sea in various degrees since 1945 but has had very mixed results in confronting irregular opponents. Always present in the spectrum of conflict, irregular warfare is the new reality in the global context, both on land and sea. This is an important point. America's Navy made the choice to become more specialized in strike power to directly influence events on land, a logical course of action if it had obtained command of the sea against other fleets or bluewater threats. Strike power in this case was designed for and is most effective against another conventional opponent. But as we have seen, the enemy is predominantly unconventional or asymmetric, against which strike power has had decidedly mixed results. Similarly on the seas the asymmetric threat is a direct challenge to the Mahanian vision of fleet power. Whereas in the past there has always been some form of "irregular" threat on the oceans, this has focused almost exclusively on some form of criminal element—piracy, slavery, etc. Now the threat is either through transnational terrorism or the shipment of WMD or some other type of strike weapon. "Command of the sea" in this regard means control of these activities—something that fleet power is not designed to do.

This is not to say that naval power is irrelevant in irregular warfare. Exactly the opposite argument can be made in terms of mobility, control, and flexibility. The sea remains the great global commons that offers tremendous benefit for a global power. But today we do not have the forces, expertise, or moreover the culture to change to meet the challenges of a new reality in conflict. This is apparent in our reaction to the wars of the GWOT. Beyond the design of a small number of specialized units—which, true to the cycle of history, are even now being marginalized in the aftermath of the irregular wars of the 21st century—assets that could meet many of the requirements of irregular conflict—littoral combat ships, coastal warfare assets, or hospital ships—are being marginalized despite the rhetoric. In asset construction and doctrine we are once again moving back to our traditional paradigm, postulating that China will be the next traditional threat—as if a new Jutland awaits.

As a traditional maritime power, the United States must change to meet the new reality of irregular war. The U.S. maintains its role of global leadership—but that role has been diminished, not by the attacks of 9/11 but by our response to the irregular threat that followed, a fact apparent not only to our enemies but also to the global community of nations. We need not to be looking back for the rise of an enemy that will fight in the traditional manner, but rather new threats, and be ready to meet that challenge with a modern theory of sea power that reflects the new reality. It is time to reassess Mahan's legacy.

Chapter Notes

Chapter One

1. U.S. Special Operations Command (SOCOM) defines irregular warfare as "...a violent struggle between state and non-state actors for legitimacy and influence over relevant populations." IW favors asymmetric and revolutionary style warfare. *Irregular Warfare DoD Directive 3000.07* (Washington, D.C: Department of Defense, 2008).

2. Edgar S. Furniss, *American Military Policy: Strategic Aspects of World Political Geography* (New York: Reinhart, 1957).

3. Max Boot, *The Savage Wars of Peace* (New York: Basic Books, 2002), xiv.

4. Russell Weigley, *The American Way of War* (Indiana University Press, 1977), 10.

5. David Tucker and Christopher J. Lamb, *United States Special Operations Forces* (New York: Columbia University Press, 2007), 107–142.

6. Joseph D. Celeski, *Operationalizing COIN*, JSOU Report 05–02 (Tampa: Joint Special Operations University, September 2005), 17.

7. Peter L. Bergen, *Holy War Inc.: Inside the Secret World of Osama Bin Laden* (New York: The Free Press, 2001), 195.

8. *Ibid.* The idea of a "generational conflict" is frequently used in Islamist terrorism, notably by ALQ and the muhajdeen in Afghanistan.

9. These trends are evident in Pakistan, Somalia, and the Sudan among others. See *Leashing the Dogs of* War, and Bergen.

10. Rupert Smith, *The Utility of Force: The Art of War in the Modern World* (New York: Vintage Books, 2005), 24. This view is not confined to those who favor land power; see also Roger Barnett, *The Navy's Strategic Culture* (Annapolis: Naval Institute Press, 2008), 106.

11. Barnett makes this point, as do many others that will be cited throughout this thesis. This is the classic navalist position.

12. T.X. Hammes, *The Sling and the Stone: On War in the 21st Century* (New York: Zenith Press, 2004), ix.

13. Harry Summers, *On Strategy: A Critical Analysis of the Vietnam War* (New York: Presidio Press, 1995).

14. Gary Hess, *Explaining America's Lost War* (Malden: Oxford Publishing, 2009).

15. *Ibid.*, 4.

16. This list is quite short as it does not address the deployment of U.S. forces in missions that are distinctly "irregular," such as peace keeping, nation building, show of force, etc. For purposes of the immediate discussion, IW focuses on deployment of combat force for actual kinetic operations.

17. As the commander of the multinational force in Bosnia, General Rupert Smith is particularly argumentative as to whether the conflict was a "victory" in the classical sense. See Rupert Smith, *The Utility of Force*, 335–374.

18. Although U.S. combat troops were withdrawn from Iraq in August 2010, 50,000 troops remained in an "advisory" role dedicated to dealing with the IW threat. How many will remain in this role after complete is unclear. See Scott Wilson, "U.S. Troops to Leave Iraq," *Washington Post World*, October 21, 2011.

19. This is reflected in a series of official USN strategies, beginning with *The Way Ahead* (Washington: Department of the Navy, 1991), released after the fall of the Soviet Union. See Chapter Six.

20. A volume of literature is available on this topic. For the navalist view of this conflict see Paul Nitze, *Securing the Seas: The Soviet Naval Challenge and Western Alliance Options* (New York: Westview Press, 1979).

21. In the 1980s both the Army's "Airland Battle" and the Navy's "Maritime Strategy" were based on this premise. See "The Maritime Strategy," USNI *Proceedings* (Annapolis: Naval Institute Press, October 1984).

22. See Smith, Hammes, Hoffman, and Kilcullen.
23. Sanjeev Gupta, Benedict Clements, Rina Bhattacharya, and Shamit Chakravarti (2002), "The Elusive Peace Dividend" at Finance & Development, a quarterly magazine of the IMF.
24. Rick Atkinson, *Crusade: The Unknown Story of the Gulf War* (New York: Mariner's Books, 1994), 540.
25. Numerous period writings stress this point, see Furniss. While both the U.S. and Russia frequently armed one or the other side, viewing them as satellites or proxies in retrospect is far too simplistic and in many cases (in hindsight) not correct.
26. Chester Crocker ed., *Leashing the Dogs of War: Conquest Management in a Divided World* (Washington D.C.: United States Institute of Peace, 2007), 15.
27. Ibid., 35.
28. Julian Zelizer, *The Arsenal of Democracy: The Politics of National Security from World War II to the War on Terrorism* (New York: Basic Books, 2010), 60.
29. Ibid., 355.
30. Hammes, 4.
31. In *True Enough*, Farhad Manjoo argues that this represents the phenomenon of "social reality"—the idea that one interprets an event largely in alignment with ideological or cultural viewpoint. The interpretation of the collapse of the Soviet Union is a case in point. See Farhad Manjoo, *True Enough* (New York: Wiley, 2008), 21.
32. Robert Suny, *The Revenge of the Past: Nationalism, Revolution, and the Collapse of the Soviet Union* (Stanford: Stanford University Press, 1993).
33. Hans Binnendjik. ed., *Transforming America's Military* (Washington: National Defense University Press, 2002), xix.
34. Ibid., xxx.
35. Hammes, 7.
36. Author experience.
37. William O'Neil, "The Naval Services: Network Centric Warfare," in *Transforming America's Military*, 155.
38. "Kinetic" operations refer to the actual use of force or firepower in combat, while "non-kinetic" refer to support or other roles.
39. Michele Flournoy ed., *QDR 2001: Strategy-Driven Choices for America's Security* (Washington: National Defense University Press, 2001), 183.
40. See Chapter Eight.
41. The Navy staff alone had at least 5 groups examining the problem of global IW and terrorism. Author experience Pentagon duty, 2004–2006.
42. The term "global war on terror" or GWOT was adopted immediately after the attacks on 9/11, first used by President Bush on October 7, 2001, in his address to the nation. It has since gone through a number of iterations, including "war versus violent extremism" and "overseas contingency operations." See http://georgewbush-whitehouse. archives.gov/news/releases/2001/10/print/ 20011007-8.html. See also Scott Wilson and Al Kamen, "Global War on Terror is Given a New Name," *The Washington Post*, March 25, 2009; Page A04.
43. SOCOM Missions Statement at http:// www.socom.mil/default.aspx, accessed April 2, 2011.
44. See "Special Operations Forces Interagency Counterterrorism Reference Manual," JSOU University, March 2009.
45. Current naval trends towards smaller, IW type combatants are tracked by Janes Publishing.
46. This was characteristic of major operations of the 1990s, notably Bosnia and Somalia. There is a strong argument from authors such as Rupert Smith that these types of conflict were and are in fact the new norm rather than mechanized warfare between States. See Smith, *The Utility of Force*, 374.
47. Athanasia Austin, "Development of U.S. Irregular Warfare Capabilities," *The Journal of the JPACC*, ed. 6, 2008.
48. *Irregular Warfare Joint Operating Concept* (Washington D.C.: Department of Defense, 2009), 2.
49. Colin Gray, "Irregular Enemies and the Essence of Strategy: Can the American Way of War Adapt?" *Strategic Studies Institute* (Washington D.C.: March 2006), 5.
50. Hammes, 2.
51. Previous theorists have touched on this point; Liddell Hart to some extent with his "strategy of the indirect approach," and Harry Summers in claiming that the tactic was used deliberately by the North Vietnamese in attempting to gain national support (through the student protest movement in the U.S.) international support for their cause during the Vietnam war. See Hart, *Strategy*, and Harry Summers, *On Strategy: A Critical Analysis of the Vietnam War* (New York: Presidio Press, 1995).
52. Frank Hoffman, "Hybrid Warfare and Challenges," *Joint Forces Quarterly*, Issue 52 (Washington: National Defense University Press, 2009), 35.
53. Ibid., 37.
54. This concept was originally articulated by Clausewitz, becoming part of the U.S. military's lexicon. See Carl von Clause-

witz, *On War* (Princeton: Princeton University Press, 1982), 144.

55. Gray, "Irregular Warfare," 7.

56. Charles Shaver, *Irregular Warfare Special Study* (Suffolk: Joint Warfighting Center (USJFCOM), March 2006), 30.

57. Hammes, 3.

58. The term was first coined by the Defense Department to characterize the global war on terror in 2005. See *Al Qaida and the Long War* (Tampa: Joint Special Operations University, April 2007).

59. The term "soft power" was coined by Joseph Nye in the late 1980s and expanded upon in his work *Soft Power: The Means to Success in World Politics* (New York: PublicAffairs 2004). The term has since come to mean many things in the post-9/11 world, but generally refers to non-kinetic means for a nation to influence events. It is a core element of irregular warfare and counterinsurgency (COIN) response operations and will be expanded upon later in this thesis as it relates to sea power operations.

Chapter Two

1. William E. Livezey, *Mahan on Sea Power* (Oklahoma: University of Oklahoma Press, 1981), 286.

2. *Ibid*.

3. Criticism and critiques of Mahan are wide ranging. One of the first was Fred Jane's *The Heresies of Sea Power* (New York: Longmans, Green, 1906), which disputed not only Mahan's historical analysis but also his various premises on the usefulness of sea power. See also Phili Crowl, "Alfred Thayer Mahan: the Naval Historian," in *Makers of Modern Strategy*, ed. Peter Paret (Oxford: Clarendon Press, 1986).

4. See Harold and Margaret Sprout, *The Rise of American Naval Power, 1776–1918* (Annapolis: Naval Institute Press, 1967), i–v, and Livezey, 39.

5. Kenneth Hagen, "Alfred Thayer Mahan: Turing America Back to the Sea" in *Makers of American Diplomacy*, Merli Wilson ed., 280. See also Charles Carlisle Taylor, *The Life of Admiral Mahan* (New York: George H. Doran, 1920), viii.

6. The term "navalists" is defined by historian Craig Symonds as "...men for whom the practical problems directly concerned with national defense were not the sole or even a primary consideration. Navalists were generally concerned with image, honor, prestige, and diplomatic clout ... navalists yearned for empire, not only for purposes of economic exploitation but also from a unique vision of what constituted national greatness. To them a naval fleet was physical evidence of national adulthood." See Craig Symonds, *The Navalists and Anti-Navalists: The Naval Policy Debate in the United States, 1785–1827* (Newark: University of Delaware Press, 1980), intr. See also Mark Russell Shulman, *Navalism and the Emergence of American Sea Power, 1882–1893* (Annapolis: Naval Institute Press, 1995), 13. Note that this definition will change over time as described in this thesis.

7. Peter Karsten, *The Naval Aristocracy: The Golden Age of Annapolis and the Emergence of Modern American Navalism* (Annapolis: Naval Institute Press, 1972), xv.

8. Phili Crowl, "Alfred Thayer Mahan: The Naval Historian," in *Makers of Modern Strategy*, Peter Paret, ed., (Princeton: Princeton University Press, 1986), 444.

9. Karsten, 30.

10. Crowl, 445.

11. Land billets during the nineteenth century were rare for "line" officers; despite poor conditions afloat, it was clearly the path to promotion. See Charles Nordhoff, *Life on the Ocean* (Cincinnati: Brown, 1874), 20, and Karsten, 52. Mahan's dislike of sea duty was well documented in a diary he kept aboard USS IRAQUOIS and USS AROOSTOOK from April 26, 1868–September 10, 1869. See *Letters and Papers of Alfred Thayer Mahan, Vol. 1, 1847–1889* (Annapolis: Naval Institute Press, 1975), 145–305.

12. Robert L. O'Connell, *Sacred Vessels: The Cult of the Battleship and the Rise of the U.S. Navy* (Oxford: Oxford University Press, 1991), 21.

13. Shulman, *Navalism and the Emergence of American Sea Power*, 46.

14. *Ibid*.

15. Feelings against steam were so virulent that for some time it was Navy policy to require captains to note in their logs in red ink any use of coal, with the implication that it would have direct impact on their future careers. This and other prejudices against steam and engineering officers continued for some time. See Frank Bennett, *The Steam Navy of the United States* (Pittsburgh: W. T. Nicholsen, 1896), 14.

16. William Livezey, *Mahan on Sea Power* (Oklahoma: University of Oklahoma Press, 1981), 224.

17. *Ibid.*, 228.

18. As quoted in Livzey, 43.

19. Mark Russel Shulman, *Navalism and the Emergence of American Sea Power*, 7.

20. A. T. Mahan, *The Influence of Sea Power Upon History* (New York: Gallery Books, 1995), 22.

21. *Ibid.*
22. Clark G. Reynolds, *Navies in History* (Annapolis: Naval Institute Press, 1998), 141.
23. Karsten, 189.
24. Shulman, *Navalism and the Emergence of American Sea Power*, 46. See also Stephen Luce, "Benefits of War," *American Review*, December 1891.
25. Ernest R. May, *American Imperialism* (New York: Brown and Root, 1968), 198. See also Letter, Theodore Roosevelt to A. T. Mahan, May 21, 1890, Mahan Papers (Washington D.C.: Naval Archives).
26. Warren Zimmerman, *The First Great Triumph: How Five Americans made Their Country a World Power* (New York: Farrar, Straus, and Giroux), 122.
27. The actual quote is from Washington's farewell address and is as follows: "The great rule of conduct for us, in regard to foreign nations, is in extending our commercial relations to have as little political connection as possible...why, by intertwining ourselves with any part of Europe, entangle our peace and prosperity in the tails of European ambition, rivalships, interest, humor or caprice? It is our true policy to steer clear of permanent alliances with any portion of the foreign world." This has often been (incorrectly) interpreted to mean that Washington was calling for isolationism. See "Washington's Farewell Address," *Senate Document 106–21*, 106th Congress (Government Printing Office, Washington D.C., 2000).
28. Livezey, *Mahan on Sea Power*, 60.
29. Zimmerman, 118. See also *Influence of Sea Power*, 26.
30. Michael Oran, *Power, Faith, and Fantasy* (New York: W.W. Norton, 2007), 25.
31. This is linked to Mahan's argument for national character. See *Influence*, 30.
32. Oran, 277.
33. James R. Reckner, *Teddy Roosevelt's Great White Fleet* (Annapolis: Naval Institute Press, 1988), 4.
34. Zimmerman, *First Great Triumph*, 112.
35. Albion, *Makers of Naval Policy*, 209.
36. Barbara Tuchman, *The Proud Tower* (New York: Macmillan, 1965), 133.
37. Albion, 211.
38. *Ibid.*, 213.
39. William Livezey, *Mahan on Sea Power*, 61.
40. This is a very Jominian approach. Mahan's father read and taught Jomini at West Point, and A. T. Mahan was well familiar with him, using his approach to the distilling of maritime "principles." See A. T. Mahan, "Practical Words: An Address Delivered at the Naval War College," Newport R.W. September 1892, in *Letters and Papers of Alfred Thayer Mahan*, Vol. 3 (Annapolis: U.S. Naval Institute, 1977), 508.
41. Theodore Roscoe, *On the Sea and in the Air* (New York: Warton, 1970), 63.
42. Admiral Haris Laning, "Big Navy," *Fortune*, March 1938.
43. Letter A. T. Mahan to Secretary of the Navy Long, 31 Jan. 1900. *Letters and Papers of Alfred Thayer Mahan*, vol. 3 (Annapolis: Naval Institute Press, 1977).
44. George W. Baer, *One Hundred Years of Sea Power* (Stanford: Stanford University Press, 1993), 41.

Chapter Three

1. William Livezey, *Mahan on Sea Power* (Norman: University of Oklahoma Press, 1981), 333.
2. A political trend that would have increasing emphasis in weapons procurement as the United States emerged as a global power that would more or less become a constant in building the national security state. See Julian Zelizer, *The Arsenal of Democracy* (New York: Basic Books, 2010).
3. Fred Jane, *Heresies of Sea Power* (London: Longmans, Green, 1906), 4.
4. Letter, Mahan to Clark, January 15, 1907, in *Letters and Papers of Alfred Thayer Mahan*, Vol. 3 (Annapolis: Naval Institute Press, 1977), 203. See also See Harold and Margret Sprout, *The Rise of American Naval Power, 1776–1918* (Annapolis: Naval Institute Press, 1967), 20.
5. Robert L. O'Connell, *Sacred Vessels: The Cult of the Battleship and the Rise of the U.S. Navy* (Oxford: Oxford University Press, 1991), 80.
6. *Ibid.*, 113.
7. *Ibid.*, 114.
8. Robert Seager, *Alfred Thayer Mahan: The Man and His Letters* (Annapolis: Naval Institute Press, 1977), 532.
9. Warren Zimmerman, *First Great Triumph: How Five Americans Made Their Country a World Power* (New York: Farrar, Strauss and Giroux, 2002), 114.
10. The original idea of "manifest destiny" was penned by journalist John O'Sullivan in 1839, who wrote "The far reaching, the boundless future will be the era of American greatness ... to establish on earth the noblest temple ever dedicated to the Most High—the Sacred and the True." The idea was fully embraced by those who supported Mahan's theories. *Ibid.*, 33.
11. Robert Albion, *Makers of Naval Policy 1798–1947* (Annapolis: Naval Institute Press, 1980) 27.

Notes—Chapter Three

12. Michael Oren, *Power, Faith and Fantasy: America in the Middle East* (New York: W.W. Norton, 2007), 30.
13. Frank Uhlig Jr., *How Navies Fight: The U.S. Navy and its Allies* (Annapolis: Naval Institute Press, 1994), 37.
14. Karsten speculates that this "hierarchy" of vessels fit very well culturally with the rigidly established hierarchy of the naval profession itself. This is a difficult thesis to prove as documentation on a distinct cultural trend is sparse. It should be noted, however, that there is no doubt that command of larger, capital ships was a distinct representation of promotion in the Service, then as in now. See Karsten, *The Naval Aristocracy*, 359.
15. The *Maritime Strategy* of the 1980s and the *Cooperative Strategy for 21st Century Sea Power* both made references to Mahan; his ideas were prevalent to some degree in all of the strategies of the 1990s. See Chapter Six.
16. The Great White Fleet, officially a force for peace, was a not so subtle announcement of the U.S. arriving on the scene as an international force and a demonstration of its new naval power—a demonstration that was significant. James Reckner, *Teddy Roosevelt's Great White Fleet* (Annapolis: Naval Institute Press, 2001), 10.
17. For purposes of this discussion the term "Mahanian" will now refer to a capital shi force doctrinally trained to seek decisive battle. Although as noted this was not strictly in accordance with Mahan, this was the popular interpretation that influenced development and remains prevalent.
18. Andrew Gordon, *The Rules of the Game: Jutland and British Naval Command* (Annapolis: Naval Institute Press, 2000), 25.
19. E.B. Potter, *Sea Power: a Naval History* (Annapolis: Naval Institute Press, 1981), 211.
20. Martin van Crevald, *Technology and War* (New York: The Free Press, 1989), 176.
21. Kenneth Davison, "Clausewitz and the Indirect Approach...Misreading the Leader," *Airpower Journal* (Maxwell AFB: Winter 1988).
22. Ibid.
23. R.A. Bowling, "The Negative Influence of Mahan on ASW," *Journal of the Royal United Service Institute for Defense Studies*, December 1977.
24. Van Crevald, *Technology and War*, 207.
25. Livezey, *Mahan on Sea Power*, 306.
26. Thomas Wildenburg, "In Support of the Battle Line: Gunnery's Influence on Carrier Aviation." *Journal of Mil. History*. Vol. 65, 657.

27. See Julian Corbett, *Some Principles of Maritime Strategy* (New York: Tredition, 2011) and James Goldrick ed., *Mahan is Not Enough.: The Proceedings of a Conference on the Works of Sir Julian Corbett and Sir Herbert Richmond* (Newport: Naval War College Press, 1993).
28. A witty and popular phrase in the U.S. in the early 1920s was "what did the war get us but death, destruction, and George M. Cohan?"
29. Albion, *Makers of Naval Policy*, 230.
30. O'Connell, *Sacred Vessels*, 240.
31. Karsten, *The Naval Aristocracy*, 370.
32. Holger Herwig, "Innovation Ignored: The Submarine Problem—Germany, Britain, and the United States, 1919–1939" in *Military Innovation in the Interwar Period* (Cambridge: Cambridge University Press, 1996).
33. Karsten argues that the Annapolis mindset was a virtual indoctrination as to the importance of overseas trade and the link to naval power. See Karsten, *The Naval Aristocracy*, 161.
34. O'Connell, *Sacred Vessels*, 240.
35. This also took a political turn; some naval officers actively campaigned against the treaty of Versailles. See Karsten, 237.
36. U.S. Senate, Naval Affairs Committee, *Navy Yearbook*, 1920–21, 872. See also *Naval Appropriations Act*, 1921, and U.S. Congress, *Act of July 12, 1921*, Section 9.
37. Trent Hone, "The Evolution of Fleet Tactical Doctrine, 1922–1941," in *The Journal of Military History*, vol. 67, October 2003, 1107–48.
38. Ibid.
39. This is the beginning of the trend that is central throughout this thesis: the rationalization of fleet power despite other challenges to naval strategic operations. See Peter Karsten, *The Naval Aristocracy*, 369.
40. Woodrow Wilson, "Declaration of War Against Germany," April 2, 1917. *Source Records of the Great War*, Vol, V, Charles F. Horne ed (Washington: National Archives, 1923).
41. John Morrow, *The Great War: An Imperial History* (New York: Routledge, 2002), 156.
42. Ermino Bagnaso, *Submarines of World War Two* (Annapolis: Naval Institute Press, 2000), 30.
43. Ibid., 45.
44. Peter Padfield, *War Beneath the Sea* (New York: John Wiley & Sons, 1995).
45. Albion, *Makers of Navy Policy*, 250.
46. Ibid.
47. Clay Blair, *Silent Victory: The U.S. Submarine War Against Japan* (New York: J.B. Lippencourt, 1975), 18.

48. The idea of the "hunter-killer" groups—small groups of destroyers patrolling on the offensive looking for U-boats—would be resurrected again during the Second World War and have similar results. See Michael Gannon, *Operation Drumbeat: The Dramatic True Story of Germany's First U-Boat Attacks Along America's Coast During WW2* (Annapolis: Naval Institute Press, 2009), 135.
49. Ibid., 156.
50. W. J. Holmes, *Undersea Victory* (New York: Doubleday, 1966), 47.
51. Karl Doenitz, *Ten Years and Twenty Days* (New York: Cassell, 2000), 120.
52. In fairness the United States was not alone in this regard. As late as 1940 some British were arguing the primary use of submarines was for reconnaissance in ports. See Commander John Creswell, *Naval Warfare* (New York: Chemical Publishing, 1942), 288.
53. It should be noted that individual submarine attacks against warships during the Second World War, despite a handful of public successes, were very ineffective. For the Americans this technique only began to show results in the latter days of the war with extensive intelligence targeting support. See Peter Padfield, *War Beneath the Sea* (New York: John Wiley & Sons, 1995), Chap. 2, for pre-war submarine theory and R. B. Watts, *Ultra Underseas: Signal Intelligence and the Submarine War Against Japan, 1941–1945* (Norfolk: Old Dominion University, 1993), 4, for warshi attacks.
54. Watts, *Ultra Underseas*, 6.
55. Geoffrey Till, "Adopting the Aircraft Carrier: The British, American, and Japanese case studies," in *Military Innovation in the Interwar Period*, 194.
56. Ibid.
57. O'Connell, *Sacred Vessels*, 2. See also Albion, *Makers of Naval Policy*, 250.
58. Ibid., 2.
59. Ibid.
60. Ibid., 262.
61. Note the argument was an international one; although the future combatants of World War II were building carriers, there was still intense discussion regarding the role of the battleship, the key focus of the Naval Disarmament conferences of the 1920s and 1930s. See Albion, *Makers of Naval Policy*, 251.
62. *At War at Sea* or *The Pacific War*.
63. Geoffrey Till, "Adopting the Aircraft Carrier: The British, American, and Japanese case studies" in *Military Innovation*.
64. Hone, "The Evolution of Fleet Tactical Doctrine."
65. By the 1920s even a venerable presence such as Sims was becoming a convert to carriers. See "Letter Sims to Fiske, January 6, 1921." *Sims Papers* (Washington: Naval Archives).
66. Thomas Wildenburg, "In Support of the Battle Line," 690.
67. This would change during the Second World War with the introduction of smaller "jeep" carriers for ASW, a practical innovation. Norman Polmar, *U.S. Aircraft Carriers* (Annapolis: Naval Institute Press, 1983).
68. Hone and O'Connell, 281.
69. The actual accuracy of battleship gunfire prior to the advent of modern range finding techniques is controversial; bigger guns did not necessarily ensure accuracy. See O'Connell, *Sacred Vessels*, 102.
70. Ibid., 253. See also Trent Hone, "Evolution of Fleet Tactical Doctrine," 45.
71. Craig Felker, *Simulation and Sea Power: the U.S. Navy Fleet Problems, 1923–1940* (Annapolis: Naval Institute Press, 1983).
72. Thomas Lowry, *The Attack on Taranto* (New York: Stackpole Books, 1995), 38.
73. Craig Felker, *Simulation and Sea Power: the U.S. Navy Fleet Problems*.
74. Polmar, *U.S. Aircraft Carriers*.
75. Michael Gannon, *Operation Drumbeat*, 230.

Chapter Four

1. Bernard Brodie, *Strategy in the Missile Age* (Princeton: Princeton University Press, 1959), Ch. 3.
2. Sources on the complexity of Cold War theory are wide ranging. For an excellent summary, see Michael Carver, "Conventional Warfare in the Nuclear Age" and Lawrence Freedman, "The First Two Generations of Nuclear Strategists," in *Makers of Modern Strategy from Machiavelli to the Nuclear Age* (Princeton: Princeton University Press), 1986.
3. As a historian emeritus Morrison was allowed unique access to Navy operations during the war, sailing with combat units in both the Atlantic and Pacific. His multivolume history of naval operations during the war is generally considered a classic work—but is decidedly pro-Navy. See Samuel Elliot Morrison, *The Two Ocean War* (Annapolis: Naval Institute Press, 2007) for an effective summary.
4. Max Hastings, *Retribution: The Battle for Japan, 1944–45* (New York: Alfred A. Knopf, 2008), 95.
5. Two of six "Iowa" class battleships, the largest in the fleet, were still in construction at the war's end. They would continue in service in various roles until the late 1980s. See Norman Friedman, *U.S. Battleships: An*

Notes—Chapter Four

Illustrated Design History (Annapolis: Naval Institute Press, 1986).

6. This transition did not occur until 1943 with the formal creation of a Deputy Chief of Naval Operations (Air). See Ronald Spector, *At War at Sea* (New York: Viking, 2001), 222.

7. The "Task Force" was an operational development. Carriers grouped in accordance with the Mahanian dictum of concentration of power were offensively strong but also vulnerable, requiring a large number of support vessels (battleships and especially fast cruisers) to defend them from air attack. See Spector, *At War as Sea*, 220.

8. Livezey, *Mahan on Sea Power*, 312.

9. Meirion and Susie Harris, *Soldiers of the Sun: The Rise and Fall of the Japanese Imperial Army* (New York: Random House, 1991), 194.

10. Spector, 201.

11. There are, of course, other factors in the fleet development, including the intense period of militarization and nationalization that occurred in Japan in the late 1800s. See Harris, *Soldiers of the Sun*, 35. This had stunning results at Tsushima in battle against the Russians in 1905, heralding the emergence of Japan as a modern naval power. R. M. Connaughton, *The War of the Rising Sun and the Tumbling Bear—A Military History of the Russo-Japanese War 1904–5* (London: John Murray), 1988.

12. *Jane's Fighting Ships* (London: Jane's Publishing, 1941).

13. The Japanese submarine fleet, trained to attack enemy warships and regarding a guerre de course as not worthy of the force was almost completely ineffective during the war compared to its German and American counterparts. See Carl Boyd and Akihiko Yoshida, *The Japanese Submarine Force in World War 2* (Annapolis: Naval Institute Press, 1995).

14. Karl Doenitz, *Memoirs: Ten Years and Twenty Days* (Annapolis: Naval Institute Press, 1990), 272.

15. Spector, *At War at Sea*, 224.

16. Michael Gannon, *Operation Drumbeat* (New York: Harper and Row, 1990).

17. *Ibid*.

18. Nathen Miller, *At War at Sea* (New York: Oxford University Press, 1995), 334.

19. *Ibid*.

20. A large number of these were "escort" or "jeep" carriers, essentially converted merchant vessels that were retrofit with a flight deck to carry a small number of aircraft. At war's end, the United States could muster 15 major carrier groups of the "fleet" variety. Hastings, *Retribution*, 101.

21. *Ibid*.

22. Jeffrey Barlow, *From Hot War to Cold: The U.S. Navy and National Security Affairs, 1945–1955* (Stanford: Stanford University Press, 2009), 35.

23. Samuel Huntington, "National Policy and the Transoceanic Navy" *USNI Proceedings*, August 1954. See also Bernard Brodie, *Naval Strategy* (Oxford: Oxford University Press, 1943).

24. Attempts to define the conflict using historical examples were not particularly successful; for years, for example, the U.S. Naval War College compared the U.S.-Soviet standoff as a reinterpretation of the Sparta vs. Athens conflict in the Peloponnesian War—an interpretation that was not particularly accurate. See Naval War College Curriculum, "Maritime Operations," (Newport: Naval War College, 1987).

25. A fact recognized by theorists and strategists at the time. See Edgar S. Furniss Jr., *American Military Policy* (New York: Reinhart, 1957).

26. Communist China had no real Navy beyond a rudimentary capability. Soviet submarines, however, were a serious threat; at war's end the Soviets possessed over 300 with a stated intention of building u to 1200. This sea denial asset could potentially dominate the waters of Europe and beyond. Michael T. Isenberg, *Shield of the Republic: The United States Navy in an Era of Cold War and Violent Peace, 1945–1962* (New York: St. Martin's Press, 1993), 130. See also Spector, *At War at Sea*, 317.

27. Zelizer, *Arsenal of democracy*, 63.

28. John Lewis Gaddis, *Strategies of Containment: A Critical Appraisal of American National Security Policy During the Cold War* (Oxford: Oxford University Press, 1982), 19.

29. Ryan, *First Line of Defense*, 8.

30. Isenberg, *Shield of the Republic*, 134.

31. Spector, *At War at Sea*, 330.

32. Jeffrey Barlow, *From Hot War to Cold: The U.S. Navy and National Security Affairs, 1945–1955* (Stanford: Stanford University Press, 2009), 162. See also Norman Polmar, *Submarines of the Russian and Soviet Navies, 1718–1900* (Annapolis: Naval Institute Press, 1991).

33. Navy Strategic Plans Study 3, "Study of Carrier Attack Force Offensive Capabilities," Op-30W, March 7, 1947, Miscellaneous Plans and Studies, Series XVII, Strategic Plans Records Division (Washington: Operational Archives, Naval Historical Center).

34. *Naval Strategic Planning Study, 1947*. NAVAL ARCHIVES.

35. Brodie, *Naval Strategy*.

36. Zelizer, *Arsenal of Democracy*, 89.
37. Isenberg, *Shield of the Republic*, 57.
38. Jeffrey Barlow, *Revolt of the Admirals: The Fight for Naval Aviation, 1945–1950* (Washington D.C.: Naval Historical Center, 1994), 24.
39. Douhet was in many respects the "air" manifestation of Mahan. Writing in the 1920s, he argued that the use of aircraft during the First World War was a premonition of things to come, when war would be decided by fleets of strategic bombers targeting enemy civilian populations. His theories were extremely popular with air power advocates and provided a basis for the development of strategic bombing aircraft and theory, much as Mahan served for the rationale for the development of the capital ship fleet. See David MacIsacc, "Voices from the Central Blue: The Air Power Theorists," in *Makers of Modern Strategy*.
40. Hastings, *Retribution*, 296.
41. The *U.S. Strategic Bombing Survey* (http://www.anesi.com/ussbs02.htm, accessed 1 December 2011) was conducted by the Army Air Corps. There is considerable debate as to whether the document is unbiased.
42. Arms production in Germany, for example, was not demonstrably effected by the bombing campaign. See Albert Speer, *Inside the Third Reich* (New York: Ishi Press, 2007).
43. The Army Air Corps formally became an independent Air Force in 1947. For purposes of this discussion the AAC will now be referred to as the Air Force.
44. Barlow, *Revolt of the Admirals*, 28. This concept would later appear in the 1990s naval strategy "From the Sea" and in the current national strategy in the Pacific toward China.
45. Barlow, *From Hot War to Cold*, 176.
46. *The National Security Act 1947* (Washington: Office of the President, 1947).
47. Isenberg, *Shield of the Republic*, 114.
48. Barlow, *Revolt of the Admirals*, 35.
49. The British had tried a similar reorganization prior to the Second World War with very poor results. See Richard Hough and Denis Richards, *The Battle of Britain: The Greatest Battle of World War II* (New York: W.W. Norton, 1989), 20.
50. *Final Report: War Department Policies and Program Review Board*, Aug. 1, 1947, (Washington: Chief of Naval Operations), 23.
51. Lawrence Freedman, *The Evolution of Nuclear Strategy* (New York: St. Martin's Press, 1983), 27.
52. The United States possessed only a handful of gravity type weapons until the 1950s. Numbers are tabulated in Barlow, 128.

53. Although this seems almost quaint today, the idea of nuclear weapons being given control to an international body such as the United Nations was considered by the Truman administration and was considered inevitable by some military planners. Freedman, *The Evolution of Nuclear Strategy*, 52.
54. The Soviets exploded an atomic bomb in 1949.
55. Furniss, *American Military Policy*, 198.
56. This was unique to the nuclear force. It was argued in government circles that the strategic and decisive nature of nuclear weapons made them far too important for policy to be relegated to military control; this led to the rise of an alliance between government and academia for atomic strategic theory. Freedman, *The Evolution of Nuclear Strategy*, 176.
57. A.E. Sokol, "Sea Power in the Next War," *U.S. Naval Institute Proceedings*, May 1952.
58. Isenberg, *Shield of the Republic*, 46.
59. It is interesting to note that the Navy's work on the bomb was almost its undoing. The Navy hierarchy was well aware of the technical limitations of the weapon and approached its potential use accordingly; the Air Force was not, and viewed the weapon far more theoretically in terms of what it "could" do. Barlow, 80.
60. *Navy Budgetary Presentations Before the JCS Fiscal Year 1951: Review of Plans, Phase II, Part I*, vol. 1, June 1, 6, 1949, (Washington: Naval Historical Center), 30.
61. Navy Strategic Plans Study 3, "Study of Carrier Attack Force Offensive Capabilities," Op-30W, March 7, 1947.
62. Ibid.
63. "Some Fundamentals Regarding Sea-Air Power and the U.S. Navy," Briefing to the Eberstadt Committee, 1948 (Washington: Naval Historical Center), 10.
64. Barlow, *From Hot War to Cold*, 21.
65. Ryan, *First Line of Defense*, 13.
66. *Employment of Carrier Forces for Strategic Atomic Attacks* (Maxwell: Air War College, 1948).
67. In a conversation with Admiral Richard L. Connally, Johnson stated, "Admiral, the Navy is on its way out. There's no reason for having a Navy and a Marine Corps. General Bradley tells me amphibious operations are a thing of the past. We'll never have any more amphibious operations. That does away with the Marine Corps. And the Air Force can do anything the Navy can do, so that does away with the Navy." See Victor Krulak, *First to Fight: An Inside View of the U.S. Marine Corps* (Annapolis: Naval Institute Press, 1999), 104.
68. http://www.history.navy.mil/photos/

sh-usn/usnsh-u/cva58.htm, accessed 12 June 2011.

69. Ryan, *First Line of Defense*, 13.

70. Defeat of the Soviet Union by long range bomber attack had been questioned by the CNO as early as 1948 on both technical and moral grounds, an issue that went to the JCS level for discussion. See "Comment on FROLIC as a Brief for Medium-Range Planning," memo from CNO to Joint Chiefs of Staff, "Planning Guidance for Medium Range Emergency Plan," Strategic Plans Division Records, 1948 (Washington: Naval Historical Center).

71. Barlow, *The Revolt of the Admirals*, 208.

72. Two of the most influential articles of the period in the popular *Reader's Digest* were Alexander de Seversky, "Peace Through Air Power," Reader's Digest 54, no. 322 (February 1949): 18–26 and William Bradford Huie, "Why We Must Have the World's Best Air Force," Reader's Digest 54, no. 323 (March 1949): 27–31.

73. Barlow, *Revolt of the Admirals*, 261. Apart from the fraternal connection, the Air Force had guaranteed the Army tactical air support in future operations prior to the hearings, a promise that was soon reneged on in favor of continued SAC development.

74. Ibid.

75. Barlow, *Revolt of the Admirals*, 291.

76. Filmed with the full support the Navy Department, the wildly popular series' thesis was that all campaigns relied to a large degree on the use of sea power. This sometimes presented an unusual interpretation of various campaigns; the "war in the desert," for example, focused almost exclusively on convoys and gives little time to the actual tank battles on land.

Chapter Five

1. The concept of "Jointness" was not mandated by law until the 1980s with the passage of the Goldwater-Nichols Act.

2. Edgar S. Furniss, Jr., *American Military Policy* (New York: Rinehart, 1957), 36.

3. Amos A. Jordan, *American National Security* (Baltimore: Johns Hopkins University Press, 1999), 274.

4. Michael Isenberg, *Shield of the Republic: The United States Navy in an Era of Cold War and Violent Peace, 1945–1962* (New York: St. Martin's Press, 1993), 249.

5. Arguably the most conventional conflict of the period was the Korean War. See David Rees, *Korea: The Limited War* (New York: St. Martin's Press, 1964).

6. It is generally held today, for example, that the Soviets were not planning an invasion of Western Europe in accordance with the classic NATO scenario. This is not to say, however, such an event could not have occurred given the myriad of political complexities of the period. U.S./NATO power was meant to negate the political influence that the USSR, with its massive conventional and nuclear power, would have exercised over Western Europe, Finlandizing it. Constantine and Vladislav Zubok, *Inside the Kremlin's Cold War from Stalin to Khrushchev* (Cambridge: Harvard University Press, 1996) and Andrew Bacevich *Washington Rules* (New York: Metropolitan Books, 2010).

7. "Navy Budgetary Presentations Before the JCS Fiscal Year 1951: Review of Plans, Phase II, Part I," Vol. 1, June 16, 1949, 30.

8. Elmo Zumwalt, *On Watch* (New York: Quadrangle, 1976), 120, and Lehman, *Command of the Seas*.

9. See Spector, *At War at Sea*.

10. The bulk of the U.S. carrier fleet was nuclear. Rickover also wanted larger ships converted or built for nuclear power; two cruisers had nuclear plants, at great cost. See Zumwalt, *On Watch*.

11. Dale O. Smith, "The Role of Air Power since World War II," *Military Affairs* (Vol. XIX, No. 2, Summer 1955).

12. A.E. Sokol, "Sea Power in the Next War," *Proceedings* (Vol. LXXVIII, No. 5, May 1952).

13. Zumwalt, 76.

14. Robert Carney, "The Principles of Sea Power," *Proceedings* (Vol. LXXIX, No. 8, Aug. 1953).

15. http://www.foreignaffairs.com/articles/35850/spurgeon-m-keeny-jr-and-wolfgang-k-h-pabofsky/nuclear-weapons-in-the-1980s-mad-vs-nuts, accessed July 5, 2011.

16. Lawrence Freedman, *The Evolution of Nuclear Strategy* (New York: St. Martin's Press, 1981).

17. Maxwell Taylor, *The Uncertain Trumpet* (New York: Harper Press, 1959), 23.

18. Anthony Buzzard, "Massive Retaliation and Graduated Deterrence." *World Politics* (Vol. III, No. 2, January 1956).

19. Clark G. Reynolds, *Navies in History* (Annapolis: Naval Institute Press, 1998), 230.

20. Joel Sokolsky, *Seapower in the Nuclear Age: The United States Navy and NATO, 1949–1980* (Annapolis: Naval Institute Press, 1991).

21. Ibid., 25.

22. "Regional Estimates of the Situation," in *North Atlantic Treaty Organization Medium Term Defense Plan*, July 1, 1954 (Washington: Naval Historical Center), 164.

23. Isenburg, *Shield of the Republic*, 595.
24. See Paul Nitze and the Atlantic Council Working Group on Securing the Seas, *Securing the Seas: The Soviet Naval Challenge and the Western Alliance Options* (Boulder: Westview Press, 1979), 45.
25. Robert Waring Herrick, *Soviet Naval Theory and Policy* (Annapolis: Naval Institute Press, 1988) and Norman Friedman, *The U.S. Maritime Strategy* (London: Jane's Publishing, 1988). It should be noted that while methods of use varied to some degree, the overwhelming viewpoint of the Soviet Navy during this period was as an offensive force.
26. Peter Huchthausen, *K-19: The Widowmaker* (Washington D.C.: National Geographic, 2002), 22.
27. Nitze, 66.
28. The Soviets eclipsed this capability with the development of the Typhoon class ballistic missile submarine in the 1980s, which could fire its missiles from protected bastions well within Soviet waters. Targeting this capability was a major focus of the Maritime Strategy of the 1980s. See Friedman.
29. Nitze, *Securing the Seas*, 66.
30. S.G. Gorshkov, *The Sea Power of the State* (English Edition. Malabar: Robert Krieger Publishing, 1983).
31. *Ibid.*, 231.
32. In terms of ballistic missile submarines, this is accurate. Soviet submarines had to approach the United States to fire their missiles; the "Yankee" class, for example, had to operate along the U.S. coastline to be effective. It was not until the 1980s with the development of the "Delta IV" and "Typhoon" class that this was rectified. See *Soviet Submarine Design: Theory and Practice*. For problems of interpretation, see Bryan Ranft and Geoffrey Till, *The Sea in Soviet Strategy* (Annapolis: Naval Institute Press, 1989), 3.
33. We must return to Mahan for this viewpoint. Recall that Mahanian inspired doctrine stressed the constant employment of naval forces to meet the enemy in decisive battle; to those in the West brought u in this tradition it was (and is) almost inconceivable that a modern battle fleet could be employed for any other purpose. This argument is being pursued today with regard to the development of the Chinese Navy; see Chapter Nine.
34. Nitze, *Securing the Seas*, 6.
35. *Ibid.*, 57.
36. *Ibid.*, 386.
37. Lawrence Kaplan, *NATO and the United States: The Enduring Alliance* (Boston: Twayne Publishers, 1988), 6.
38. Sokolsky, 67.
39. *Ibid.*, 69. Note that even through the 1980s various "limited war at sea" scenarios were still actively part of the curriculum at the U.S. Naval War College. Author's experience.
40. Isenburg, *Shield of the Republic*, 691.
41. Nitze, *Securing the Seas*, 391.
42. Zumwalt, *On Watch*, 123.
43. Sokolsky, *Seapower in the Nuclear Age*.
44. It is important to note that these upgrades made many previously smaller combatants capital ships in their own right. "Cruisers," for example, ultimately possessed strike power and capability equal to or greater than the battleships of the World War II generation. A Spruance class "Destroyer" possessed advanced air search radar and both surface and land strike missiles (variants of which had nuclear capability) in addition to their ASW capability and were enormous platforms in their own right, a far cry from the smaller specialized ASW variant of World War II. See *Jane's Fighting Ships*, 1960–1980, and Norman Polmar, *Ships of the U.S. Fleet*.
45. Isenberg, *Shield of the Republic*, 691.
46. *Jane's Fighting Ships* of the period reflect this trend in its description of the U.S. fleet. See *Jane's Fighting Ships* (London: Jane's Publishing, 1950–1970).
47. Robert McNamara, *In Retrospect: The Tragedy and Lessons of Vietnam* (New York: Vintage Books, 1996). See also Max Boot, *The Savage Wars of Peace* (New York: Basic Books, 2002).
48. Edward Marolda and Oscar Fitzgerald, *The United States Navy and the Vietnam Conflict, Vol. 2: From Military Assistance to Combat, 1959–1965* (Washington D.C.: Department of the Navy, 1986), 20.
49. *Jane's Fighting Ships, 1960*.
50. See Chapter One.
51. Marolda, 94. See also Oscar Fitzgerald, "U.S. Naval Forces in the Vietnam War: the Advisory Mission, 1961–65," in *Changing Interpretations and New Sources in Naval History: Papers from the Third United States Naval Academy History Symposium* (New York: Garland, 1980).
52. George Baer, *One Hundred Years of Sea Power: The U.S. Navy, 1890–1990* (Stanford: Stanford University Press, 1993), 384.
53. Secretary McNamara, for example, knew full well and appreciated the power of aircraft carriers but refused to build new ones until 1966, causing the Navy to once again engage with the public on the value of carriers in all wars. See James Roherty, *Decisions of Robert B. McNamara: a Study of the Role of the Secretary of Defense* (Miami: University of Miami Press, 1970), 151–172.
54. David McDonald, "Carrier Employment Since 1950," *USNI Proceedings*, Vol. 90 (November 1964), 26–33.

55. Clodfelter, *The Limits of Air Power*.
56. Korea cannot be characterized as a classic "irregular" conflict in the modern vernacular, as early operations were distinctly conventional. However, as the war went on it became a *limited* conflict in that application of power was considerably restricted. See David Ree, *Korea: The Limited War* (New York: Natraj Pub., 1985).
57. Isenburg, *Shield of the Republic*, 184.
58. Spector, *At War At Sea*, 329.
59. Spector, 318.
60. Max Hastings, *The Korean War* (New York: Simon & Schuster, 1987), 266.
61. Reynolds, 220.
62. Hastings, 266.
63. Frank Manson, *The Sea War in Korea* (Annapolis: Naval Institute Press, 1957), 281–284.
64. Frank Uhlig Jr., *How Navies Fight: The U.S. Navy and its Allies* (Annapolis: Naval Institute Press, 1994), 306.
65. Mahan, *The Influence of Sea Power on History*, 225.
66. Hastings, 330.
67. Isenburg, 220.
68. A common term referring to America's hesitancy to commit military force following the war is "Vietnam syndrome." See Arnold Issacs, *Vietnam Shadows: The War, Its Ghosts, and Its Legacy* (Baltimore: Johns Hopkins University Press, 1997). This would change after the first Gulf War and the implementation of the so called "Powell Doctrine." See Andrew Basevich, *Washington Rules: America's Path to Permanent War* (New York: Metropolitan Books, 2011).
69. Max Boot, *The Savage Wars of Peace* (New York: Basic Books, 2002), 304.
70. Neil Sheehan, *A Bright and Shining Lie: John Paul Vann and America in Vietnam* (New York: Vintage Books, 1989), 300.
71. Baler, *One Hundred Years of Sea Power*, 387.
72. Mark Clodfelter, *The Limits of Air Power: The American Bombing of North Vietnam* (New York: The Free Press, 1989).
73. Robert McNamara, *In Retrospect*, 171.
74. Spector, *At War at Sea*, 367.
75. The degree to which the North supplied the insurgency using the sea is controversial. General consensus by modern historians is that this was in fact minimal. See Spector, Brown Water, and Reynolds.
76. Thomas Cutler, *Brown Water, Black Berets* (Annapolis: Naval Institute Press, 2000).
77. Baer, 389.
78. Don Sheppard, *Riverine* (New York: Presidio, 1992) and Spector, 359. Interestingly, the "brown water" force viewed itself in an entirely different light, the caliber of its operations generating an elite status within the small community.
79. The most famous of these vessels was the Destroyer Escort (DE) VANCE, the seat of the famous "Arnheiter affair," the only near mutiny in U.S. Navy history. See Neil Sheehan, *The Arnheiter Affair* (New York: Random House, 1972).
80. Multiple sources agree on the failure of this metric. See Karnow, *Vietnam: A History* (Chap. 10), Sheehan, *A Bright and Shining Lie* (Chap. 3) and Basevich *Washington Rules* (Chap. 3).
81. Don Shepard, *Destroyer Skipper: A Memoir of Command at Sea* (New York: Presidio, 1996), 18.
82. Baer, *One Hundred Years of Sea Power*, 390.
83. Spector, 360.
84. *Ibid.*, 363.
85. In the recriminations following the war there was considerable debate surrounding the "limitations" placed on airpower and how if these limitations had been lifted the war could have taken a different course. Although most of this debate centered on the use of Air Force strategic bombing, it also extended to the use of naval air power, which was extensive. Mark Clodfelter, *The Limits of Air Power*.
86. The Navy lost 421 aircraft shot down during the 37 months of the "Rolling Thunder" campaign. Frank Uhlig, *How Navies Fight: The U.S. Navy and Its Allies* (Annapolis: Naval Institute Press, 1994), 327.
87. The North Vietnamese, at war's end, possessed one of the most sophisticated AAW networks in the world. *Ibid.*, 326.
88. The Army, for example, began to study the IW concept seriously during Vietnam and continued at its Special Operations Centers in North Carolina and Panama until the present day. See http://www.soc.mil/swcs/_pdf/AcademicHandbook.pdf, accessed June 1, 2011.
89. The exception to this was the SEAL community which was fairly well established in the special operations world.
90. Zumwalt, 519. Zumwalt was particularly insistent on this point. In testimony, he noted that Soviet naval construction from 1966–1970 was 237 percent higher than the U.S., broken down as follows:

	U.S.	U.S.S.R.	Difference
Major combatants	9	20	222%
Minor combatants	28	138	490%
Amphibious	24	10	42%
Subs	27	152	152%
Total	88	209	237%

91. Zumwalt, 60.
92. *Ibid.*, 72.

93. Geoffrey Till, *Maritime Strategy in the Nuclear Age* (New York: St. Martin's Press, 1982), 63.
94. The "unions" in the Navy are generally recognized as Surface, Submarine, and Air—all of whom compete within the bureaucracy for funding and influence. The Sea Control Shi was resisted by the Air union as it employed VSTOL technology that (at the time) was unproven—and generally disdained by the strike fighter community. Zumwalt, 75.
95. The rationale was that these ships—which were relegated to counter-narcotics patrol and other special missions in the Caribbean—used too much fuel to be effective. Author experience.
96. Stansfield Turner, "The Missions of the U.S. Navy," (Newport: *Naval War College Review*, Fall 1975).
97. See Navy Capstone documents *Strategic Concepts of the U.S. Navy* (Washington: Chief of Naval Operations 1978) and *The Future of U.S. Sea Power* (Washington: Chief of Naval Operations, reprinted in USNI Proceedings, October 1979).

Chapter Six

1. The Navy's budget doubled from 1980–1985. Naval Department Library/Naval Historical Center/www.history.navy.mil/library/online/budget.htm.
2. Michael D. Wormser ed., *U.S. Defense Policy: Congressional Quarterly* (Washington D.C.: Congressional Quarterly Inc., 1983), 27.
3. The first iteration of the Maritime Strategy was a classified document issued in 1982. John Hattendorf, *The Evolution of the U.S. Navy's Maritime Strategy, 1977–1986* (Newport: NWC Newport Papers 19, 2004), 194.
4. Ibid., 89.
5. John Lehman, "The 600 Ship Navy," (Annapolis: USNI *Proceedings*, January 1986).
6. The plan ultimately called for the expansion from to 1, 2, 15, Carrier battle groups, an increase of roughly 150 ships. Note that unlike air or land systems, ship service life is roughly 20 years or longer. This was a fleet designed for strategic duration. See Wormser, 27.
7. Ronald Reagan, *National Security Strategy of the United States* (The White House, National Security Strategy, January 1987), 29–30.
8. John Lehman, *Command of the Seas* (New York: Scribner's, 1988). See also Michael A. Palmer, *Origins of the Maritime Strategy: American Naval Strategy in the First Postwar Decade* (Washington D.C.: Naval Historical Center, 1988).
9. Norman Friedman, *The U.S. Maritime Strategy* (London: Jane's Publishing, 1988), 141.
10. George W. Baer, *One Hundred Years of Sea Power*, 402.
11. Lehman, "The 600 Ship Navy," 37.
12. Stansfield Turner, "Sea Control," 2. See also Paul Nitze, *Securing the Seas: The Soviet Naval Challenge and Western Alliance Options* (Boulder: Westview Press, 1979).
13. Frederick H. Hartmann, *Naval Renaissance: The U.S. Navy in the 1980s* (Annapolis: Naval Institute Press, 1990), 27–30.
14. Daniel Deudney, "Pushing and Pulling: The Western System, Nuclear Weapons, and Soviet Change," *International Politics* (Vol 48, July–September 2011), 498.
15. Michael Cox, "Western Capitalism and the Cold War System," in *War, State, and Society* (M. Shaw, ed. London: Macmillan, 1984), 136–94. See also Julian Zelizer, *The Arsenal of Democracy: The Politics of National Security from World War II to the War on Terrorism* (New York: Basic Books, 2010), 303.
16. Lehman, *Command of the Seas*.
17. Keith L. Shimko, "Reagan on the Soviet Union and the Nature of International Conflict," (Political Psychology, Vol. 13, No. 3. Sep., 1992), 353–377. Article Stable URL: http://www.jstor.org/stable/3791603.
18. Edward Luttwak, *The Pentagon and the Art of War* (New York: Simon & Schuster, 1985), 255.
19. Linton Brooks, "Naval Power and National Security: The Case for the Maritime Strategy" (Boston: MIT Press, *International Security*, Vol. II, No. Autumn 2, 1986), 59.
20. Mahan was cited in the sense of his focus on decisive battle. Like previous uses of (and modification) of Mahanian theory, his other elements such as development of merchant power, colonies, etc., were ignored. *The Maritime Strategy* (Annapolis: USNI *Proceedings* supplement January 1986).
21. Friedman, *The Maritime Strategy*, 138.
22. Zbigniew, Brzezinski, "Game Plan: The Geostrategic Framework for the Conduct of the U.S.-Soviet Contest," (Boston: Atlantic Monthly Press, 1986), 191–192.
23. The Navy was very clear on this element of the strategy. See Baer, 425.
24. Ronald Spector, *At War at Sea* (Annapolis: Naval Institute Press, 2001).
25. Layered defense of high value assets (carriers) was first developed and perfected during the Second World War. See Wayne Hughes, *Fleet Tactics* (Annapolis: Naval Institute Press, 1989).
26. Prior to the release of the Maritime Strategy professional writing on naval strategy was extremely sparse; in "An Examina-

tion of the Professional Concerns of Naval Officers as Reflected in Their Professional Journal," (NWC Review Vol. No 3, 3, 1, January–February 1988), Linton Brooks notes that in a 25 year history of USNI *Proceedings* on 3 articles were written by flag officers on strategy—of 719 articles written from 1964–68, there were only 2. Conversely after the publication of the *Maritime Strategy* there were hundreds; see Peter Schwartz, *The Maritime Strategy Debates* (Newport: Naval War College Papers 19, 2004).

27. Baer, 442.

28. The first combatant developed for irregular operations, the PC-179, was launched in 1993—to be met with considerable controversy. See http://www.navy.mil/navydata/fact_display.asp?cid=4200&tid=2000&ct=4, accessed June 1, 2011; and Chapter Eight.

29. Watkins, James. "Current Strategy of the U.S. Navy" (*Los Angeles Times*, June 21, 1984), 22. See also Floyd Kennedy, "From SLOC Protection to a National Maritime Strategy," in *Peace and War* (Kenneth Hagen, ed., Westport: Greenwood, 1984), 304–326.

30. *The Maritime Strategy.*

31. Alan Zimm, "The First Salvo" (Annapolis: USNI *Proceedings*, February 1985), 55–60.

32. Joel Sokolsky, *Sea Power and the Nuclear Age: The United States Navy and NATO, 1949–1980* (Annapolis: Naval Institute Press, 1991).

33. These efforts largely failed. U-boats were defeated through a variety of means, most notably through the use of intelligence and signals analysis. Submarine bases, however, were always a prime target. See *Undersea Warfare*.

34. Submarine operations during the Cold War were (and are) highly classified. A number of works have been written on these operations; the first was Sherry Sontag's *Blind Man's Bluff* (New York: Harper Books, 2000). Criticized when it was first published for research, additional works have followed that confirm the "cat and mouse" submarine games played between U.S. and Soviet submarines.

35. The LA class was designated a "direct support" submarine in its design concept. See John Collins, *U.S.-Soviet Military Balance, 1980–1985* (Washington: Pergamon, 1985).

36. Most sources of the period assumed that Soviet forces (and doctrine) all were offensive. See Phillip Karber, "The Battle of Unengaged Military Strategies," in *Soviet Power and Western Negotiating Policies* (Cambridge: Ballinger Publishing, 1983), 226. See also Steven Miller, "The Northern Seas in Soviet and U.S. Strategy," in *Nuclear Disengagement in Europe* (London: Taylor and Francis, 1983), 117–137.

37. This was a common NATO planning assumption, voiced by Lehman in "A 600 Ship Navy," 36.

38. Office of the Chief of Naval Operations, *Understanding Soviet Naval Developments, 5th ed.*, (Washington D.C., U.S. Government Printing Office, 1985). See also T. Fitzgerald, "Blitzkreig at Sea," (Annapolis: USNI *Proceedings*, January 1986), 12–16.

39. This reflected standard NATO planning. See Steven Biddle, "Strategy in War," (*Political Science and Politics*, Vol. 40, No. 3 July, 2007), 461–466.

40. John Lehman, *Command of the Seas.* See also Zumwalt, *On Watch.*

41. Baer, 443.

42. Swartz, *The Maritime Strategy Debates.*

43. Passed in 1985, the act mandated Joint Duty for flag promotion.

44. Peter Schwartz, "Evolution of Navy Strategy," unclassified briefing to USN Chief of Naval Operations Staff (N35), March 2005.

45. Fred Ikle, "The Reagan Defense Program: A Focus on the Strategic Imperatives," (*Strategic Review*, Spring 1982), 11–18.

46. James L. George ed., *Problems of Sea Power as We Approach the Twenty-First Century* (Washington D.C.: American Enterprise Institute for Public Policy Research, 1978), 195.

47. Gene R. LaRouche, "Commentary," in *Problems of Sea Power,* 197.

48. See *The Maritime Strategy.*

49. John Lehman, *Aircraft Carriers: The Real Choices* (Beverly Hills: Sage, for the Center for Strategic and International Studies, 1978), 76–86.

50. *Soviet Naval Strategy and Programs through the 1990s: National Intelligence Estimate* (Washington D.C.: Central Intelligence Agency, 1983).

51. A classic statement of this is contained in Hans Morgenthau, "The United States and Europe in a Decade of Détente," in *The United States and Western Europe: Political, Economic and Strategic Perspectives* (Cambridge: Winthrop, 1974. W. Handreider, ed.), 1–7.

52. Baer, 438.

53. Federal Minister of Defense, Federal Republic of Germany, *White Paper 1985: The Situation and Development of the Federal Armed Forces,* 27–29.

54. D. Rivkin, "No Bastions for the Bear," (Annapolis: USNI *Proceedings,* April 1984), 36–43.

55. John J. Mearsheimer, "A Strategic Misstep: The Maritime Strategy and Deterrence in Europe" (International Security Vol. 11, No. 2, Autumn, 1986), 3–57.

56. Barry Posen, "Inadvertent Nuclear War? Escalation and NATO's Northern Flank," (*International Security*, Fall 1982), 28–54.
57. Michael Gannon, *Operation Drumbeat* (Michigan: University of Michigan Press, 193), 510.
58. S. Landersman, "Naval Protection of Shipping: A Lost Art?" (Newport: *Naval War College Review*, March–April 1986), 23–34.
59. R. Watts, "Defending our Shores," (Annapolis: USNI *Proceedings*, September 1987).
60. http://www.globalsecurity.org/military/agency/dot/mdz.htm.
61. *Maritime Defense Zone: Concept of Operations* (New York: Coast Guard Atlantic Area, 1987).
62. "OCEAN SAFARI '85: Meeting the Threat in the North Atlantic," (*All Hands*, January 1986), 20–29.
63. Mobile Undersea Warfare (MIUW) units, for example, were manned entirely by naval reservists with no identified role overseas.
64. *Maritime Defense Zone: Concept of Operations*.
65. The ensuing confusion in coordinating operations was a direct factor in the passage of the Goldwater-Nichols Act of 1986 which mandated the development of "jointness." Ronald H. Cole, "Grenada, Panama, and Haiti: Joint Operational Reform," Joint Forces Quarterly (Washington: NDU University Press, Fall 2003).
66. In this case the operation is classified as "irregular" as Grenada was not the enemy, but rather a small group of revolutionaries, many of whom were not professional soldiers.
67. http://www.history.navy.mil/faqs/faq95-2.htm, accessed September 12, 2011.
68. Fred Hiatt, "Accidents, 'Friendly Fire' Blamed for Many U.S. Casualties in Grenada," *Washington Post*, November 1, 1983.
69. Edward Luttwak, *The Pentagon and the Art of War* (New York: Simon & Schuster, 1985), 54.
70. In the immediate aftermath the threat was exaggerated, given the casualties suffered by the U.S. during the operation. Richard Halloran, *New York Times*, October 30, 1983.
71. Luttwak, 56.
72. Reporter George Wilson who was on scene speculates that the battleship did not demonstrate the proper "resolve" that would be demonstrated by an airstrike. George Wilson, *Super Carrier* (New York: Berkley Books, 1988), 163.
73. *Ibid*. See also Ki Cooper, "Admiral Blames Washington for Loss of 2 Planes over Syria," San Diego Union, May 12, 1984, 4–5.
74. Max Boot, *The Savage Wars of Peace: Small Wars and the Rise of American Power* (New York: Basic Books, 2002), 320.
75. *Ibid*.
76. Lehman, *Command of the Seas*, 119.
77. Zelizer, *Arsenal of Democracy*, 303.
78. *Ibid*., 354.

Chapter Seven

1. Amos Jordan, William Taylor, and Michael Mazarr, *American National Security* (Baltimore: Johns Hopkins University Press, 1999), 545.
2. Eugene Russell, "Low Intensity Conflict in a Changed and Changing World," National Security Papers: GAO Conference on Worldwide Threats, *GAO International Affairs Policy 92–104S* (Washington D.C.: April 1992), 126.
3. Chris Lawson, "Battle for 12 ARGs Gathers New Steam" (Washington: Navy Times, 812/94, Vol 4. Issue 3, 46), 6.
4. Fleet composition is noted in *Jane's Fighting Ships* 1980–1990. See also Norman Polmar, *Ships and Aircraft of the U.S. Fleet* (Annapolis: Naval Institute Press, 1987).
5. Chester A. Crocker, ed., *Leashing the Dogs of War: Conflict Management in a Divided World* (Washington D.C.: United States Institute of Peace, 2007), 7.
6. *Budgeting for Naval Forces: Structuring Tomorrow's Navy at Today's Budget Levels* (Washington D.C.: Congressional Budgeting Office, October 2000), 2.
7. H. Gaffney ed., *U.S. Naval Response to Situations, 1970–1999* (Alexandria: Center for Naval Analyses, December 2000), 54.
8. *Ibid*., 55.
9. Steve Yetiv, *The Persian Gulf Crisis* (Westport: Greenwood Press, 1997), 6.
10. David Johnson, *Learning Large Lessons: The Evolving Power of Ground Power and Air Power in the Post-Cold War Era* (Santa Monica: Rand, 2007), 32. See also John Ballard, *From Storm to Freedom: America's Long War with Iraq* (Annapolis: Naval Institute Press, 2010), 51.
11. Ronald Post, *Sealift in Operations Desert Shield and Desert Storm, August 7, 1990–February 17, 1991* (Washington D.C.: Center for Naval Analysis, 1998), 10.
12. Joy Gordon, "Economic Sanctions and Global Governance: the Case of Iraq" (Routledge: *Global Crime*, Vol. 10. No. 4, November 2009), 360.
13. J. Lukas, "Lessons from Desert Storm"

(Quantico: *Marine Corps Gazette*, May 1998), 78.

14. *Iraqi Naval Strength*, at www.globalsecurity.org/military/world/iraq/navy.htm.

15. Richard Stewart, *War in the Persian Gulf: Operations Desert Shield and Desert Storm* (Carlyle: Center for Military History, 2010), 71.

16. Katherine Schinesi, "Naval Mine Warfare: Plans to Improve Countermeasures Unclear," *NSIAD 980135* (Washington D.C.: Government Accounting Office, 1998), 2.

17. Ballard, 35.

18. Norman Schwarzkopf, "Press Briefing," *Military Review*, Vol. 71, Issue 9, 96–108.

19. John Hattendorf ed., *U.S. Naval Strategy in the 1990s: Selected Documents* (Newport: Naval War College Papers 27, September 2006), 10.

20. Ultimately the Navy would only have 12 carriers, with one in reserve for a total of 13.

21. "Arleigh Burke FL 1 & 2 Class," *Jane's Defense and Security Analysis*, March 24, 2011, 1. See also Robert Holzer, "Navy Scrutinizes Greater Variety of DDG-51 Alternatives," *Defense News*, October 28, 1991, 42.

22. Gaffney, *U.S. Naval Responses*, 154.

23. The first Arleigh Burke cost close to a billion dollars. Subsequent models were cheaper but still were extremely expensive combatants. See Carlyle Trost, "A Report on the Posture and Budget of the U.S. Navy, Fiscal Year 1991," Statement to the House Armed Services Committee, February 20, 1990.

24. Senator Sam Nunn, "Implementing a New Military Strategy: The Budget Decisions," remarks prepared for delivery, April 20, 1990, 1.

25. Stan Zimmerman, "Talk of Mission Consolidation Grows in the Senate," *Navy News and Undersea Technology*, May 14, 1990, 1–3.

26. Carlyle Trost, "A Maritime Strategy for the 1990s," USNI *Proceedings* (Annapolis: Naval Institute Press, May 1990), 92–100.

27. Frank Kelso, "The Way Ahead," *USNI Proceedings* (Annapolis: Naval Institute Press, April 1991), 36.

28. Although considered friendly to the Navy as a whole, the Naval Institute is an independent forum for sea power widely respected for its willingness to publish on topics that do not necessarily agree with policy. It was (and is) frequently used by the Navy to publish various positions on strategy and policy—and, equally, employed by critics.

29. Kelso, 37.

30. The Navy shipbuilding plan for capital ships FY 1993 (projected to FY 2000) was as follows:

Ship Class	FY 1993	FY 2000 Projection
Ticonderoga-class cruiser	17	22
Spruance-class destroyer	23	31
Arleigh-Burke-class destroyer	1	33

Note that although the carrier force was reduced from 14 to 12, this reflected the retirement of most conventional carriers and the future addition of 2 new nuclear vessels. The building of the new Arleigh-Burke DDG—a capital platform designed specifically for strike—almost doubled the size of the capital ship fleet. See *Navy Carrier Battle Groups: The Structure and Affordability of the Future Force*, GAO/NSIAD-93-74 (Washington D.C.: U.S. General Accounting Office Report to Congress, February 1993), 35.

31. B. Duffy, "The Shrinking of the Pentagon," *U.S. News and World Report*, Vol. 104, Issue 9, March 7, 1988, 34.

32. "One, Two, Many Wars" (*Progressive*, Vol. 10, October 1993), 57.

33. Within the Pentagon there was actually a movement supported by the new neoconservative movement to make the U.S. the world's dominant superpower as opposed to move away from the Cold War model. When leaked a document describing this proposal caused considerable embarrassment in the administration. See Julian Zelizer, *Arsenal of Democracy* (New York: Basic Books, 2010), 381.

34. Maj. Francis G. Hoffman, "Comment and Discussion on 'The Way Ahead,'" USNI *Proceedings*, June 1991, 14.

35. William H. McMichael, *The Mother of All Hooks: the Story of the U.S. Navy's Tailhook Scandal* (Brunswick: Transaction Publications, 1997), 20.

36. Melissa Healy, "Pentagon Blasts Tailhook Probe, Two Admirals Resign," *Los Angeles Times*, September 25, 1992.

37. Zelizer, *The Arsenal of Democracy*, 383.

38. Hattendorf, *Naval Strategies of the 1990s*, 39.

39. Ernani Lacson, *TQL As It Applies to the Surface Navy* (Monterey: Naval Post Graduate School Monterey, 1998), 34.

40. J.M. Boorda, "From the Sea," *USNI Proceedings* (Annapolis: Naval Institute Press, September 1992), 2.

41. Hattendorf, 87.

42. The Marines have always had a finely tuned public relations program designed to constantly illustrate the Corps' values, ranging from Commandant Vandegraft's "bended

knee" speech to Congress in 1946 (widely credited with saving the Marines from merging with the Army) to its current strategy. See *U.S. Marine Corps Strategic Communications Plan* (Quantico: U.S. Marine Corps, 2010).

43. http://articles.latimes.com/1991-02-01/news/mn-362_1_gulf-war, accessed November 11, 2011. The actual defense budget was reduced by 60 billion dollars in the 1990s.

44. Boorda, "From the Sea," 3.

45. *Ibid.*

46. *Ibid.*

47. See Chapter Six.

48. A remarkable assumption given the capability of modern diesel submarines, as demonstrated in the Falklands conflict as well as in practical demonstrations of deployment capability. See Richard Scott, "New Submarine Concepts Ready to Break Surface" (London: *Jane's Defense and Security Review*, May 2008), 9.

49. Diesel submarines are exceptionally good at exploiting the variable underwater environmental conditions of the littoral. *Ibid.*

50. David Miller, "The Silent Menace: Diesel Submarines in 1993" (London: *Jane's International Defense and Security Review*, Vol. 26/008, August 1993), 15.

51. Hattendorf, *Naval Strategies of the 1990s*, 50.

52. Ziegler, 386.

53. Gaffney, *U.S. Naval Responses to Situations*, 56.

54. This retrenchment ultimately became known as "the Blackhawk down effect." See John Hirsch, "The Blackhawk Down Effect," *Foreign Policy* (Washington: August 12, 2011), 5.

55. Boorda, "Forward, From the Sea," 1.

56. Hattendorf, *Naval Strategies of the 1990s*, 65.

57. Boorda, 3.

58. *Budgeting for Naval Forces*, 36.

59. Admiral Jay Johnson, "Forward from the Sea ... the Navy Operational Concept," *USNI Proceedings* (Annapolis: Naval Institute Press, March 1997), 20.

60. Admiral Jay Johnson, "Anywhere, Anytime: A Navy for the 21st Century," *USNI Proceedings* (Annapolis: Naval Institute Press, November 1997), 42.

61. Jack Levy, "International Sources of Interstate and Intrastate War," in *Leashing the Dogs of War* (Washington D.C.: United States Institute of Peace, 2008), 28.

62. Gaffney, *U.S. Naval Responses*, 63.

63. The move to the F-18 began in the mid–1990s with the retirement of a number of mission specific aircraft, including the A-36 "Prowler" fighter-bomber and the ASW/ASUW S-3 "Viking." Officially this was an increase in capability, although the point is debatable as the new plane carried far less ordinance than those it was replacing. It was, however, faster, leading to an internal argument that the change was driven by the fighter "union." Author experience, Pentagon, 2006.

64. Gaffney, *U.S. Naval Responses*, 75.

65. *Ibid.*

66. *Ibid.*, 64.

67. Author experience.

68. Gaffney, 73.

69. Abuh Shah, "Effects of Iraq Sanctions," Global Issues at www.globalissues.org, accessed October 15, 2010.

Chapter Eight

1. This was a theory postulated in a famous article of the same name by Francis Fukyama who speculated that the triumph of liberal democracy represented the ultimate political development and would naturally herald peace. See Francis Fukyama, "The End of History" in *The National Interest*, October 1989.

2. Joseph Collins, *Understanding War in Afghanistan* (Washington: National Defense University Press, 2011), 46.

3. A broad survey of reports compiled by the Government Accounting Office during the pre–9/11 period indicate that the overwhelming concern regarding terrorism was its potential use against American targets overseas. See Status of DOD Efforts to Protect Forces Overseas, *GAO/NSIAD-97-207 (Washington: Government Accountability Office, 2007).*

4. Karlyn Browning, *Attitudes Toward Terror and the War on Afghanistan: A Ten Year Review* (Washington D.C.: American Enterprise Institute Center for Public Policy, 2011), 9.

5. *Homeland Security: Management Challenges Facing Federal Leadership*, GAO-03-26 (Washington D.C.: Government Accounting Office, December 2002), 22.

6. T.X. Hammes, *The Sling and the Stone: On War in the 21st Century* (St. Paul: Zenith Press, 2004), 195.

7. See Bruce Hoffman, *Inside Terrorism* (Columbia: Columbia University Press, 2006). See also A.J. Rapin, "What is Terrorism?" in *Behavioral Sciences of Terrorism and Political Aggression* (Vol. 3. Issue 3, September 9, 2011), 161.

8. Henry Eccles, *Military Power in a Free Society* (Honolulu: University Press of the Pacific, 1979), 55.

9. Zelizer, *The Arsenal of Democracy*, 446.

10. Stephen Flynn, *America the Vulnerable* (New York: HarperCollins, 2004), 10.

11. Ibid., 17.

12. While on Pentagon duty, for example, the author was tasked with examining the likelihood of the use of Al Qaida submarines, cruise missiles, and attacks against such esoteric targets as fish stocks.

13. "Homeland Security Generates Multi-Billion Dollar Business," USA TODAY, September 16, 2006, accessed at http://www.usatoday.com/money/industries/2006-09-10-security-industry_x.htm.

14. David Walker, Comptroller General of the United States. *Homeland Security: A Framework for Addressing the Nation's Efforts*, Statement Before Congress (Washington D.C.: General Accounting Office, GAO-01-1158T, September 21, 2001), 4.

15. T.X. Hammes, "Rethinking the Principles of War: The Future of Warfare," in *Rethinking the Principles of War* (Annapolis: Naval Institute Press, 2005), 270.

16. Henry Eccles, *Military Concepts and Philosophy* (Rutgers: Rutgers University Press, 1967), 66.

17. Glenn Kent, *Thinking About America's Defense: An Analytical Memoir* (Santa Monica: Rand, 2008), 105.

18. Ziegler, *The Arsenal of Democracy*, 300. See also Bacevich, *Washington Rules* (Chap. 1).

19. Joseph Jockel and Joel Sokolsky, "Canada's Cold War Nuclear Experience," *Pondering NATO's Nuclear Options* (Kingston: Queen's Quarterly, 1999), 108.

20. Bacevich, *Washington Rules*, 30. See also Bacevich, *American Empire*, 36.

21. Douglas Feith, *War and Decision: Inside the Pentagon at the Dawn of the War on Terrorism* (New York: Harper, 2008), 9. Note Baseovich disagrees with this in Washington Rules.

22. James Loy, "Meeting the Homeland Security Challenge: A Principled Strategy for a Balanced and Practical Response" (Washington D.C.: U.S. Coast Guard, October 2001), 2.

23. For methodology prior to and after 9/11, see S. Hrg. 107-1086: Joint Inquiry into Intelligence Community Activities Before and After the Terrorist Attacks of September 11, 2001. *Hearings before the Select Committee on Intelligence, U.S. Senate and the Permanent Select Committee on Intelligence, House of Representatives*, Vol. I, September 18, 19, 20, 24, and 26, 2002.

24. See Martha Crenshaw, "Terrorism, Strategies, and Grand Strategies," in *Attacking Terrorism: Elements of a Grand Strategy*, Audrey Cronin, ed., (Washington: Georgetown University Press, 2004), 74. See also Bruce Hoffman, *Inside Terrorism* (New York: Columbia University Press, 2006), 175.

25. Colin Gray, "Thinking Asymmetrically in Times of Terror," *Parameters*, U.S. Army War College Quarterly, Spring 2002, 8.

26. The most common being the smuggling of WMD through various maritime conveyances such as containers. See Stephen Flynn, *America the Vulnerable* (New York: Vintage, 2005).

27. Hoffman, 34.

28. The point here is not that terrorist groups do not desire these weapons; Laqueur argued as early as 1996 that some groups (such as ALQ) would seek to do so. The point is the American public saw this as almost certain rather than unlikely. See Walter Laqueur, "Postmodern Terrorism," *Foreign Affairs* 75, 5 (September–October 1996): 34.

29. Robert J. Art, "Geopolitics Updated: The Strategy for Selective Engagement," *International Security* 23, 3 (Winter 1998–99): 85.

30. Hoffman, *Inside Terrorism*, 229.

31. Graham Allison, *Nuclear Terrorism: the Ultimate Preventable Catastrophe* (New York: Times Books, 2004), 4.

32. See Dennis Gormley, "Unmanned Air Vehicles as Terror Weapons: Real or Imagined?" (Global Security Newswire, www.nti.org, July 1, 2005). Also author experience, threat analysis USN liaison, Pentagon, 2004.

33. David Smigielski, "Review of the Suitcase Nuclear Bomb Controversy," (Washington D.C.: Russian American Nuclear Security Advisory Council, September 2003), 11.

34. See the Gilmore Commission, *Towards a National Strategy for Combating Terrorism* (Washington D.C.: Government Printing Office, December 15, 2000), 5.

35. U.S. Coast Guard, *Maritime Strategy for Homeland Security* (Washington D.C.: U.S. Coast Guard, 2002), 7.

36. The first unit dedicated exclusively to maritime IW, a riverine force, was deployed to Iraq in 2007, almost 4 years after the start of war. See Ronald O'Rourke, *Navy Irregular Warfare and Counterterrorism Operations: Background Issues for Congress* (Washington D.C.: Congressional Research Service, November 2011), 8.

37. Rebecca Grant, *Battle-Tested: Carrier Aviation in Afghanistan and Iraq* (Washington D.C.: IRIS Press, 2005), 2.

38. Benjamin Lambeth, *American Carrier Air Power at the Dawn of a New Century* (Santa Monica: Rand, 2005), 12.

39. William A. Arkin, "A Week of War," *Washington Post*, October 14, 2001.

40. Lambeth, 15.
41. *Ibid.*, 16.
42. Steve Vogel, "Gas Stations in the Sky Extend Fighters' Reach," *Washington Post*, November 1, 2001.
43. Lambeth, 13.
44. Rumsfeld, Donald. *Annual Report to the President and Congress* (Washington, D.C.: Department of Defense, December 2002), 30. See also Benjamin Lambeth, *Air Power Against Terror: Operation Enduring Freedom* (Santa Monica: Rand, 2001), 138.
45. J.D. Oliver, "Use the Carriers or Lose Them," USNI *Proceedings*, September 1993, 70.
46. Grant, 74.
47. *Sea Power Magazine* (Washington D.C.: Dept. of the Navy, March 2002), 5.
48. Tony Capaccio, "Sixty Percent of Bombs Dropped on Afghanistan Precision-Guided," Bloomberg.com, November 20, 2001.
49. Lambeth, *American Carrier Air Power*, 34.
50. Admiral Vern Clark, *Sea Power 21: Projecting Decisive Joint Capability* (Annapolis: USNI *Proceedings* (insert), October 2002).
51. "Military Transformation: Navy Efforts Should be More Integrated and Focused," *United States General Accounting Office Report to Congressional Committees*, GAO-01-853 (Washington D.C.: General Accounting Office, August 2001), 23.
52. Clark, *Waging Modern War*, 9.
53. *Ibid.*, 7.
54. Thomas Hone, "Sea Basing: Poised for Takeoff" (Washington, D.C.: Office of Transformation, Dept. of Defense, February 2005), 7.
55. Clark, 5.
56. Vice Admiral Mike Mullen, in "Sea Shield: Projecting Global Defensive Assurance," *Sea Power 21: Projecting Decisive Joint Capabilities* (Washington: U.S. Navy, 2003), 14.
57. "Navy Transformation: Hearing Before the Readiness Sub-Committee of the Committee of Armed Services, House of Representatives, 109th Congress" (Washington, D.C.: House of Representatives, April 2006), 8.
58. This was a frequent criticism of Secretary of Defense for Homeland Defense Paul McHale. Paul McHale, speech to the Naval War College, March 2005.
59. Secretary Donald Rumsfeld Interview with Georgie Anne Geyer, UPS, November 11, 2001. WMD were never found in Iraq and by all accounts the Iraqi WMD program was at best in its infancy.
60. Bob Woodward, *Plan of Attack* (New York: Simon & Schuster, 2004), 7.
61. Feith, *War and Decision*, 395.
62. Lambeth, *American Carrier Air Power*, 43.
63. *Ibid.*, 45.
64. Grant, 144.
65. Lt Gen Michael Mosely, *Operation Iraqi Freedom: By the Numbers* (Shaw AFB: Assessment and Analysis Division, U.S. Central Command, April 30, 2003), 6–10.
66. Grant, 158.
67. The President landing in flight suit on a carrier to make this pre-mature announcement of victory in Afghanistan seemed to further emphasize the decisive role of sea-based airpower, although it was widely regarded later as a political gaffe.
68. For one of the best accounts of the Iraq devolution see Dexter Filkins, *The Forever War* (New York: Vintage Press, 2009).
69. Jonathan Steele, *Ghosts of Afghanistan* (Berkeley: Counterpoint Publishing, 2011), 203.
70. Preventative war was the fundamental premise of the "Bush Doctrine" further articulated in the *National Security Strategy of the United States* (Washington D.C.: The White House, 2002).
71. Paul Parfomak, *Liquified Natural Gas (LNG) Infrastructure Security: Background and Issues for Congress* (Washington D.C.: Congressional Research Service, September 9, 2003), 20.
72. "The Cruise Missile Threat: Prospects for Homeland Defense," *National Security Watch* (Arlington: Institute of Land Warfare, 2006), 2.
73. Michael McNicholas, *Maritime Security* (New York: Elsevier, 2008), 116.
74. *National Plan to Achieve Maritime Domain Awareness*, Office of the Secretary of Defense for Homeland Defense, Washington D.C., 2005, 9.
75. Flynn, *America the Vulnerable*, 74.
76. McNicholas, *Maritime Security*, 225.
77. James Carafano, "Small Boats, Big Worries: Thwarting Terrorist Attacks from the Sea," *Backgrounder* (Washington D.C.: Heritage Foundation, June 11, 2007), 2.
78. This was validated to some extent by the Mumbai terrorist attack. See Joseph Trindull, "The Mumbai Attacks: Lessons for the Western World," in *Dompre Journal*, Issue V, vol. 1, January 2009.
79. James Wylie, "North American Maritime Homeland Security and Defense," (Washington D.C.: Center for Naval Analyses, January 16, 2004), 4.
80. David Chase, "Posse Comitatus: A Nineteenth Century Law Worthy of Review for the Future," (Carlyle: U.S. Army Command and Staff College, 2001), 5.

Notes—Chapter Eight

81. The reality of Posse Comitatus is far more complicated; it was originally written to prevent Northern troops from enforcing the law against Southerners after the Civil War, specifically voting rights for free slaves, but it has since come to be viewed as a cornerstone of the idea that U.S. citizens will be free of civil military interference in law enforcement. See Gary Felicetti and John Luce, "The Posse Comitatus Act: Liberation from the Lawyers," *Parameters* no. 3 (Fall 2004) 34.

82. The Navy first became involved in LE support missions during the Reagan administration with assistance to the counternarcotics effort; a mission that was never fully embraced. See *Drug Control: Assets DOD Contributes to Reducing the Illegal Drug Supply Have Declined* (Washington D.C.: Government Accounting Office, Report to Congressional Requestors, 1999), 15.

83. Clark McCauley, "Psychological Issues in Understanding Terrorism and the Response to Terrorism," in *Psychology of Terrorism* (Oxford: Oxford University Press, 2007), 15.

84. George W. Bush, *The National Security Strategy of the United States of America* (Washington, D.C.: The White House, September 2002), 6.

85. George W. Bush, *National Strategy for Homeland Security* (Washington, D.C.: The White House, July 2002), 2.

86. Gordon England. *Strategy for Homeland Defense and Civil Support* (Washington, D.C.: Department of Defense, June 2005), 10.

87. *National Strategy for Homeland Security*, 13.

88. Ibid.

89. *Unconventional Operational Concepts and the Homeland*, A Panel Report of the Defense Science Board 2007 Summer Study on Challenges to Military Operations in Support of U.S. Interests (Washington D.C.: Office of the Under Secretary of Defense for Acquisition, Technology, and Logistics, March 2009), xv.

90. *America's Maritime Guardian: U.S. Coast Guard Pub 1* (Washington D.C.: U.S. Coast Guard, January 2002), 3.

91. High seas are defined as waters beyond 12 nautical miles of the coastline. *Maritime Law Enforcement Manual*, Washington D.C.: U.S. Coast Guard, 2004).

92. National Commission on Terrorist Attacks, *The 9/11 Commission on Terrorist Attacks Upon the United States* (Washington D.C.: W.W. Norton, 2004).

93. U.S. Coast Guard, *Maritime Strategy for Homeland Security* (Washington D.C.: U.S. Coast Guard, 2002), 5.

94. As commercial facilities subject to limited protection ports were a special concern, notably "strategic" ports responsible for large areas of commerce. See S. Hrg. 107–309: Weak Links: Assessing the Vulnerability of U.S. Ports and Whether the Government is Adequately Structured to Safeguard Them: Hearing before the Committee on Governmental Affairs, United States Senate, One Hundred Seventh Congress, First Session, December 6, 2001.

95. *National Plan to Achieve Maritime Domain Awareness* (Washington D.C.: Department of Homeland Security, 2006), 5.

96. R. B. Watts, *Implementing Maritime Domain Awareness* (Monterey: Naval Post Graduate School, 2006), 2.

97. Ibid., 27.

98. *National Plan for Maritime Domain Awareness*, 6.

99. George Bush, *National Security Presidential Directive 41* (Washington D.C.: The White House, December 2004), 13.

100. *National Strategy for Maritime Domain Awareness*, CONOPS, 1.

101. George Bush, *Homeland Security Presidential Directive 13* (Washington D.C.: The White House, April 2005).

102. Flynn, *American the Vulnerable*, 64.

103. Jeffrey High, "How Better Coordination can Improve Maritime Domain Awareness" (Washington D.C.: National Research Council Transportation Security Board, November 2004), 7.

104. Robert Ackerman, "Pace of Change Accelerates for U.S. Navy," *Signal*, December 2004.

105. Author experience, MDA negotiations for operational experience, Pentagon, 2004.

106. *National Strategy for Maritime Domain Awareness*, CONOPS. William Wimmer, "Maritime Domain Awareness Concept of Operations (Action Officer-Level Draft)." 2005.

107. Statement by Honorable Paul McHale, Assistant Secretary of Defense for Homeland Defense, Before the 109th Congress, Subcommittee on Terrorism, Unconventional Threats and Capabilities, Committee on Armed Services, United States House of Representatives, March 15, 2005.

108. NORTHCOM technically controlled all maritime defense operations for the homeland—but like other COCOMs, it controlled no actual assets; rather, ships were assigned by the Navy on an "as needed" basis. Timothy Keating, *CDRNORTHCOM-CDR NORAD Strategic Guidance* (Colorado Springs: U.S. Northcom, 2006).

109. http://www.navy.mil/navydata/cno/mullen/speeches/mullen050816.txt.

110. *Intelligence, Surveillance, and Reconnaissance: DOD Needs a Strategic, Risk-Based Approach to Enhance its Maritime Domain Awareness*, GAO Report to Congress, GAO-11-621 (Washington D.C.: General Accounting Office, June 2011), 2.
111. John Morgan and Charles W. Martoglio. "The 1,000-ship Navy: Global Maritime Network." U.S. Naval Institute *Proceedings*. (November 2005): 14–18.
112. *Ibid*.
113. Harlan Ullman, "The 1,000-Ship Navy—Turning a Slogan into a Strategy," U.S. Naval Institute Proceedings (October 2006): 10.
114. Author experience, MDA negotiations, Pentagon, 2005.
115. *Inaugural Global Maritime Information Sharing Symposium* (Kings Point: U.S. Dept. of Justice, 2008), 6.
116. Mary Beth Nikitin, *Proliferation Security Initiative: CRS Report for Congress* (Washington D.C.: Congressional Research Service, 2008), 2.
117. Jin Kim, "Influence of PSI on North Korea," *Strategic Insights*, Vol. 5 no. 7, August 2006.
118. U.S. Customs and Border Protection, *Container Security Initiative, Strategic Plan 2006–2011* (Washington, D.C.: U.S. Customs and Border Protection Service, 2006). See also "S. Hrg. 109-186: The Container Security Initiative and the Customs-Trade Partnership against Terrorism: Securing the Global Supply Chain or TroJanuaryHorse?" Hearing before the Permanent Subcommittee on Investigations of the Committee on Homeland Security and Governmental Affairs, United States Senate, One Hundred Ninth Congress, First Session, May 6, 2005.
119. Charles Mauney, "The Navy's Role in Homeland Defense," *U.S. Navy N3/N5 Strategic Briefing*, February 2004, 30.
120. R. B. Watts, *Implementing Maritime Domain Awareness* (Monterey: Naval Post Graduate School, 2006), 65.
121. Ronald O'Rourke, *Navy Irregular Warfare and Counterterrorism Operations: Issues for Congress* (Washington D.C.: Congressional Research Service, November 2011), 8.
122. *Ibid*., 11.
123. *Ibid*.
124. "The Current Readiness of U.S. Forces," Hearing before the Subcommittee on Readiness and Management Support of the Committee on Armed Service, U.S. Senate, 111th Congress, April 14, 2010.
125. "As NECC Stands Up, Navy Prepares Riverine Forces for 2007 Iraq Mission," Jason Ma. Inside the Navy, www.insidedefense.com.

126. "Protecting the Maritime Borders: Leveraging New Enforcement Cooperation to Enhance Security Along America's Coasts," Hearing before the U.S. House of Representatives, Committee on Homeland Security, Sub-Committee on Border and Maritime Security, July 12, 2011.
127. U.S. Coast Guard, *Maritime Strategy for Homeland Security* (Washington D.C.: U.S. Coast Guard, July 2002).
128. Anthony Pate, *Protecting America's Ports: Promising Practices* (Washington D.C.: Report to the Department of Justice, January 2008), 12.
129. This was a policy decision. Staffing for JHOCs with Navy personnel was reduced as was future plans for additional facilities. In addition, fleet assets that coordinated operations (mainly frigates) were assigned other missions. Author experience, Pentagon, 2005.
130. These "conversations" were a series of "town hall" style meetings held by the CNO to discuss elements of the strategy with various civilian communities as part of a public relations campaign prior to the strategy's release. See Karl Walling, "Why a Conversation with the Country?" *Joint Forces Quarterly*, Issue 50, 3rd Quarter 2008 (Washington: NDU Press, 2008), 139.
131. *Ibid*.
132. *A Cooperative Strategy for 21st Century Sea Power* (Washington D.C.: Department of the Navy, October 2007), 2.
133. Note this did not include response to domestic disasters (at least initially), such as Katrina, where the Navy deployed late and only after tremendous public pressure. Author experience, Pentagon, 2006.
134. USNI *Proceedings*, November 2007.
135. Michael Bruno, "New Maritime Strategy Plan Meets Congressional Doubts," Aerospace Daily & Defense Report, December 14, 2007.
136. Robert O'Wok, "A Cooperative Strategy for 21st Century Sea Power: An Assessment," (Washington D.C.: Center for Strategic and Budgetary Assessments, March 2008), 4.
137. *Ibid*., 17.

Chapter Nine

1. Jonathan Steele, *Ghosts of Afghanistan: Hard Truths and Foreign Myths* (Berkeley: Counterpoint Publishing, 2011), 150.
2. See http://voices.washingtonpost.com/44/2009/03/23/the_end_of_the_global_war_on_t.html, accessed December 24, 2011.

Notes—Chapter Nine

3. Anthanasia Austin, "Development of U.S. Irregular Warfare Capabilities," *The Journal of the Joint Air Power Coordination Center* (NV: USAF, 2008). See also Eliot Cohen ed., *U.S. Government Counterinsurgency Guide* (Washington: U.S. Government Interagency Counterinsurgency Initiative, 2009), 24.

4. Ronald O'Rourke, *Navy Role in Irregular Warfare and Counterterrorism* (Washington: Congressional Research Service, 2010), 5. Whether this implies permanence for the NECC remains to be seen.

5. A. Fritz, *The Navy Role in Confronting Irregular Challenge: Implementing the Navy Vision for CNC* (Washington: Center for Naval Analysis, 2011), 15.

6. *Highlights of the Department of the Navy FY 2012 Budget* (Washington: Dept. of the Navy, February 2011) 2–1, 2–4.

7. U.S. Coast Guard, *Maritime Law Enforcement Manual* (Washington: U.S. Coast Guard, 2006), 20.

8. Frank Hoffman, "Conflict in the 21st Century: The Rise of Hybrid Wars," *Small Wars Journal*, March 2006.

9. See Ronald O'Rourke, CRS Report RL32665, *Potential Navy Force Structure and Shipbuilding Plans: Background and Issues for Congress* (Washington: Congressional Research Service, 2004), and Christopher J Castelli, "DOD Develops Homeland Defense Strategy, Advocates for Maritime NORAD," *Inside the Navy*, August 2, 2004, 1. Ultimately NORTHCOM was designated as the maritime component commander for homeland defense—meaning that ships had to be requested for this duty, a request that was rarely honored. Author experience Pentagon duty, 2005.

10. Cohen, *U.S. Government Counterinsurgency Guide*, 34.

11. Ibid. See also Richard Armitage and Joseph Nye, *CSIS Commission on Smart Power* (Washington: Center for Strategic and International Studies, 2007).

12. A. Fritz, *The Navy Role in Confronting Irregular Challenges*, 18.

13. Ibid.

14. Ibid., 19.

15. See http://www.huffingtonpost.com/2011/12/20/old-coast-guard-cutters-r_n_1161268.html, accessed December 30, 2011.

16. This point is controversial within the surface fleet, as this mission can be performed by amphibious Expeditionary Strike Forces (ESFs). See RAND unclassified briefing, Expeditionary Strike Group Five, "Fast-Forward-Flexible," October 20, 2011.

17. O'Rourke, *Navy Irregular Warfare and Counterterrorism Operations*, 6.

18. Ronald Spector, *At War at Sea: Sailors and Naval Combat in the Twentieth Century* (New York: Viking, 2001), 359.

19. A. Fritz, *The Navy Role in Confronting Irregular Challenges*, 3.

20. Charles Moore, "Revitalizing the Cooperative Strategy for 21st Century Sea Power," *Parameters* (Carlisle: U.S. Army War College, 2011), 30.

21. John Lehman, *Aircraft Carriers: The Real Issue* (Washington: Policy Papers, 1978).

22. A. Fritz, *The Navy Role in Confronting Irregular Challenges*, 23. See also USNI Proceedings debate.

23. Interestingly this operation was classic HA/DR which was, as noted, a point of contention as to whether this type of mission should be classified as falling under IW.

24. O'Rourke, *Navy Irregular Warfare and Counterterrorism*, 15.

25. Ibid., 16.

26. The "179" in this case refers to the length of the vessel. Commanded by a Navy LT or LCDR, these were littoral warships in the classic sense, possessing considerable power, speed, and irregular capability (list of weapons), source. See http://www.globalsecurity.org/military/systems/ship/pc-1.htm, accessed December 27, 2011).

27. Milan Vigo, "No Need for High Speed," USNI *Proceedings* (Annapolis: U.S. Naval Institute, September 2009), 47.

28. Author experience as battle group operations officer, UNITAS 1998.

29. See http://www.navytimes.com/news/2011/08/navy-patrol-boats-coast-guard-081511w/, accessed January 4, 2012.

30. For an analysis of the numbers versus capabilities method of naval analysis, see Robert Work, *Know When to Hold 'em, Know When to Fold 'em: A New Transformation for the Navy's Surface Battle Line* (Washington: Center for Strategic and Budgetary Assessments, 2007), 49.

31. *Navy Acquisitions: Improved Littoral Warfighting Capabilities Needed*, Report to the Chairman and Ranking Minority Member, Subcommittee on Military Research and Development on Armed Services, House of Representatives, GAO-1–493 (Washington D.C.: Government Accounting Office, March 2001), 3.

32. See *GAO 1–493* and http://www.marsec4.com/2011/09/waterborne-ied-threats-and-the-straits-of-hormuz/, accessed January 4, 2012.

33. See http://www.navy.mil/navydata/fact_display.asp?cid=4200&tid=1200&ct=4, accessed January 4, 2012.

34. Martin Murphy, *Littoral Combat Ship: An Examination of its Possible Concepts of*

Operation (Washington: Center for Strategic Budgetary Assessments, 2010), 5.

35. *Defense Acquisitions: Navy's Ability to Overcome Challenges Facing LCS Will Determine Capabilities* (Washington: Government Accounting Office, August 2010), 10.

36. Ibid.

37. *Defense Acquisitions: Assessment of Selected Programs*, GA)-10-388S (Washington D.C.: Government Accounting Office, March 2010). See also Otto Kriesher, "Checkered Past, Uncertain Future," in USNI *Proceedings* (Annapolis: Naval Institute Press, Vol. 13, January 5, 2009).

38. Vigo, "No Need for High Speed," *Proceedings*, September 2009.

39. Christopher Cravas, "The Road From Promise to Reality," *Navy Times*, April 23, 2012, 28.

40. Thomas Henderschedt and Chad Sbragia, "Clearing u China's Naval Intentions," *Navy Times*, September 20, 2010, 32.

41. Bud Cole, *The Great Wall At Sea: China's Navy in the 21st Century* (Annapolis: Naval Institute Press, 2010).

42. Taiwan has always been a contingency for the Navy; for current policy see transcript, "Admiral Willard Delivers Asian Pacific Military Overview Briefing," Foreign Press Center with Admiral Robert Willard, Commander, U.S. Pacific Command, The Washington Foreign Press Center, Washington, D.C. September 27, 2011. Available at http://www.pacom.mil/web/Site_Pages/Media/News_2011/09/27-Willard-Delivers-Overview.shtml, accessed January 5, 2012.

43. China has recently become the focus of the Naval War College graduate curriculum, and fostered the creation of a number of China and Asia focused think tanks at the National Defense University.

44. Nan Li, "The Evolution of China's Navy Strategy and Capabilities: From 'Near Coast' and 'Near Seas' to 'Far Seas,'" in *The Chinese Navy: Expanding Capabilities, Expanding Roles* (Washington: Center for the Study of Chinese Military Affairs, National Defense University Press, 2011), 110.

45. Ronald O'Rourke, "PLAN Force Structure: Submarines, Ships and Aircraft," in *The Chinese Navy: Expanding Capabilities, Modern Roles* (Washington: National Defense University Press, 2011), 161. See also Issues for Congress.

46. Ibid., 149.

47. Cole, *The Great Wall at Sea*.

48. The Chinese have a tendency to view cycles of history in far greater time frames than the West. When asked about the impact of the French Revolution, for example, Chinese Premier Zhou Enlai was quoted as saying "it's too early to tell." See Richard McGregor, "Zhou's cryptic caution lost in translation," *Financial Times*, June 10, 2011.

49. Peter Swartz, "Rising Powers and Naval Power," in *The Chinese Navy: Expanding Capabilities, Modern Roles*.

50. Niu Baocheng, "From Rights and Interests at Sea to Military Rights and Interests at Sea," *Modern Navy*, no s1, 32. Chinese source quoted from M. Taylor Fravel and Alexander Liebman, "Beyond the Moat: the PLAN's Evolving Interests and Potential Interests," in *The Chinese Navy: Expanding Capabilities, Modern Roles* (Washington: National Defense University Press, 2011), 41.

51. Nan Li, "The Evolution of China's Naval Strategy and Capabilities: From 'Near Coast' and 'Near Seas' to 'Far Seas,'" in *The Chinese Navy*, 109.

52. Cole, *The Great Wall at Sea*.

53. Swartz, "Rising Powers and Naval Power."

54. http://www.nationalreview.com/articles/285685/air-sea-battle-jim-lacey, accessed December 30, 2011.

55. Ibid.

56. See Chapter Four. The analogy is the author's.

57. Department of Defense, *Quadrennial Defense Review Report* (Washington, D.C.: Department of Defense, 2010), 55.

58. Andrew Krepinevich, *Why Air-Sea Battle?* (Washington, D.C.: Center for Strategic and Budgetary Assessments, 2010), 8.

59. http://www.usni.org/magazines/proceedings/2010-08/whats-new-about-airsea-battle-concept, accessed December 30, 2011.

60. Januaryver Tol, *Air-Sea Battle: A Point of Departure Operational Concept* (Washington D.C.: Center for Strategic and Budgetary Assessments, 2010), xi.

61. O'Rourke, "Force Structure: Submarines, Ships, and Aircraft," in The Chinese Navy, 166.

62. The Japanese Maritime Defense Force, for example, has an overall compliment of 110 major warships. See http://www.globalsecurity.org/military/world/japan/jmsdf.htm, accessed January 6, 2012.

63. Secretary Leon Panetta, "Sustaining U.S. Global Leadership: Priorities for 21st Century Defense," (Washington D.C.: Statement on Defense Strategic Guidance, December 2011).

Bibliography

History

Adams, Chris. *Inside the Cold War*. Montgomery: Air War College University Press, 1999.

Addington, Larry. *The Patterns of War Since the 18th Century*. Bloomington: Indiana University Press, 1984.

Alach, Zhivan. *Slowing Military Change*. Washington D.C.: Strategic Studies Institute, 2008.

Albion, Robert. *Makers of Naval Policy, 1798–1947*. Annapolis: Naval Institute Press, 1980.

_____. *Sea Lanes in Wartime: The American Experience*. New York: Archon Books, 1968.

Arkin, William. "A Week of War." *Washington Post*, Oct. 14, 2001.

Atkinson, Rick. *Crusade: The Unknown Story of the Gulf War*. New York: Mariner's Books, 1994.

Bacevich, Andrew. *American Empire: The Reality and Consequences of U.S. Diplomacy*. Boston: Harvard University Press, 2004.

_____. *Washington Rules*. New York: Metropolitan Books, 2010.

Baer, George. *One Hundred Years of Sea Power*. Stanford: Stanford University Press, 1993.

Bagnaso, Ermino. *Submarines of World War II*. Annapolis: Naval Institute Press, 1980.

Ballard, John. *From Storm to Freedom: America's Long War with Iraq*. Annapolis: Naval Institute Press, 2010.

Barlow, Jeffrey. *From Hot War to Cold: The U.S. Navy and National Security Affairs, 1945–1955*. Stanford: Stanford University Press, 2009.

_____. *Revolt of the Admirals: The Fight for Naval Aviation, 1945–1950*. Washington D.C.: Brasseys, 1998.

Barnett, Roger. *The Navy Strategic Culture*. Annapolis: Naval Institute Press, 2009.

Bennett, Frank. *The Steam Navy of the United States*. Pittsburg: W. T. Nicholsen, 1896.

Blair, Clay. *Silent Victory: The U.S. Submarine War Against Japan*. New York: Lippincott, 1975.

Blank, Stephen, ed. *Culture, Conflict and History*. Montgomery: Air War College University Press, 2006.

Bobbit, Phillip. *The Shield of Achilles: War, Peace, and the Course of History*. New York: Random House, 2002.

Boot, Max. *The Savage Wars of Peace: Small Wars and the Rise of American Power*. New York: Basic Books, 2002.

Bowling, R. A. "The Negative Influence of Mahan on ASW." *Journal of the Royal United Service Institute for Defense Studies*. London: Dec. 1977.

Boyd, Carl. *The Japanese Submarine Force in World War 2*. Annapolis: Naval Institute Press, 1995.

Brodie, Bernard. *War and Politics*. New York: Macmillan, 1973.

Builder, Carl. *The Masks of War: American Military Styles in Strategy and Analysis*. Baltimore: Johns Hopkins University Press, 1989.

Capaccio, Tony. "Sixty Percent of Bombs Dropped on Afghanistan Precision-Guided." Bloomberg.com, Nov. 20, 2001.

Clark, Wesley. *Waging Modern War*. New York: PublicAffairs, 2002.

Clodfelter, Mark. *The Limits of Air Power: The American Bombing of North Vietnam*. New York: The Free Press, 1989.

Connaughton, R. M. *The War of the Rising Sun and the Tumbling Bear: A Military History of the Russo-Japanese War, 1904–1905*. London: John Murray, 1988.

Cooper, Kip. "Admiral Blames Washington for Loss of 2 Planes over Syria," *San Diego Union*, May 12, 1984.

Corbett, Julian. *Some Principles of Maritime Strategy*. New York: Tredition, 2011.

Creswell, John. *Generals and Admirals*. New York: Greenwood Publishing, 1976.

———. *Naval Warfare*. Brooklyn: Chemical Publishing, 1942.

Crevald, Martin. *Technology and War*. New York: The Free Press, 1989.

Cutler, Thomas. *Brown Water, Black Berets*. Annapolis: Naval Institute Press, 2000.

Davison, Kenneth. "Clausewitz and the Indirect Approach: Misreading the Leader." *Air Power Journal*. Maxwell: Air University Press, Winter 1988.

Doenitz, Karl. *Ten Years and Twenty Days*. Annapolis: Naval Institute Press, 1958.

Felker, Craig. *Simulation and Sea Power: the U.S. Navy Fleet Problems, 1923–1940*. Annapolis: Naval Institute Press, 1983.

Filkins, Dexter. *The Forever War*. New York: Vintage Press, 2009.

Fiske, Bradley. *The Navy as a Fighting Machine*. New York: Budge Press, 2010.

Fitzgerald, Oscar. "U.S. Naval Forces in the Vietnam War: the Advisory Mission, 1961–1965." *Changing Interpretations and New Sources in Naval History: Papers from the Third United States Naval Academy History Symposium*. New York: Garland Press, 1980.

Freeman, Lawrence. *The Evolution of Nuclear Strategy*. New York: St. Martin's Press, 1981.

Friedman, Norman. *U.S. Battleships: An Illustrated Design History*. Annapolis: Naval Institute Press, 1986.

Gaddis, John. *Strategies of Containment: A Critical Appraisal of American National Security Policy During the Cold War*. Oxford: Oxford University Press, 1982.

Gaffney, H. (ed.). *U.S. Naval Response to Situations: 1970–1999*. Alexandria: Center for Naval Analysis, Dec. 2000.

Gannon, Michael. *Operation Drumbeat: The Dramatic True Story of Germany's First U-Boat Attacks Along America's Coast During World War 2*. Annapolis: Naval Institute Press, 2009.

Goldrick, James. *Mahan is Not Enough: The Proceedings of a Conference on the Works of Sir Julian Corbett and Sir Herbert Richmond*. Newport: Naval War College Press, 1993.

Gordon, Andrew. *The Rules of the Game: Jutland and British Naval Command*. Annapolis: Naval Institute Press, 2000.

Gordon, Joy. "Economic Sanctions and Global Governance: the Case of Iraq." *Global Crime*, Vol. 10. Rutledge: Nov. 2009.

Grant, Rebecca. *Battle-Tested: Carrier Aviation in Afghanistan and Iraq*. Washington D.C.: IRIS Press, 2005.

Gray, Colin. *The Leverage of Sea Power*. New York: Macmillan, 1992.

Harries, Meirion and Harries, Susie. *Soldiers of the Sun: The Rise and Fall of the Imperial Japanese Army*. New York: Random House, 1991.

Hattendorf, John. *The Evolution of the U.S. Navy's Maritime Strategy, 1977–1986*. Newport: Naval War College, 2004.

——— (ed.). *U.S. Naval Strategy in the 1990s: Selected Documents*. Newport: Naval War College, Sept. 2006.

Hartmann, Frederick. *Naval Renaissance: The U.S. Navy in the 1980s*. Annapolis: Naval Institute Press, 1990.

Hastings, Max. *The Korean War*. New York: Simon & Schuster, 1987.

———. *Retribution: The Battle for Japan, 1944–1945*. New York: Alfred A. Knopf, 2008.

Healy, Melissa. "Pentagon Blasts Tailhook Probe, Two Admirals Resign." *Los Angeles Times*, Sept. 25, 1992.

Herman, Arthur. *To Rule the Waves: How the British Navy Shaped the Modern World*. New York: Harper, 2004.

Hiatt, Fred. "Accidents, 'Friendly Fire' Blamed for Many U.S. Casualties in Grenada," *Washington Post*, 1 Nov. 1983.

Hickam, Homer. *Torpedo Junction*. Annapolis: Naval Institute Press, 1989.

Hirsch, John. "The Blackhawk Down Effect." *Foreign Policy*, Aug. 12, 2011.

Holmes, W. J. *Double-Edged Secrets*. Annapolis: Naval Institute Press, 1979.

———. *Undersea Victory*. New York: Doubleday, 1966.

Hone, Trent. "The Evolution of Fleet Tactical Doctrine, 1922–1941." *Journal of Military History* Vol. 67, Oct. 2003.

Horne, Charles, ed. *Source Records of the*

Great War. Washington: National Archives, 1923.

Hought, Richard. *The Battle of Britain: The Greatest Air Battle of World War 2.* New York: W.W. Norton, 1989.

Howard, Michael. *War in European History.* Oxford: Oxford University Press, 1972.

Huchthausen, Peter. *K-19: The Widowmaker.* Washington D.C.: National Geographic, 2002.

Huie, William. "Why We Must have the World's Best Air Force," *Reader's Digest,* March 1949.

Isenberg, Michael *Shield of the Republic: The United States Navy in an Era of Cold War and Violent Peace, 1945–1962.* New York: St. Martin's Press, 1993.

Issacs, Arnold. *Vietnam Shadows: The War, its Ghosts, and its Legacy.* Baltimore: Johns Hopkins University Press, 1997.

Jane, Fred T. *Heresies of Sea Power.* London: Longmans, Green, 1906.

____. *Jane's Fighting Ships.* London: Jane's Publishing, 1941.

Jessup, John. *A Guide to the Study and Use of Military History.* Washington D.C.: U.S. Government Printing Office, 1982.

Johnson, Robert Erwin. *Guardians of the Sea: the History of the U.S. Coast Guard.* Annapolis: Naval Institute Press, 1987.

Jordon, Amos, and Taylor, William. *American National Security: Policy and Process.* Baltimore: Johns Hopkins University Press, 1984.

Karsten, Peter. *The Naval Aristocracy: The Golden Age of Annapolis and the Emergence of Modern American Navalism.* Annapolis: Naval Institute Press, 1972.

Kent, Glenn. *Thinking About America's Defense: An Analytical Memoir.* Santa Monica: Rand, 2008.

Khong, Yuen Foong. *Analogies at War.* Princeton: Princeton University Press, 1992.

Krulak, Victor. *First to Fight: An Inside View of the U.S. Marine Corps.* Annapolis: Naval Institute Press, 1999.

Lambert, Nicholas. *Sir John Fisher's Naval Revolution.* Columbia: University of South Carolina Press, 1999.

Layton, Edwin. *"And I Was There": Pearl Harbor and Midway, Breaking the Secrets.* New York: Quill, 1985.

Lehman, John. *Command of the Seas.* New York: Scribner's, 1988.

Livezey, William. *Mahan on Sea Power.* University of Oklahoma Press, 1981.

Lowry, Thomas. *The Attack on Taranto.* New York: Stackpole Books, 1995.

Lukas, J. "Lessons from Desert Storm." *Marine Corps Gazette.* Quantico: May 1998.

Lynn, John. *Battle: A History of Culture and Conflicts.* Boulder: Westview Press, 2003.

Mahan, A. T. *The Influence of Sea Power on History.* New York: Dover, 1987.

____. *The Interest of America in Sea Power.* Annapolis: Naval Institute Press, 1970.

____. *Letters and Papers of Alfred Thayer Mahan.* Annapolis: Naval Institute Press, 1975.

Manson, Frank. *The Sea War in Korea.* Annapolis: Naval Institute Press, 1957.

Marolda, Edward. *The United States Navy and the Vietnam Conflict: From Military Assistance to Combat, 1959–1965.* Washington D.C.: Dept. of the Navy, 1986.

May, Ernest. *American Imperialism.* New York: Brown and Root, 1968.

McMaster, H.R. *Dereliction of Duty: Lyndon Johnson, Robert McNamara, the Joint Chiefs of Staff, and the Lies that Led to Vietnam.* New York: Harper, 1998.

McMichael, W. *The Mother of all Hooks: The Story of the U.S. Navy's Tailhook Scandal.* Brunswick: Transaction Publications, 1997.

McNamara, Robert. *In Retrospect: The Tragedy and Lessons of Vietnam.* New York: Vintage Books, 1996.

Miller, Nathen. *At War at Sea.* Oxford: Oxford University Press, 1995.

Morrison, Samual Elliot. *The Two Ocean War.* Annapolis: Naval Institute Press, 2007.

Morrow, John. *The Great War: An Imperial History.* New York: Routledge, 2002.

Mosley, Michael. *Operation Iraqi Freedom: By the Numbers.* Shaw AFB: U.S. Central Command, April 2003.

Murray, Williamson, ed. *Military Innovation in the Interwar Period.* Cambridge: Cambridge University Press, 1996.

____. *The Past as Prologue.* Cambridge: Cambridge University Press, 2006.

Nordhoff, Charles. *Life on the Ocean.* Cincinnati: Brown, 1874.

O'Connell, Robert. *Sacred Vessels: The Cult of the Battleship and the Rise of the*

U.S. Navy. Oxford: Oxford University Press, 1991.
Oran, Michael. *Power, Faith and Fantasy: America in the Middle East*. New York: W.W. Norton, 2007.
Padfield, Peter. *War Beneath the Sea*. New York: John Wiley & Sons, 1995.
Palmer, Michael. *Origins of the Maritime Strategy: American Naval Tradition in the First Postwar Decade*. Washington D.C.: Naval Historical Center, 1988.
Paret, Peter, ed. *Makers of Modern Strategy from Machiavelli to the Nuclear Age*. Princeton: Princeton University Press, 1986.
Polmar, Norman. *Submarines of the Russian and Soviet Navies*. Annapolis: Naval Institute Press, 1991.
_____. *U.S. Aircraft Carriers*. Annapolis: Naval Institute Press, 1983.
Post, Ronald. *Sealift in Operations Desert Shield and Desert Storm, 7 Aug 1990-17 Feb 1991*. Washington D.C.: Center for Naval Analysis, 1998.
Reckner, James. *Teddy Roosevelt's Great White Fleet*. Annapolis: Naval Institute Press, 1988.
Ree, David. *Korea: The Limited War*. New York: Natraj Publishing, 1985.
Renshon, Stanley, ed. *Good Judgment in Foreign Policy*. New York: Rowman and Littlefield, 2006.
Reynolds, Clark. *Navies in History*. Annapolis: Naval Institute Press, 1998.
Ricks, Tom. *Fiasco: The American Military Adventure in Iraq*. New York: Penguin Books, 2006.
Roherty, James. *Decisions of Robert B. McNamara: a Study of the Role of the Secretary of Defense*. Miami: University of Miami Press, 1970.
Roosevelt, Theodore. "Letter to A. T. Mahan, 12 May, 1890." Washington D.C.: Naval Archives.
Roscoe, Theodore. *On the Sea and in the Air*. New York: Warton, 1970.
Russet, Bruce. *The Prisoners of Insecurity: Nuclear Deterrence, the Arms Race, and Arms Control*. San Francisco: W.H. Freeman, 1983.
Ryan, Paul. *First Line of Defense: The U.S. Navy Since 1945*. Stanford: Hoover Institution Press, 1981.
Schwartz, Peter. *The Maritime Strategy Debates*. Newport: Naval War College, 2004.

Schwarzkopf, Norman. "Press Briefing." *Military Review*, Vol. 71. 1996.
Seagar, Robert. *Alfred Thayer Mahan: The Man and His Letters*. Annapolis: Naval Institute Press, 1977.
Seversky, Alexander. "Peace Through Air Power." *Reader's Digest*, Feb. 1949.
Sheehan, Neil. *The Arnheiter Affair*. New York: Random House, 1972.
_____. *A Bright and Shining Lie: John Paul Vann and America in Vietnam*. New York: Vintage Books, 1989.
Sheppard, Don. *Destroyer Skipper*. Nevado: Presidio Press, 1996.
_____. *Riverine*. Nevado: Presidio Press, 1992.
Shulman, Mark. *Navalism and the Emergence of American Sea Power, 1882-1893*. Annapolis: Naval Institute Press, 1995.
Sims, William. "Letter Sims to Fiske, 6 Jan. 1921." *Sims Papers*. Washington D.C.: Naval Archives.
Smith, Dale. "The Role of Air Power Since WW2." *Military Affairs*, vol. xix. Summer 1955.
Sokolsky, Joel. *Sea Power in the Nuclear Age: The U.S. Navy and NATO, 1949-80*. Annapolis: Naval Institute Press, 1991.
Spector, Ronald. *At War at Sea*. New York: Viking Press, 2001.
Sprout, Harold, and Sprout, Margaret. *The Rise of American Naval Power, 1776-1918*. Annapolis: Naval Institute Press, 1967.
Steele, Jonathan. *Ghosts of Afghanistan: Hard Truths and Foreign Myths*. Berkeley: Counterpoint Publishing, 2011.
Stevenson, Charles. *Congress at War: The Politics of Conflict since 1789*. Washington D.C.: National Defense University Press, 2007.
Stewart, Richard. *War in the Persian Gulf: Operations Desert Shield and Desert Storm*. Carlyle: Center for Military History, 2010.
Summers, Harry. *On Strategy: A Critical Analysis of the Vietnam War*. New York: Presidio Press, 1995.
Suny, Robert. *The Revenge of the Past: Nationalism, Revolution, and the Collapse of The Soviet Union*. Stanford: Stanford University Press, 1993.
Symonds, Craig. *The Navalists and the Anti-Navalists: The Naval Policy Debate in the United States 1785-1827*.

Newark: University of Delaware Press, 1980.

Taylor, Charles. *The Life of Admiral Mahan.* New York: George H. Doran, 1920.

Thompson, Roger. *Lessons not learned: the U.S. Navy's Status Quo Culture.* Annapolis: Naval Institute Press, 2007.

Townsend, Charles, ed. *The Oxford History of Modern War.* Oxford: Oxford University Press, 2005.

Tuchman, Barbara. *The Proud Tower.* New York: Macmillan, 1965.

Uhlig, Frank Jr. *How Navies Fight.* Annapolis: Naval Institute Press, 1994.

U.S. Congress. *Naval Appropriations Act 1921.* Washington D.C.: 1921.

———. *Act of 12 July 1921.* Washington D.C.: 1921.

U.S. Navy. *Final Report: War Department Policies and Program Review Board, 11 Aug 1947.* Washington: Chief of Naval Operations, 1971. Naval Historical Center.

———. *Navy Budgetary Presentations Before the JCS Fiscal Year 1951: Review of Plans, Phase II, Part 1, Vol.1.* Washington: Chief of Naval Operations, 1949. Naval Historical Center.

———. *Navy Strategic Plans Study 3, Study of Carrier Attack Force Offensive Capabilities.* Op30W, March 7, 1947, Miscellaneous Plans and Studies, Series XVII, Strategic Plans Records Division. Washington: Operational Archives, Naval Historical Center.

———. "Regional Estimates of the Situation" in *North Atlantic Treaty Organization Medium Term Defense Plan,* 1 July 1954. Washington: Naval Historical Center.

U.S. Senate. *Navy Yearbook.* Naval Affairs Committee. Washington D.C.: 1921.

Van de Vat, Dan. *The Atlantic Campaign.* New York: Harper and Row, 1988.

Vogel, Steve. "Gas Stations in the Sky Extend Fighters' Reach." *Washington Post,* Nov. 1, 2001.

Washington, G. "Washington's Farewell Address." *Senate Document 106–21,* 106th Congress. Washington D.C.: Government Printing Office, 2000.

Watts, R. B. *Ultra Underseas: Signal Intelligence and the Submarine War Against Japan, 1941–1945.* Norfolk: Old Dominion University, 1993.

Weigley, Russel. *The American Way of War.* Bloomington: Indiana University Press, 1973.

White, E.B. *Sea Power.* Annapolis: Naval Institute Press, 1972.

Wildenburg, Thomas. "In Support of the Battle Line: Gunnery's Influence on the Development of Carrier Aviation in the U.S. Navy." *Journal of Military History,* Vol. 65, 2001.

Wilson, George. *Super Carrier.* New York: Berkley Books, 1988.

Woodward, Bob. *Plan of Attack.* New York: Simon & Schuster, 2004.

Yetiv, Steve. *The Persian Gulf Crisis.* Westport: Greenwood Press, 1997.

Zelizer, Julian. *The Arsenal of Democracy: The Politics of National Security—from World War II to the War on Terrorism.* New York: Basic Books, 2010.

Zimmerman, Warren. *First Great Triumph: How Five Americans Made Their Country Into a World Power.* New York: Farrar, Straus, and Giroux, 2002.

Zubok, Vladislav. *Inside the Kremlin's Cold War from Stalin to Khrushchev.* Cambridge: Harvard University Press, 2010.

Zumwalt, Elmo. *On Watch.* New York: New York Times Books, 1976.

Strategy

"Admiral Willard Delivers Asian Pacific Military Overview Briefing." Washington D.C.: The Washington Foreign Press Center, Sept. 2011.

Alberto, David, ed. *Complexity, Global Politics, and National Security.* Washington D. C.; National Defense University Press, 1999.

Arleigh Burke FL 1& 2 Class. Jane's Defense and Security Analysis, 24 Mar. 2011.

Art, Robert. "Geopolitics Updated: The Strategy for Selective Engagement." *International Security* 23, Winter 1998.

Biddle, Steven. "Strategy in War." *Political Science and Politics,* Vol. 40, July 2007.

Binnendjik, Hans (ed.). *Transforming America's Military.* Washington: National Defense University Press, 2002.

Bolt, Paul, ed. *American Defense Policy.* Baltimore: Johns Hopkins University Press, 2005.

Boot, Max. *The Savage Wars of Peace.* New York: Basic Books, 2002.

Boyer, Pellham, ed. *Strategic Transforma-*

tion and Naval Power in the 21st Century. Newport: Naval War College Press, 1998.
Breemer, Jan. Soviet Submarines: Design, Development, and Tactics. London: Jane's Information Group, 1989.
Bremmer, Ian. The J Curve: A New Way to Understand Why Nations Rise and Fall. New York: Simon & Schuster, 2006.
Brodie, Bernard. Strategy in the Missile Age. Princeton: Princeton University Press, 1959.
Brooks, Linton. "Naval Power and National Security: the Case for the Maritime Strategy." International Security Vol. II, Autumn 1986.
Bruno, Michael. "New Maritime Strategy Plan Meets Congressional Doubts." Aerospace Daily & Defense Report, Dec. 14, 2007.
Brzezinski, Zbigniew. Game Plan: How to Conduct the U.S.-Soviet Contest. Boston: Atlantic Monthly Press, 1986.
Bush, George W. Homeland Security Presidential Directive 13. Washington D.C.: The White House, 2005.
_____. National Security Presidential Directive 41. Washington D.C.: The White House, 2004.
_____. The National Security Strategy of the United States. Washington D.C.: The White House, Sept. 2002.
_____. National Strategy for Homeland Security. Washington D.C.: The White House, 2002.
Buzzard, Anthony. "Massive Retaliation and Graduated Deterrence." World Politics Vol. III, January 1956.
Cable, James. Diplomacy at Sea. Annapolis: Naval Institute Press, 1988.
Carney, Robert. "The Principles of Sea Power." USNI Proceedings, August 1953.
Chase, David. "Posse Comitatus: A Nineteenth Century Law Worthy of Review for the Future." Carlyle: U.S. Army Command and Staff College, 2001.
Clausewitz, Carl. On War. Princeton: Princeton University Press, 1982.
Coakley, Thomas P. (ed.) C3I: Issues of Command and Control. Washington D.C.: National Defense University Press, 1991.
Cole, Bud. The Great Wall At Sea. Annapolis: Naval Institute Press, 2010.
Cole, Ronald. "Grenada, Panama, and Haiti: Joint Operational Reform," Joint Forces Quarterly. Washington D. C.: NDU University Press, Fall 2003.
Collins, John. U.S.-Soviet Military Balance, 1980–1985. Washington D.C.: Pergamon Press, 1985.
Congressional Budget Office. Budgeting for Naval Forces: Structuring Tomorrow's Navy at Today's Budget Levels. Washington D.C.: Congressional Budgeting Office, Oct. 2000.
Corbett, Julian. Some Principles of Maritime Strategy. Annapolis: Naval Institute Press, 1988.
Deibel, Terry. Foreign Affairs Strategy. Cambridge: Cambridge University Press, 2007.
Department of Defense. Quadrennial Defense Review Report. Washington D.C.: Department of Defense, 2010.
_____. Soviet Naval Strategy and Programs through the 1990s: National Intelligence Estimate. Washington D.C.: Central Intelligence Agency, 1983.
Department of Homeland Security. National Plan to Achieve Maritime Domain Awareness. Washington D.C.: Dept. of Homeland Security, 2006.
Deudney, Daniel. "Pushing and Pulling: The Western System, Nuclear Weapons, and Soviet Change." International Politics, Vol. 48, July 2011.
Duffy, B. "The Shrinking of the Pentagon." U.S. News and World Report, Vol. 104 Iss. 9, March 1988.
Eccles, Henry. Military Concepts and Philosophy. New York: Rutgers University Press, 1965.
_____. Military Power in a Free Society. Honolulu: University of Pacific Press, 1979.
England, Gordon. Strategy for Homeland Defense and Civil Support, Washington D.C.: Department of Defense, 2005.
Feith, Douglas. War and Decision: Inside the Pentagon at the Dawn of the War on Terrorism. (New York: Harper and Row, 2008).
Felicetti, Gary. "The Posse Comitatus Act: Liberation from the Lawyers, Enforcement." Parameters, no. 3. Fall 2004.
Fiske, Bradley. The Navy as a Fighting Machine. New York: Scribner's, 1916.
Fitzgerald, T. "Blitzkrieg at Sea." USNI Proceedings, Jan. 1986.
Flanagan, Stephen. Strategic Challenges: America's Global Security Agenda. Wash-

ington D.C.: National Defense University Press, 2006.
Flourney, Michele (ed.). *QDR 2001: Strategy-Driven Choices for America's Security*. Washington D.C.: National Defense University Press, 2001.
Freedman, Lawrence. *The Evolution of Nuclear Strategy*. New York: St. Martin's Press, 1981.
Freier, Nathan. *Knowing Unknowns: Unconventional Strategic Shocks in Defense Strategy Development*. Washington D.C.: Strategic Studies Institute, 2008.
Friedman, George and Meredith. *The Future of War*. New York: St. Martin's, 1996.
Friedman, Norman. *The U.S. Maritime Strategy*. London: Jane's Publishing, 1988.
Fullbright, William. *The Arrogance of Power*. New York: Random House, 1966.
Furniss, Edgar. *American Military Policy: Strategic Aspects of World Geography*. New York: Reinhart, 1957.
George, James (ed.). *Problems of Sea Power as We Approach the Twenty-First Century*. Washington D.C.: American Enterprise Institute for Public Policy Research, 1978.
Goldrick, James (ed.) *Mahan Is Not Enough*. Newport: Naval War College Press, 1993.
Goldstein, Joshua. *International Relations*. New York: HarperCollins, 1994.
Gongora, Thierry ed., *Toward a Revolution in Military Affairs: Defense and Security Strategy in the 21st century*. Westport: Greenwood Press, 2000.
Gorshkov, S. G. *The Sea Power of the State*. Malabar: Robert Keiger Pub., 1983.
Government Accounting Office. *Navy Carrier Battle Groups: The Structure and Affordability of the Future Force*. GAO/NSIAD-93-74. Washington D.C.: Feb. 1993.
Gray, Colin. *Explorations in Strategy*. Westport: Praeger, 1996.
_____. *Modern Strategy*. London: Oxford University Press, 1999.
_____. *The Navy in the Post-Cold War World*. University Park: Pennsylvania State University Press, 1994.
Green, Robert. *The 33 Strategies of War*. New York: Viking Press, 2006.
Grove, Eric. *The Future of Sea Power*. Annapolis: Naval Institute Press, 1990.
Gupta, Sanjeev, and Clements, Benedict, and Bhattacharya, Rina, and Chakravarti, Shamit. "The Ellusive Peace Dividend," *Finance and Development* 39:4, International Monetary Fund, 2002.
Haffa, Robert. *Planning U.S. Forces*. Washington D.C.: National Defense University Press, 1988.
Hagen, Kenneth (ed.). *In Peace and War*. Westport: Greenwood Press, 1984.
Handreider, W. (ed.). *The United States and Western Europe: Political, Economic, and Strategic Perspectives*. Cambridge: Winthrop Publishing, 1974.
Henderschedt, Thomas. "Clearing up China's Naval Intentions." *Navy Times*, Sept. 20, 2010.
Herrick, Robert. *Soviet Naval Theory and Policy: Ghorskov's Inheritance*. Annapolis: Naval Institute Press, 1988.
High, Jeffrey. "How Better Coordination can Improve Maritime Domain Awareness." Washington D.C.: National Research Council Transportation Security Board, November 2004.
Highlights of the Department of the Navy FY 2012 Budget. Washington D.C.: Department of the Navy, Feb. 2011.
Hill, J. R. *Anti-Submarine Warfare*. Annapolis: Naval Institute Press, 1984.
Hoffman, F. "Comment and Discussion on 'The Way Ahead.'" *USNI Proceedings*, June 1991.
Holzer, Robert. "Navy Scrutinizes Greater Variety of DDG-51 Alternatives," *Defense News*, 28 Oct. 1991.
Hone, Thomas. "Sea Basing: Poised for Takeoff." Washington D.C.: Office of Transformation, Dept. of Defense, Feb. 2005.
Hugues, Wayne. *Fleet Tactics*. Annapolis: Naval Institute Press, 1986.
_____. *The New Navy Fighting Machine: A Study of the Connections Between Contemporary Policy, Strategy, Sea Power, and the Composition of the United States Fleet*. Monterey: Naval Postgraduate School, 2009.
Huntington, Samuel. "National Policy and the Transoceanic Navy." *USNI Proceedings*, Aug. 1954.
Ikenberry, John. *After Victory: Institutions, Strategic Restraint, and the Rebuilding of Order After Major Wars*. Princeton: Princeton University Press, 2001.
Ikle, Fred. "The Reagan Defense Program: A Focus on the Strategic Imperatives." *Strategic Review*. Spring 1982.

Johnson, David. *Learning Large Lessons: The Evolving Power of Ground Power and Air Power in the Post-Cold War Era*. Santa Monica: Rand, 2007.

The Joint Staff Officer's Guide. Washington, D.C.: National Defense University Press, 2000.

Jordan, Amos. *American National Security*. Baltimore: Johns Hopkins University Press, 1999.

Kaplan, Lawrence. *NATO and the United States: The Enduring Alliance*. Boston: Twayne Publishers, 1988.

Karber, Phillip. *Soviet Power and Western Negotiating Policies*. Cambridge: Ballinger Publishing, 1983.

Kelso, Frank. "The Way Ahead." *USNI Proceedings*, May 1990.

Knorr, Klaus, ed. *Economic Issues and National Security*. Lawrence: University of Kansas Press, 1982.

Kobb, Lawrence. *Integrated Power: A National Security Strategy for the 21st Century*. Washington D.C.: Center for American Progress, 2009.

Krepinevich, Andrew. *Why Air-Sea Battle?* Washington D.C.: Center for Strategic And Budgetary Assessments, 2010.

Kugler, Richard. *Policy Analysis in National Security Affairs*. Washington D.C.: National Defense University Press, 2006.

Laird, Robbin. *The Soviet Union and Strategic Arms*. New York: Westview Press, 1984.

Lake, Anthony, ed. *Forging a World of Liberty Under Law: U.S. National Security Strategy in the 21st Century*. Princeton: Princeton Project for National Security, 2006.

Lambeth, Benjamin. *Air Power Against Terror: Operation Enduring Freedom*. Santa Monica: Rand, 2001.

_____. *American Carrier Air Power at the Dawn of a New Century*. Santa Monica: Rand, 2005.

_____. *The Transformation of American Air Power*. Ithaca: Cornell University Press, 2000.

Landersman, S. "Naval Protection of Shipping: A Lost Art?" Newport: *Naval War College Review*, March 1986.

Lascon, Ernani. *TQL as It Applies to the Surface Navy*. Monterey: Naval Post Graduate School, 1998.

Lehman, John. *Aircraft Carriers: The Real Choices*. Georgetown University: Center for Strategic and International Studies, 1978.

_____. "The 600 Ship Navy." *USNI Proceedings*. Jan. 1986.

_____. *Command of the Seas*. New York: Scribner's, 1988.

Lloyd, Richard, ed. *Defense Strategy and Forces: Setting Future Directions*. Newport: Naval War College, 2007.

Luce, Stephen. "Benefits of War." *American Review*, Dec. 1891.

Luttwak, Edward. *The Grand Strategy of the Soviet Union*. New York: St. Martin's Press, 1984.

_____. *The Pentagon and the Art of War*. New York: Simon & Schuster, 1985.

_____. *The Political Uses of Sea Power*. Washington D.C.: The Washington Center for Foreign Policy Research, Johns Hopkins University Press, 1974.

Mahan, A. T. *Mahan on Naval Strategy*. Annapolis: Naval Institute Press, 1991.

Manjoo, Farhad. *True Enough*. New York: Wiley Publishing, 2008.

May, Ernest R. (ed.) *American Cold War Strategy: Interpreting NSC 68*. New York: St. Martin's Press, 1993.

McGregor, Richard. "Zhou's Cryptic Caution Lost in Translation." *Financial Times*, June 10, 2011.

McNicholas, Michael. *Maritime Security*. New York: Elsevier, 2008.

MDZ: Coastal Defense Planner's Guide. New York: Coast Guard Atlantic Area, 1988.

Mearsheimer, John. "A Strategic Misstep: The Maritime Strategy and Deterrence in Europe." *International Security* Vol. 11, Autumn 1986.

Melanson, Richard. *American Foreign Policy Since the Vietnam War*. New York: M.E. Sharpe, 1996.

Middlebrook, Martin. *Task Force*. London: Penguin Books, 1987.

Miklaucic, Michael, ed. *Commanding Heights: Strategic Lessons from Complex Operations*. Washington D.C.: National Defense University Press, 2009.

Miller, David. "The Silent Menace: Diesel Submarines in 1993." London: *Jane's Defense and Security Review*, Aug. 1993.

Miller, Steven. *Nuclear Disengagement in Europe*. London: Taylor and Francis, 1983.

Moore, Charles. "Revitalizing the Cooperative Strategy for 21st Century Sea

Power." *Parameters*, U.S. Army War College, 2011.
Morrison, Samuel Eliot. *The Two Ocean War*. New York: Little, Brown, 1963.
Mrazek, James. *The Art of Winning Wars*. New York: Walker, 1968.
Naval War College. *Maritime Operations*. Newport: Naval War College Press, 1987.
Nerlich, Uwe. *Soviet Power and Western Negotiating Policies, Vol.1: The Soviet Asset: Military Power in the Competition over Europe*. New York: Ballinger Publishing, 1983.
Nitze, Paul. *Securing the Seas: The Soviet Naval Challenge and the Western Alliance Options*. Boulder: Westview Press, 1983.
Nunn, Sam. "Implementing a New Military Strategy: The Budget Decisions." Washington D.C.: Remarks prepared for delivery, 20 April 1990.
O'Rourke, Ronald. *Potential Navy Force Structure and Shipbuilding Plans: Background and Issues for Congress*. CRS Report RL32665. Washington D.C.: Congressional Research Service, 2004.
O'Wok, Robert. "A Cooperative Strategy for 21st Century Sea Power: An Assessment." Washington D.C.: Center for Strategy and Budgetary Assessments, March 2008.
Panetta, Leon. "Sustaining U.S. Global Leadership: Priorities for 21st Century Defense." Washington D.C.: Statement on Defense Strategic Guidance, 2011.
Patterson, Thomas G. *American Foreign Policy: A History Since 1900*. New York: D.C. Heath, 1983.
Posen, Barry. "Inadvertent Nuclear War? Escalation and NATOs Northern Flank." *International Security*, Fall 1982.
Ranft, Bryan, and G. Till. *The Sea in Soviet Strategy*. Annapolis: U.S. Naval Institute, 1989.
Reagan, Ronald. *National Security Strategy of the United States*. Washington D.C.: The White House, Jan. 1987.
Rivkin, D. "No Bastions for the Bear." *USNI Proceedings*, April 1984.
Ross, Dennis. *Statecraft*. New York: Farrar, Straus and Giroux, 2007.
Rumsfeld, Donald. *Annual Report to the President and Congress*. Washington D.C.: Department of Defense, 2002.
Saunders, Phillip (ed.). *The Chinese Navy: Expanding Capabilities, Evolving Roles*. Washington D.C.: Center for the Study of Chinese Military Affairs, National Defense University Press, 2011.
Schinesi, Katherine. "Naval Mine Warfare: Plans to Improve Countermeasures Unclear." *NSIAS 980135*. Washington D.C.: Government Accounting Office, 1998.
Schneider, Barry, ed. *Battlefields of the Future: 21st Century Warfare Issues*. Montgomery: Air War College University Press, 1998.
Schwartz, Peter. "Evolution of Naval Strategy." Unclassified briefing to USN Chief of Naval Operations Staff N-35, March 2005.
Scott, Richard. "New Submarine Concepts Ready to Break Surface." London: *Jane's Defense and Security Review*, May 2008.
Shah, Abuh. "Effects of Iraq Sanctions." *Global Issues*, 15 Oct. 2010.
Shaw, Alan. *Costs of Expanding and Modernizing the Navy's Carrier Based Air Forces*. Washington, D.C.: Congressional Budget Office, May 1982.
Shaw, M. (ed.). *War, State, and Society*. London: Macmillan, 1984.
Shiffman, Gary. *Economic Instruments of Security Policy*. New York: Palgrave Macmillan, 2006.
Smith, Rupert. *The Utility of Force*. New York: Vintage Books, 2005.
Sokel, A. E. "Sea Power in the Next War." *USNI Proceedings*. Annapolis: Naval Institute Press, May 1952.
Speed, Roger. *Strategic Deterrence in the 1980s*. Stanford: Hoover Institution Press, 1983.
Swicker, Charles. *Theater Ballistic Missile Defense from the Sea: Issues for the Maritime Component Commander*. Newport: Naval War College, 1998.
Tactics for MDZ Operations. New York: Coast Guard Atlantic Area, 1988.
Tammen, Ronald. *Power Transitions: Strategies for the 21st Century*. New York: Chatham House, 2000.
Taylor, Maxwell. *The Uncertain Trumpet*. New York: Harper Press, 1959.
Till, Geoffrey. *Maritime Strategy and the Nuclear Age*. New York: St. Martin's, 1982.
Trost, Carlyle. "A Maritime Strategy for the 1990s." *USNI Proceedings*, April 1991.
———. "A Report on the Posture and Budget of the U.S. Navy, Fiscal Year

1991." Washington D.C.: Statement to the House Armed Services Committee, 20 Feb. 1990.

Turner, Stansfield. "Missions of the U.S. Navy." *Naval War College Review*, Fall 1975.

U.S. Coast Guard. *America's Maritime Guardian: U.S. Coast Guard Pub 1.* Washington D.C.: U.S. Coast Guard, 2002.

———. *Maritime Defense Zone: Concept of Operations.* New York: Coast Guard Atlantic Area, 1987.

———. *Maritime Law Enforcement Manual.* Washington D.C.: U.S. Coast Guard, 2002.

———. *Maritime Strategy for Homeland Security.* Washington D.C.: U.S. Coast Guard, 2002.

U.S. Customs Service. *Container Security Initiative Strategic Plan 2006–2011.* Washington D.C.: U.S. Customs and Boarder Protective Service, 2008.

U.S. Marine Corps. *U.S. Marine Corps Strategic Communications Plan.* Quantico: U.S. Marines, 2010.

U.S. Navy. *Understanding Soviet Navy Developments, 5th ed.* Washington D.C.: Office of the Chief of Naval Operations, 1985.

U.S. Navy Capstone documents: (Washington, D.C.: Dept. of the Navy):
Missions of the U.S. Navy, 1974.
Strategic Concepts of the U.S. Navy, 1975/1978.
Future of U.S. Sea Power, 1979.
The Maritime Strategy, 1982.
The Way Ahead, 1991.
The Navy Policy Book, 1992
From the Sea, 1992.
Naval Doctrine Pub 1: Naval Warfare, 1994.
Forward: From the Sea, 1994.
The Navy Operational Concept, 1997.
Anywhere, Anytime, 1997.
Navy Strategic Planning Guidance, 1999.
Naval Power 21: A Naval Vision, 2002.
Naval Operating Concept for Joint Operations, 2002.
Sea Power 21, 2002.
Fleet Response Plan, 2003.
3/1 Strategy, 2005.
Cooperative Strategy for 21st Century Sea Power, 2007 (published jointly with the U.S. Coast Guard and U.S. Marines).
Naval Operations Concept 2010: Implementing the Maritime Strategy.
U.S. Pacific Command Strategic Guidance, 2011.

Ver Tol, Jan. *Air-Sea Battle: A Point of Departure Operational Concept.* Washington D.C.: Center for Strategic and Budgetary Assessments, 2010.

Walling, Karl. "Why a Conversation with the Country?" *Joint Forces Quarterly*, Issue 50. Washington D.C.: NDU University Press, 2008.

Wardak, Ghulam. *The Voroshilove Lectures: Materials from the Soviet General Staff Academy.* Washington D.C.: National Defense University Press, 1989.

Watkins, James. "Current Strategy of the U.S. Navy." *Los Angeles Times*, June 21, 1984.

Watson, Cynthia. *U.S. National Security Policy.* Santa Barbara: ABC-CLIO, 2008.

Watts, R. B. "Defending Our Shores." *USNI Proceedings*, Sept. 1987.

———. *Implementing Maritime Domain Awareness.* Monterey: Naval Post Graduate School, 2006.

Wormser, Michael. *U.S. Defense Policy.* Washington D.C.: Congressional Quarterly Inc., 1983.

Zimm, Alan. "The First Salvo." *USNI Proceedings*, Feb. 1985.

Irregular Warfare

Ackerman, Robert. "Pace of Change Accelerates for U.S. Navy." *Signal*, Dec. 2004.

Alexander, John. *Africa: Irregular Warfare on the Dark Continent.* JSOU Report 09–5. Tampa: Joint Special Operations University, May 2009.

———. *The Changing Nature of Warfare, the Factors Mediating Future Conflict, and Implications for SOF.* JSOU Report 06–1. Tampa: Joint Special Operations University, April 2006.

Allison, Graham. *Nuclear Terrorism: The Ultimate Preventable Catastrophe.* New York: Times Books, 2004.

Armitage, Richard. *CSIS Commission on Smart Power.* Washington D.C.: Center for Strategic and International Studies, 2007.

Art, Robert, ed. *International Politics: En-*

during Concepts and Contemporary Issues. New York: Longham, 2003.
Austin, Athanasia. "Development of U.S. Irregular Warfare Capabilities," The Journal of The JPACC, ed. 6, 2008.
Bangor, Bruce (ed.). The Psychology of Terrorism. Oxford: Oxford University Press, 2007.
Barnett, Roger. Asymmetrical Warfare. Washington D.C.: Brassey's Inc., 1993.
Bellany, Alex. Understanding Peacekeeping. Malden: Polity Press, 2004.
Bergen, Peter. Holy War Inc.: Inside the Secret World of Osama Bin Laden. New York: The Free Press, 2001.
Binnendijk, Hans, ed. Transforming America's Military. Washington D.C.: National Defense University Press, 2002.
_____. Transforming for Stabilization and Reconstruction Operations. Washington D.C.: National Defense University Press, 2004.
Browning, Karlyn. Attitudes Toward Terror and the War in Afghanistan: A Ten Year Review. Washington D.C.: American Enterprise Institute for Public Policy, 2011.
Buffaloe, David. Defining Asymmetric Warfare. Arlington: Institute of Land Warfare, Sept. 2006.
Bullock, Jane, ed. Homeland Security. New York: Butterworth-Heinemein, 2008.
Carafano, James. "Small Boats, Big Worries: Thwarting Terrorist Attacks from the Sea." Backgrounder. Washington D.C.: Heritage Foundation, June 2007.
Castelli, Christopher. "DOD Develops Homeland Defense Strategy, Advocates for Maritime NORAD." Inside the Navy, Aug. 2, 2004.
Cavas, Christopher. "The Road From Promise to Reality." Navy Times, April 23, 2012.
Celski, Joseph. Hunter-Killer Teams: Attacking Enemy Safe Havens. Joint Special Operations University Report 10-1. Tampa: Joint Special Operations University, Sept. 2005.
_____. Operationalizing COIN. Joint Special Operations University Report 05-2. Tampa: Joint Special Operations University, Sept. 2005.
Chester, Crocker, ed. Leashing the Dogs of War: Conflict Management in a Divided World. Washington D.C.: U.S. Institute of Peace, 2007.

Cohen, Eliot (ed.). U.S. Government Counterinsurgency Guide. Washington D.C.: U.S. Government Interagency Counterinsurgency Initiative, 2009.
Collins, Joseph. Understanding War in Afghanistan. Washington D.C.: National Defense University Press, 2011.
Crawford, George. Manhunting: Counter-Network Organization for Irregular Warfare. Joint Special Operations University Report 09-07. Tampa: Joint Special Operations University, Sept. 2009.
Cronin, Audrey (ed.). Attacking Terrorism: Elements of a Grand Strategy. Washington D.C.: Georgetown University Press, 2004.
_____. How Terrorism Ends: Understanding the Decline and Demise of Terrorist Campaigns. Princeton: Princeton University Press, 2011.
"The Cruise Missile Threat: Prospects for Homeland Defense." National Security Watch. Arlington: Institute of Land Warfare, 2006.
Defense Acquisitions: Assessment of Selected Programs. Washington D.C.: Government Accounting Office, March 2010.
Defense Acquisitions: Navy's Ability to Overcome Challenges Facing LCS Will Determine Capabilities. Washington D.C.: Government Accounting Office, August 2010.
Dobbins, James, ed. America's Role in Nation Building from Germany to Iraq. Washington D.C.: Rand, 2003.
_____. The UN's Role in Nation Building from the Congo to Iraq. Washington D.C.: Rand, 2005.
Dunnigan, James. How to Make War. New York: Quill, 1982.
Flynn, Stephen. America the Vulnerable. New York: HarperCollins, 2004.
Freeman, Chas. Arts of Power: Statecraft and Diplomacy. Washington D.C.: U.S. Institute of Peace, 1997.
Fritz, A. The Navy Role in Confronting Irregular Challenge: Implementing the Navy Vision for CNC. Washington D.C.: Center for Naval Analysis, 2011.
Galula, David. Counterinsurgency Warfare: Theory and Practice. Westport: Praeger Security International, 1964.
Gilmore Commission. Towards a National Strategy for Combating Terrorism. Wash-

ington D.C.: Government Printing Office, Dec. 15, 2000.
Gompert, David. *Battle-Wise: Seeking Time-Information Superiority in Networked Warfare*. Washington D.C.: National Defense University Press, 2006.
Gormley, Dennis. "Unmanned Air Vehicles as Terror Weapons: Real or Imagined?" *Global Security Newswire*, July 1, 2005.
Government Accounting Office. *Drug Control: Assets DOD Contributes to Reducing the Illegal Drug Supply Have Declined*. Report to Congressional Requestors. Washington D.C.: Government Accounting Office, 1999.
_____. *Homeland Security: Management Challenges Facing Federal Leadership*. GAO-03-26. Washington D.C.: Government Accounting Office, 2002.
_____. *Military Transformation Efforts Should be More Focused and Integrated*. GAO-01-853. Washington D.C.: Government Accounting Office, 2001.
_____. *Status of DOD Efforts to Protect Forces Overseas*. GAO/NSIAD-97-207. Washington D.C.: Government Accountability Office, 2007.
Gray, Colin. "Irregular Enemies and the Essence of Strategy: Can the American Way of War Adapt?" Washington D.C.: *Strategic Studies Institute*, 2006.
_____. "Thinking Asymmetrically in Times of Terror." *Parameters*. Carlyle: U.S. Army War College, Spring 2002.
Greenberg, Michael. *Maritime Terrorism: Risk and Liability*. Washington D.C.: Rand, Center for Terrorism Risk Management Policy, 2006.
Hammes, Thomas. "Rethinking the Principles of War." *Rethinking the Principles of War*. Annapolis: Naval Institute Press, 2005.
_____. *The Sling and the Stone: On War in the 21st Century*. St. Paul: Zenith Press, 2006.
Hoffman, Bruce. *Inside Terrorism*. New York: Columbia University Press, 2006.
Hoffman, Frank. "Conflict in the 21st Century: The Rise of Hybrid Wars." *Small Wars Journal*, March 2006.
_____. "Hybrid Warfare and Challenges," *Joint Forces Quarterly*, Issue 52. Washington: National Defense University Press, 2009.
Hollander, Paul, ed. *Understanding Anti-Americanism*. Chicago: Ivan R. Dee, 2004.
Inaugural Global Maritime Information Sharing Symposium. Kings Point: U.S. Dept. of Justice, 2008.
Irregular Warfare DOD Directive 3000.07. Washington D.C.: Department of Defense, 2008.
Irregular Warfare Joint Operating Concept. Washington D.C.: Department of Defense, 2009.
Keating, Timothy. *CDRNORTHCOM-CDR NORAD Strategic Guidance*. Colorado Springs: U.S. NORTHCOM, 2006.
Klare, Michael. *Rising Powers, Shrinking Planet*. New York: Metropolitan Books, 2008.
_____. *Resource Wars*. New York: Henry Holt, 2001.
Kim, Jim. "Influence of PSI on North Korea." *Strategic Insights* v.5, Aug. 2006.
Kriesher, Otto. "Checkered Past, Uncertain Future." *USNI Proceedings*, Jan. 2009.
Latimer, Jon. *Deception in War*. New York: Overlook Press, 2003.
Lawson, Chris. "Battle for 12 ARGs Gathers New Steam." *Navy Times*, Iss. 46 Dec. 1994.
Lewis, Ware. *LIC in the 3rd World*. Montgomery: Air War College Press, 1988.
Lord, Canes, ed. *Political Warfare and Psychological Operations*. Washington D.C.: National Defense University Press, 1989.
Loy, James. "Meeting the Homeland Security Challenge: A Principled Strategy for a Balanced and Practical Response." Washington D.C.: U.S. Coast Guard, Oct. 2001.
Ma, Jason. "As NECC Stands Up, Navy Prepares Riverine Forces for 2007 Iraq Mission." *Inside the Navy*, 2006.
Mahnken, Thomas. *The Limits of Transformation: Officer Attitudes Toward the Revolution in Military Affairs*, Newport: Naval War college Newport papers 17, 2003.
Mauney, Charles. "The Navy's Role in Homeland Defense." *U.S. Navy N3/N5 Strategic Briefing*, Feb. 2004.
McMahon, Michael, ed. *2006 JSOU/NDIA SO/LIC Chapter Essays*. JSOU Report 06-7. Tampa: Joint Special Operations University, June 2006.
McNicholas, Michael. *Maritime Security*. Boston: Elsevier, 2008.

Metz, Stephen. *Asymmetry and U.S. Military Strategy: Definitions, Background, and Strategic Concepts*. Carlisle: U.S. Army Strategic Studies Institute, Jan. 2001.

Morgan, John. "The 1000-Ship Navy: Global Maritime Network." USNI *Proceedings*, Nov. 2005.

Murphy, Martin. *Littoral Combat Ship: An Examination of its Possible Concepts of Operation*. Washington D.C.: Center for Strategic Budgetary Assessments, 2010.

Nagel, John. *Learning to Eat Soup with a Knife*. Chicago: University of Chicago Press, 2005.

National Commission on Terrorist Attacks. *The 9/11 Commission Report*. Washington D.C.: W.W. Norton, 2004.

Newton, Richard. *Contemporary Security Challenges: Irregular Warfare and Indirect Approaches*. JSOU Report 09–03. Tampa: Joint Special Operations University, Feb. 2009.

Nikitin, Mary Beth. *Proliferation Security Initiative: CRS Report for Congress*. Washington D.C.: Congressional Research Service, 2008.

Nye, Joseph. *Soft Power*. New York: PublicAffairs, 2004.

———. *Understanding International Conflicts*. New York: Longbow, 2003.

O'Neill, Bard. *Insurgency and Terrorism*. Washington: Potomac Books, 2005.

O'Rourke, Ronald. *Navy Irregular Warfare and Counterterrorism Operations: Background Issues for Congress*. Washington D.C.: Congressional Research Service, Nov. 2011.

———. *The Navy Role in Confronting Irregular Challenges*. Washington D.C.: Center for Naval Analysis, 2011.

Orr, Robert, ed. *Winning the Peace: an American Strategy for Post-Conflict Reconstruction*. Washington D.C.: CSIS Press, 2004.

Parfomak, Paul. *Liquified Natural Gas (LNG) Infrastructure Security: Background and Issues for Congress*. Washington D.C.: Congressional Research Service, 2003.

Pate, Anthony. *Protecting America's Ports: Promising Practices*. Washington D.C.: Report to the Dept. of Justice, Jan. 2008.

Perito, Robert, ed. *Guide for Participants in Peace, Stability, and Relief Operations*. Washington D.C.: U.S. Institute for Peace, 2007.

Rand Unclassified Briefing. *Expeditionary Strike Group Five: Fast, Forward, Flexible*. Oct. 20, 2011.

Russel, Eugene. "Low Intensity Conflict in a Changed and Changing World," *GAO International Affairs Policy 92–104S*. Washington D.C.: Government Accounting Office, 1992.

Sanger, David. *The Inheritance: The World Obama Confronts and the Challenges to American Power*. New York: Harmony Books, 2009.

Sen, Amartya. *Development as Freedom*. New York: Anchor Books, 1999.

Shaver, Charles. *Irregular Warfare Special Study*. Suffolk: Joint Warfighting Center, March 2006.

Smigielski, David. "Review of the Suitcase Nuclear Bomb Controversy." Washington D.C.: Russian American Nuclear Advisory Council, Sept. 2003.

Special Operations Forces Interagency Counterterrorism Reference Manual. Tampa: Joint Special Operations University, March 2009.

Stiglitz, Joseph. *Making Globalization Work*. New York: W.W. Norton, 2006.

Tammen, Robert (ed.). *Power Transitions: Strategies for the 21st Century*. Washington D.C.: CQ Press, 2000.

Tangredi, Sam, ed. *Globalization and Maritime Power*. Washington D.C.: National Defense University Press, 2002.

Trindull, Joseph. "The Mumbai Attacks: Lessons for the Modern World." *Domprep Journal*, Iss. V, Jan. 2009.

Tucker, David. *U.S. Special Operations Forces*. New York: Columbia University Press, 2007.

Ullman, Harlan. "The 1000 Ship Navy-Turning a Slogan into a Strategy." USNI *Proceedings*, Oct. 2006.

Unconventional Operational Concepts and the Homeland. A Panel Report of the Defense Science Board 2007 Summer Study on Challenges to Military Operations in Support of U.S. Interests. Washington D.C.: Office of the Under Secretary Of Defense for Acquisition, Technology, and Logistics. March 2009.

U.S. House of Representatives. Hrg. 107–1086: Joint Inquiry into Intelligence Community Activities Before and After the Terrorist Attacks of September 11,

2001: Hearings before the Select Committee on Intelligence, U.S. Senate and the Permanent Select Committee on Intelligence, House of Representatives, Volume 1, September 18, 19, 20, 24, and 26, 2002.
_____. *Navy Acquisitions: Improved Littoral Warfighting Capabilities Needed*, Report to the Chairman and Ranking Minority Member, Subcommittee on Military Research and Development on Armed Services, House of Representatives, GAO-1-493, Washington D.C.: Government Accounting Office, March 2001.
_____. "Navy Transformation: Hearing Before the Readiness Sub-Committee of the Committee of Armed Services, House of Representatives, 109th Congress." Washington, D.C.: House of Representatives, April 2006.
_____."Protecting the Maritime Borders: Leveraging New Enforcement Cooperation to Enhance Security Along America's Coasts," Hearing before the U.S. House of Representatives, Committee on Homeland Security, Sub-Committee on Border and Maritime Security, July 12, 2011.
_____. Statement by Honorable Paul McHale, Assistant Secretary of Defense for Homeland Defense, Before the 109th Congress, Subcommittee on Terrorism, Unconventional Threats and Capabilities, Committee on Armed Services, United States House of Representatives, March 15, 2005.
U.S. Senate. "The Current Readiness of U.S. Forces," Hearing before the Subcommittee on Readiness and Management Support of the Committee on Armed Service, U.S. Senate, 111th Congress, 14 April 2010.
_____. S. Hrg. 109–186: "The Container Security Initiative and the Customs-Trade Partnership against Terrorism: Securing the Global Supply Chain or Trojan Horse?" Hearing before the Permanent Subcommittee on Investigations of the Committee on Homeland Security and Governmental Affairs, United States Senate, One Hundred Ninth Congress, First Session, May 6, 2005.
"U.S. Troops to Leave Iraq," *Washington Post World*, Oct. 21, 2011.
Vigo, Milan. "No Need for High Speed." USNI *Proceedings*, Sept. 2009.
Walker, David. *Homeland Security: A Framework for Addressing the Nation's Efforts*. Statement by the Comptroller General of the Unite States before Congress. Washington D.C.: General Accounting Office, GAO-01-1158T, Sept. 21, 2001.
Watson, Cynthia. *Nation Building and Stability Operations*. New York: Praeger Security International, 2008.
Wilson, Scott. "Global War on Terror is Given a New Name," *The Washington Post*, March 25, 2009.
Work, Robert. *Know When to Hold 'em, Know When to Fold 'em: A New Transformation for the Navy's Surface Battle Line*. Washington D.C.: Center for Strategic and Budgetary Assessments, 2007.
Wylie, James. "North American Maritime Homeland Security and Defense." Washington D.C.: Center for Naval Analysis, Jan. 2004.
Zakaria, Fareed. *The Post-American World*. New York: W.W. Norton, 2008.

Index

USS *Abraham Lincoln* 168
Achille Lauro 112
adaptation 74
AEGIS 80, 99, 120, 145
Afghanistan 16, 18, 23–24, 95, 133, 141, 142–143, 148, 159, 162, 163
Africa 130
Air Force 69, 83, 143, 174; Desert Storm 118; revolt of the admirals 70
Air-Sea Battle (ASB) 174–175
Air War College 70
aircraft (at sea) 51
aircraft carrier 2, 10, 104; conventional role 77; culture 148; deterrent effect 118; development as capital ship 51; HLD 148; HLS/HLD 151; Iraq 146; Mahanian theory 53; North Korea 84–85; Nuclear strike 75–76; numbers post 9/11 146; post war 68, 70; risk to 1990s 120, 121; role in Desert Storm 118; role in irregular warfare 110–113; strike ops 117–118; support of the gun line 53; *see also* capital ships, Navy
Al Qaida 5, 14, 16, 23, 25, 133, 135, 142, 148, 151, 162, 132
Allied Force 132
USS *America* 110
American way of war 15
amphibious power 132
amphibious ready group 129
amphibious ships 110, 118
Annapolis 32–33
anti-access 174
anti-ship missiles 174
anti-terrorist force protection 160
Anywhere, Anytime 129
Arctic 100
ARG 132, 147
Arleigh Burke (destroyer) 120
arms race 31
Army Air Corps 65
ASDIC 50
ASW 53, 66, 81, 97, 125, 169; campaign 60; coastal 107
asymetric threat 133, 137–138, 153

Atlantic bridge 107
Atlantic Theater 57
atomic bomb 66, 67
atomic weapons 57
automatic identification system (AIS) 158

B-1 bomber 93
B-36 70
balanced fleet 89
ballistic missile submarine 11
Baocheng, Niu 173
Barbary pirates 35
Ba'thists 26
battleships 10, 47, 52, 71
Beirut 111
Bekka valley 112
Berlin 61, 117
Berlin Wall 109, 120
Beverridge, Albert 35
Bikini Atoll 68
"big gun club" 13, 43, 53, 58
bi-polar 62, 73
blockade 128
blue water 10, 31
BMD 145
bombing 65
Bosnia 18, 128
Bradley, Omar 71
breakout 108
Bridges at Toko-Ri (film) 72
briefcase nuke 140
British Navy 34; officers 43
brushfire wars 20
Burke, Arleigh 71, 81
Bush, George 120, 121, 127; administration 146

capabilities 138
capital ships 10–11; adaptability 115–116; carrier deep strike 124; cuts 128; economic benefit 42; fear of loss 44; forward from the sea 129; investment 72; multi-dimension 51; Navy policy book 123; role in crisis operations 125; strategic application WWI 48; in strategy 132;

217

Index

theory 120, 177; vulerability to technology 44; WWI 43–44; WWII 57
carrier battle group 98
carrier war 58
Carter, Jimmy: administration 95, 104; technological developments 98
CENTCOM 119, 144, 146
Center for Naval Analysis 132
center of gravity 27, 111
Central Europe 99
China 59, 162; aircraft carrier 173; economy 173; Naval expansion 174; Navy 173; peer rival 173; relation to North Korea 84–85; threat 175
civil authority 152
Civil War 7, 9, 32
civilian morale 65
CIWS 99
Clark, Vern 170
Clausewitz, Carl von 10, 26, 44–45, 106, 113
Clinton, Bill 127
CNN 119
CNO 71, 119, 129, 146
Coast Guard 1, 107, 150, 152, 165; leadership 155, 158, 159
COIN 15, 164, 167, 175
Cold War 2, 3, 19, 62, 114, 115; budget 121; end 122; mindset 123; Naval 92; threat analysis 138; threat vs. irregular warfare 136
USS *Cole* 150
Cole, Bud 174
command of the sea 61, 81
Commercy raiding 48
common operating picture (COP) 154, 157
Communism 66, 71
Communist Bloc 153
Congress 47, 48, 103, 123, 146, 162, 169, 175
consolidation 125
Container Security Initiative 158
containment 65
contingencies 76
contingency ops 132
control of the sea 85, 118
conventional power 26–28
conventional war 6, 115
Cooperative Strategy for 21st Century Sea Power 161
Corbett, Julian 45, 106, 178
cost of fleet 41
counter-dispersion (doctrine) 98
counter-force 105
counter-insurgency 121
counter-narcotics 121
coup de main 111
crisis contingency ops 14
crisis response 121
critical infrastructure 150
CRS 168

cruise missiles 118, 170
CSP 21, 167
Cuba 109, 110
Cuban missile crisis, 78
culture 8, 12, 14
culture war 33
CVBG 132

Darwin, Charles 31
Davies, Thomas 70
DDG 125
DDG-51 171
DD(x) 145
decade of war 3, 12, 13, 14, 41, 47, 62, 178
deep strike 124
demilitarization 116
Denefield, Louis 71
Department of Defense (DOD) 19, 20–22, 66, 127, 145, 150
Department of Homeland Security (DHS) 135
Department of the Navy 103
Desert One 94
Desert Shield 118–120, 147
Desert Storm 118–120, 125, 126, 127, 129, 147
détente 95
deterrence 123, 161
deterrent effect 118
deterrent force 74
DHS 150
dive bombing 54
doctrine 8, 10, 171
Doenitz, Karl 50
Doolittle, James 68
Douhet 10
dreadnaughts 51
drug war 151
"drumbeat" 60, 107
Druze 111

East Germany 79
economic warfare 54
EEZ 173
Eisenhower, Dwight 47
El Salvador 117
"end of history" 133
England 12, 54
EOD 108, 159
escorts 50, 104
expeditionary strike groups 146
Exxon Valdez 167

F-14 99
F-18 99, 142, 143
Falklands 99
Fallujah 148
far seas 173
"fleet in being" 45, 78
Fleet Response Plan 146
flexible response 77

Index

force packages 125
Forrestal, James 70
forward deployment 84, 124, 126, 128
forward presence 123, 161
4GW 25
4th generation warfare 6
freedom of the seas 48, 157, 175
frigates 42
From the Sea 124–126, 128

Gaddafi, Muammar 112
Gates, Robert 174
"Gato" class 49
genocide 130
Germany 65, 117; Naval officers 43
Glasnost 114
Global Maritime Initiative 162
global policeman 57
global power 43, 58
global war 82
globalization 128
Goldwater–Nichols 113
Gorshkov, Sergei 78
Great Britain 10
Grenada 109
Gulf of Sidra 112
Gulf War 123
"guns or butter" 20
GWOT 23–24, 135, 141, 145, 146, 148, 150, 154, 158, 163, 164, 178,

HADR 162, 165
Haiti 128
Hammes, T.X. 25
Hampton Roads 32
harpoon 80, 99
Hart, Lidell 10
Hawk revisionism 18
Hay, John 35
hierarchy of vessels 38
high seas 10
high-low 89, 104, 120; theorist reaction 90
Hobson, Pearson 37
Hoffman, Frank 165
Holmes, James 174
homeland 13, 135, 136, 138; threat 148
homeland defense (HLD) 134, 146, 151; threat 149; vs. HLS 150
homeland security (HLS) 28, 150, 151
Hoover, Herbert 48
hospital ships 48
humanitarian operations 121, 157
hunter-killer group 50, 61
Hussein, Saddam 115, 117, 128, 132, 146
hybrid war 6, 26, 165
hydrofoil (PHM) 90

IA program 159
illegal immigration 151
IMO 149, 158
Impeccable 172

Imperial Japan 174
Imperial Russia 77
Inchon 84
USS *Independence* 110
India 173
intentions 138
Iran 95, 112
Iraq 16, 18, 23–24, 95, 112, 126, 132, 141, 146–148, 159; Army 117; Navy 119
ironclads 32
irregular warfare 3, 6, 7, 13–14, 15; assets 167; challenge of conventional forces 82; conflicts, 1980s 94; definitions 24–25; domestic challenges 83; enemy 60; forms 26–27; future role of USN 168; history 18, 21; missions 164; naval forces 82; naval threat 126; 1990s 130; reduction in force 176; relation to sea power 28; rhetoric 163; role of aircraft carriers 83; role of capital ships 83; sea/air dominance 144; shift away 175; small boats 82; strengths 17; theory, operations 109; threat 136; units 141
ISIS 17, 23–24

Japan 59–60, 65
JDAMs 142
JHOCs 160
Johnson, Louis 70
"joint" 66
joint chiefs 71
jointness 103
Jomini 106
Jutland 43–44, 79, 179

Kelso, Frank 123
Kennan, George 63
USS *Kennedy* 111
Kennedy, John F.: administration, 15
Khrushchev, Nikita 78
kinetic 22, 29
USS *Kitty Hawk* 142, 143, 172
Korea 81
Korean War 172

law enforcement 151
layered defense 156
LCS 170–171
Lebanon 18, 111–112
Lehman, John 113, 162
Le May, Curtis 67, 68
Liberia 112
limited war at sea 79
littoral warfare 125, 126, 159, 167, 169
LNGs 149
Lodge, Henry Cabot 35
London Naval Disarmament Conference 48
"long telegram" 63
"long war" 16, 162
Los Angeles 155

low intensity conflict 18–20
Loy, James 155

MAD (mutual assured destruction) 76, 138
Mahan, Alfred Thayer, 2, 3, 9, 106, 177; background 30–32; civilian support 42; command of the sea 38; critique 41; expansionism 35; forward basing 84, 85; impact on naval profession 38; influence of sea power on history 34; influence overseas 37; judgment of history 39; legacy 132, 140; loss of influence 42; loss of sea control 85; manipulation of theory 40; maritime strategy 93, 115; modern operations 164; nuclear power 75; popularity 36; principles 113; role of capital ships 39; theoretical writing 33; theory 12; U.S. superpower 75; use of fleet 34; vision, 32, 57–61, 64; The Way Ahead 121; World War I 40
Mahan, Dennis 31
Manifest Destiny 35
Marine barracks bombing 111
Marine Corps 124–125, 128, 147
maritime defense zone (MDZ) 107; design 108, operations 108, political impact 108
maritime domain awareness (MDA) 153–158, 160
maritime dominance 164
maritime security 164
maritime stability 164
maritime strategy 92, 97, 125; coastal defense/homeland defense 106–109; concentration of force 98; decisive battle 97; defensive posture 99; deterrence 105; forward deployment rationale 100; irregular warfare 106; modified 120; NATO reponse 105; operations vs. strategic forces 105; public relations 102; reliance on technology 100–101; resistance to 104; risk 94; role in NATO 100; role of aircraft carriers 93; role of the Air Force 103; role of the Army 103; Soviet Navy action 101; Soviets 93; strike operations 100; submarine fleet 97; use of carriers forward 97
Marshal Plan 63
massive retaliation 77
McCullough, Barry 168
McHale, Paul 155, 157
MDA 165
MDZ 145
Mediteranean 97
MEU 110
Midway 11
military industrial complex 47, 137
military sealift command 118
mines 9, 107, 119, 126, 170
mission creep 167
Mitchell, Billy 51

MIUW 108
Monroe Doctrine 36, 42
Morrison, Samuel Elliot 58, 177
Mullen, Mike 157
MX missile 93, 105

nation building 121
national defense strategy 176
National Guard 152
National Performance Review 127
national security state 58
national strategy 7
NATO 64, 76, 100, 101–102, 130, 157; maritime alliance 77; 1970 scenario 104; Soviet/sea contingencies 79
Naval Expeditionary Combat Command (NECC) 159
Naval War College 2, 54, 89, 91
Naval War College Review 90
Naval Warfare Publication 1, 91
Navalists, 11, 31, 34, 42, 47, 51, 57n113, 62, 122, 123, 141, 171
Navy Policy Book, 123
Navy 7, 8, 10–11; adaptability 124; air-sea battle 174; aircraft carriers 53, 168, 172 (*see also* aircraft carriers); arms race 38, 43; Atlantic campaign, 60–61; capital ships 130, 168 (*see also* capital ships); challenge from non-traditional warfare 136; challenge/threat 57; China 162; coastal operations 152, 159–161; cooperation with Coast Guard 160; cooperative strategy 161; culture 126; deployment philosophy 131; development of irregular forces 83; expansion 43; force structure 115; global role 73; history 30, 32, 178; HLD operating areas 153; irregular warfare 29, 159, 164–167, 169–170; Korean operations 84–85; littoral operations 126, 170; Mahan China 174; MDA 153; mini-containment 131; missions 12, 104; nuclear strategy 75; OEF 146; 1000 ship Navy 157; operating concept 129; Pacific 58–59; patrol craft 169; post graduate school 2; post-war concerns 61–62; post-WWI 47; public backlash to WWI 44; reaction to Soviet collapse 117; renaissance 104; response 46; return to tradition 164; riverine forces 159; role in coastal defense 107; senior leadership 132; strategic goals 82; submarines 49; support 42; theory 101, 140; three dimensions 44; vs. Air Force 69; vs. air power debate 65; vessels, cost 47; Way Ahead 124
NECC 163, 169
NEO 112, 132
net centric warfare 22, 129
neutrality patrols 53
New Jersey 111
New World Order 117, 124

Index

Nicaragua 117
Nitze, Paul 77
no-fly 131
non-kinetic 22
Norfolk 160
Normandy 77, 110
North Korea 83
North Sea 97
NORTHCOM 157
Norway 98, 99
nuclear power vs. conventional 75
nuclear theory 105
Nunn, Sam 121
NUTS 76, 138

Obama, Barack: administration 175
offensive battle 53
oil rigs 112, 159
Oliver Hazard Perry (class) 90, 108, 170
Operation Anaconda 144
Operation Earnest Will 112
Operation Enduring Freedom (OEF) 142
Operation Iraqi Freedom (OIF) 147
Operation Just Cause 113
operational concept 171
OPNAV 123
outload operations 107
overseas contingency operations 163

Pacific 97
Panama 113
Patriot Act 137
Pax Americana 58
PC 179, 169
peace dividend 2, 123, 143
peace keeping 111, 121
Pearl Harbor 54
peer competitor 162
Pentagon 66, 103, 174
Persian Gulf 112, 118, 128, 159, 170
piracy 154, 157
PLAN 173
Poland 79
Polaris 75
Polmar, Norman 174
Posse Comitatus 150, 151
Powell, Colin 119
Power projection 90, 97, 161
presence ops 90, 111
preventative war 148
private sector 158
proceedings 121, 128
proliferation security initiative (PSI) 158
protection of shipping 107
PSI 165
public relations 119, 127–129

QDR 22, 174

Reagan, Ronald 21, 92, 113–114, 120; administration 93, 107, 105–106, 109;

agenda 86; budget 103; defense buildup 110; shipbuilding 98
Red Star over the Pacific 174
re-flagging 112
regional war 81
Republican Guard 147
Republicans 95
"revolt of the admirals" 69–70, 75, 82, 103
revolution in military affairs 21
Rickover, Hyman 75, 126
Ridge, Tom 155
riverine forces 159
Roosevelt, Theodore 35, 47; Great White Fleet 43
Royal Naval College 45
Royal Navy aircraft carriers 51
Rubicon 69
Rumsfeld, Donald 22, 155
Russia 61, 173
Rwanda 130

sabotage 136
SAC 67, 75
sail power 9
Salamis 11
San Diego 160
Sandanistas 26
Saudi Arabia 118
Scapa Flow 45
Schwarzkopf, Norman 119
scouting 66
SCUD missiles 140
SDI 21
sea basing 144, 145
sea control 90, 97, 100, 101, 122, 128
sea fighter 170
Sea Plan 2000 94
sea power 2, 7, 8, 12, 17, 21, 28–29, 30, 135, 144
sea shield 144, 145
sea strike 144, 145
seaborne threat 140
SEALs 110, 169
Second World War (World War II) 11, 18, 54, 57, 65, 101, 135, 151
sectors 108; command center 161
security assistance 121
Seebee 82
Senate Armed Services Committee 121
September 11 (9/11) 3, 5, 7, 13, 16, 24–25, 28, 117, 132, 133, 135, 137, 139, 140, 148, 149, 150, 153, 163, 170
SES (vessel) 90
Shiite 111
shock and awe 129, 138, 147
show of force 88, 131
Sierra Leone 112
Sims, William 113, 132
Singapore 155
Sino-Soviet split 172
600 ship navy 97, 122

small combatants 168
smuggling 154
Social Darwinism 34, 36
SOF 24, 142–143, 148
soft power 7, 13, 28, 165
Somalia 18, 128
SOSUSS 101
South Africa, apartheid 117
Soviet Union 19–20, 62, 85, 65, 107, 109, 120, 138; agenda 95; ballistic missile submarines 98, 100; collapse 115, 122; composition, history 78–79; confrontation 82; Europe 69; fleet 126; focus on 1980, 91; land/air bases 98; land space 102; Navy 101; 1970s 89; nuclear parity 76; power, Pacific 105; submarines 107; submarines 64; threat 73
special interest vessels 153
SSBNs 105
Stalin, Josepf 77
standing military 57
USS *Stark* 112
state department 63
Stealth 93
Strategic Air Command (film) 72
strategic bombing 67, 71; survey 66
strategic deterrence 90
strategic ports 107
strategy 8, 10–11
submarines 47–48, 50, 53
Summers, Harry 18
superpower 64, 73
supply side economics 95
Syria 111

tactical nuclear weapons 101
Tailhook 122, 123
Taiwan 172
Taliban 122, 123, 133, 141, 142–144, 172
tankers 143
Taranto 54
terrorism 13, 136, 137, 156; cruise missiles 149; threat analysis 140
theory 8, 12–13, 24, 46, 108; adaptation to irregular warfare 83; Cold War 74; force design 74; procurement 80; sea superiority 80
thousand ship navy 157
Tiananmen square 173
Title 10 104
Tomahawk 80, 99, 129, 131, 146
torpedo planes 54
torpedoes 9
TQL 123
traditionalists 33, 39
Trafalgar 11

transformation 22
Trost, Carlyle 121
Truman, Harry 63, 64
tsunami relief 167, 168
Turner, Stansfield 91, 94
two ocean war 58

U-boats 48–49, 51, 60, 107, 151
unification hearings 73
unions (air, surface, submarine) 75, 93
United Nations 146
U.S. Code Title 14, 156, 160
US–Soviet conflict 130
USS *United States* 70
Uphold Democracy 132
Urgent Fury 109–111
USSOCOM 23

Versailles 46
Victorious 172
HMS *Victory* 12
Victory at Sea (film) 72
Vietnam 15, 18, 81, 110, 141, 144, 159; "brown water" 86–87; carrier ops 86, 88; Gulf of Tonkin 86; irregular warfare 86; lessons ignored 88; market time 87; North Vietnam, power 86
USS *Vincennes* 112
VSTOL 90

War Department 66
war games 51
War Plan Orange 174
wars of choice 130
warship 12
wartime economy 95
The Way Ahead, 121, 123
weapons of mass destruction (WMD) 135, 137, 138, 146, 149, 152, 165
Western tier 107
Western way of war 27
Westmoreland, William 88
wolfpack tactics 50
World War I 43, 44, 60
World War II 11, 18, 54, 57, 65, 101, 135, 151
worst case scenario 138
Worth, Cedric 70

Yemen 170
Yoshihara, Toshi 174
Yost, Paul 108

zealots 43
Zumwalt, Elmo 80, 91, 104, 120, 145, 170